The New Economy in Transatlantic Perspective

What's left from the *new economy*? This book takes an unfashionable perspective and shows that despite all the mistaken ideas and exaggerations, the technological changes of the 1990s still have important effects today. Economic history shows that technological revolutions tend to generate deep economic and social crises before a temporary state of equilibrium is reached.

The established modes of accumulation and regimes of regulation of national capitalisms and international capitalism have been undermined by the collapse of the high tech asset bubble. Financial markets are still in disarray. What can be observed, however, is that some national economies are better positioned to tackle the crisis than others. Why is this?

This and other important questions are tackled by an international team of contributors including Daniele Archibugi, Harald Hagemann, Bruno Amable, Martin Heidenreich and David Gibbs. This volume should be of great interest to all those working at the intersection of international politics and economics.

Kurt Hübner is professor of Political Science and the director of the Canadian Center for German and European Studies, York University, Toronto.

Routledge studies in governance and change in the global era

The New Economy in Transatlantic Perspective

Spaces of innovation

Edited by Kurt Hübner

Routledge
Taylor & Francis Group

LONDON AND NEW YORK

First published 2005
by Routledge

Published 2017 by Routledge
2 Park Square, Milton Park, Abingdon, Oxon OX14 4RN
605 Third Avenue, New York, NY 10017

*Routledge is an imprint of the Taylor & Francis Group,
an informa business*

Typeset in Times by Wearset Ltd, Boldon, Tyne and Wear

British Library Cataloguing in Publication Data
A catalogue record for this book is available from the British Library

Library of Congress Cataloging in Publication Data
A catalog record for this book has been requested

ISBN 13: 978-0-415-33608-6 (hbk)
ISBN 13: 978-0-415-40692-5 (pbk)

Contents

Illustrations

Figures

Tables

Contributors

Bruno Amable is professor of economics at the University of Paris X Nanterre, MODEM. He is the director of DEA Macroéconomie et Analyse Quantitative and a research associate with CEPREMAP's project URA 922 Régulation, Ressources Humaines et Économie Publique.

Daniele Archibugi is technological director at the Italian National Research Council in Rome. He has worked and taught at the universities of Sussex, Naples, Cambridge and Rome and he is currently Leverhulme visiting professor at the London School of Economics and Political Science.

Neil Brenner is assistant professor of Sociology and Metropolitan Studies, New York University. His research and teaching focus on critical urban and regional political economy, state theory and sociospatial theory.

Alberto Coco is currently completing a PhD at the Université Catholique de Louvain la Neuve, Belgium and works for the Bank of Italy. He has worked on data analysis and forecasting for Italian Telecom.

Georg Erber is research associate at the German Institute for Economic Research (DIW) and has held various professorships in the PR China and Thailand. His main research activities are in the field of industrial organization in information and communication industries as well as economics of networks and regulation of network industries.

Michael Fritsch is professor of Economics at the Technical University Bergakademie Freiberg, where he holds the Chair for Economic Policy. He is research professor at the German Institute for Economic Research (DIW), Berlin, and at the Max-Planck-Institute for Research into Economic Systems, Jena.

David Gibbs is professor of Human Geography in the Department of Geography at the University of Hull. His main research interests are in the field of local and regional economic development, with a particular focus on the environmental implications of such development and the impact of information and communication technologies (ICTs).

Harald Hagemann is professor of Economic Theory at the University of Hohenheim. His research focuses on macroeconomic theory and policy and technological change and employment as well as on history of economic thought.

Martin Heidenreich is professor of European Studies in Social Sciences at the University of Bamberg (Germany). His research interests are regional and national patterns of work, management and innovation. He is currently conducting a research project on growth and employment consequences of the new information and communication technologies.

Kurt Hübner is professor of Political Science and director of the Canadian Center for German and European Studies, York University, Toronto. His research focuses on the political economy of Germany and Europe; he is currently working on the economic, social, spatial and ecological dimensions of the regime of accumulation and mode of regulation due to changes in the currency relationships in the global economy.

Gerhard Krauss is associate professor in Sociology, University of Lille 1 and researcher at the CLERSE (Centre lillois d'études et de recherches sociologiques et économiques). His main research areas are innovation sociology, organization sociology and economic sociology.

Stefan Krätke is professor of Economic and Social Geography at the European University Viadrina in Frankfurt-on-Oder. He has written various books and articles on urban and regional development in Germany and Europe.

Martin Zagler is associate professor of Economics at the Vienna University of Economics and Business Administration and visiting professor at the Free University of Bozen/Bolzano. His research interests are economic growth theory, growth policy, labor markets and public finance.

Acknowledgments

This book is the offspring of the fortunate encounter of a research project on the first crisis of the *New Economy* and an international conference on the *Regional Divide* generated by the launch of new Information and Communication Technologies. The report on the first crisis of the *New Economy* and its aftermath got generous financial funding and intellectual support from the Hans Böckler Foundation, the research institute of the Deutsche Gewerkschaftsbund. Preliminary results of this research laid the ground for the design of an interdisciplinary international conference on the *New Economy* on both sides of the Atlantic, held in 2002 at York University in Toronto. This conference was mainly made possible by the Canadian Center for German and European Studies (CCGES) at York University. CCGES is one of the rare lucky cases where students, staff and faculty share their enthusiasm about the understanding of transforming trends in the contemporary world.

It goes without saying that neither the conference nor this volume would have happened without the willingness of the scholars to contribute to this endeavor. As it is often the case, as the organizer of this event I had to make a hard choice which pieces should be included in this volume. I hope to have made the right choices.

Special thanks goes to Martin G. Fischer, a graduate student at York's political science department, who acted as my managing editor and had to deal with the whole shebang I tried to escape from. Frederick Peters, another of our great graduate students at CCGES, helped masterfully to bring the chapters into readable format. This book would not have been possible without the strong intellectual and emotional support of my friend and colleague Daniel Drache.

As always, all remaining errors are mine.

Kurt Hübner
Toronto, June 2004

Part I

Macroeconomics of innovation

1 Spaces of innovation

Introductory remarks on the comparative analysis of the *new economy*

Kurt Hübner

The *new economy* and beyond

Reports on the death of the new economy are widely exaggerated. A couple of years after the failure of the so-called new economy, the drama of the burst of the dot.com bubble of 2001, it takes little courage for a statement like this. A closer inspection of the pre- as well as the post-bubble literature shows that today's condemnation of *project new economy* is as strong and widespread as was its praise during the 1990s. Both attitudes are understandable, at least to some degree, but nevertheless misleading. The expectation that the new information and communication technologies (ICTs)[1] would fundamentally change the nature of a capitalist money economy and prepare the way to a *nirvana economy* were unfounded from the beginning, at least if one takes the historical experiences of previous fundamental technological changes as well as the well-established knowledge of economic theory as measuring rods.

New technologies have neither banished the business cycle nor have they abolished inflation and unemployment. However, there is no doubt that ICTs have shaken the trajectories of developed capitalist economies in fundamental ways. New lead sectors have been established and existing sectors have undergone technical and to some degree organizational transformations: skill profiles of employees have been changed and the technical content of physical capital goods has been altered.

In a longer perspective, the economic surge in the 1990s and the years since the burst of the financial bubble should be understood as two sides of a deep-seated structural change of the given regime of accumulation and mode of regulation that are driven by the launch of fundamental technological changes. The appellation *new economy,* therefore, should not be taken literally but as a preliminary name for a growth regime that will or will not ultimately establish a compatible regime of accumulation and mode of regulation with the potential for a renewed *golden age of capitalism*. When exactly such a regime will evolve and where this will happen only time will tell.

From today's perspective it seems to many observers that there is only one answer to those questions: the new growth regime will be established in the US.[2] This proposition carries at least one implicit thesis, namely that Europe will fall back in the global race for innovations. Even though the financial meltdown was area-wide, the financial and technological resources that are still available in the US seem more than sufficient for the resurrection of ICT activities. While good reasons for such a perspective exist, the same perspective holds for some of the European economies. The burst of the bubble may not have changed the race totally but reshuffled the pole positions. What used to be mainly a US-dominated game has turned into a competition between spaces of innovations on both sides of the Atlantic.

Economies that have the capacity to generate fundamental technological innovations or have immediate access to them have the advantage of reaping the economic fruits of this fundamental change, usually in above-average growth rates of GDP and productivity. In this respect it seems almost dramatic that the economies of the European Union not only experienced a stop of their catch-up process with the US since 1995 but lost until 2003 one-fifth of their gain in output per hour relative to the US from the period 1950 to 1995 (Gordon 2004). This reversal in growth dynamics has raised not only political concern in European capitals but also started an intense academic debate about the reasons for this relative decline.

In contrast to the mainstream analysis of European growth of GDP and employment,[3] the contributors of this volume underline the centrality of innovations for economic growth. While the analytical connection between innovations and economic growth is very well established, there is an enduring discussion about the numerical impact of specific technologies on growth dynamics. Usually, three channels of influence are distinguished. (i) Innovations trigger investments, which improve the quality of the capital stock and generate increases in productivity. (ii) Innovations lead to new sectors of production which enhance employment. (iii) The use of product and process innovations shapes the methods of production on the company level and contributes to the improvement of competitiveness.[4]

As most of the chapters of this book show, such a Schumpeterian approach has to come with a distinct institutional flavor if it wants to overcome the blind spots of growth accounting practices. Technical innovations can be the motor of economic growth, but there is urgent need for good brakes, a navigation system as well as a developed infrastructure to allow for a sustainable drive. It is a well-established fact that not all economies have the same capacity to generate or access technological change at the same pace at the same point in time. Sometimes forgotten seems to be the further insight that not all national economies possess the *social capabilities* (Abramovitz 1986) to create the institutional matrix for successful innovatory activities.

There exists not only a huge gap in the distribution of ICTs between the club of the OECD economies and the rest of the world, buzzed as the *digital divide*, but this gap also exists inside the OECD club. A few fore-runners and a host of latecomers divide the pie unevenly.[5] It would be a simplification, however, to draw a picture of North American ICT-haves and European ICT-have-nots. The reality is highly nuanced. Although it is true that the US is leading the pack and Europe fell behind decisively during the 1990s, such a picture only gives a rough and cloudy image. Aside from the many practical problems for comparisons that arise out of highly different methods of measurement of ICT-activities in national accounts statistics,[6] OECD research teams have been relatively successful in gathering a pool of data that allows a comparative analysis of ICT between those two economic blocs (OECD 2004; van Ark *et al.* 2003).

Those data show that a small group of European economies have been very successful in installing, developing and exploiting ICTs; Nordic coun-tries such as Finland, Denmark and Sweden, also economies such as the British, for some indicators show an even better performance than the forerunner the US. Based on a back-of-the-envelope calculation using data on the share of ICT investment in overall gross capital formation, the share of ICT value-added in overall private business value-added and for the IT capital stock per hour worked,[7] the Nordic countries (Sweden, Finland and Denmark) are very close to the US. A second group consist-ing of the biggest European economies Germany and France on the one side and the two small economies of the Netherlands and Ireland on the other side follow those forerunners. They tried hard to keep up with the US and the European lead economies in ICT but only with mediocre results so far. The third group of the laggard economies consists of Greece, Spain, Portugal and Italy, which lag far behind with respect to every single indicator. It is this *olive belt* which makes the image of a digital transat-lantic divide.

While only sketched in charcoal, this picture is pretty much similar to other empirical attempts to measure the technological capabilities of capitalist market economies.[8] More concise calculations of the impact of ICTs show that the *usage hypothesis* which has been brought forward by analyses of the US case, is not very convincing in the case of Europe. First, the US user industries (finance, wholesale and retail trade) that show the highest growth rates of productivity during the 1990s have no counterparts in Europe. Second, improvements in productivity in Europe mainly came from the production side of ICTs. Both findings refer to the fact that dif-fusion processes seem to be far more developed in the US regime of growth than in its European counterparts (von Ark *et al.* 2003; Daveri and Silva 2004).[9] As Amable argues in this volume, the degree of usage and production of new technologies in a given economy depends very much on the institutional base of a growth regime.

If one accepts the argument that the capacity to generate and access cutting-edge technologies is the "single most important force driving the secular process of economic growth" (Bresnahan and Trajtenberg 1995: 1),[10] then the uneven spatial distribution of this capacity seems to be one of the keys to understanding the halt of the secular convergence process that occurred during the 1990s. Contrary to the arguments of mainstream economics, it is not technological progress *per se* but the ingenious *coupling* of technological and institutional changes that drives economic growth in the medium term.[11] Viewed from this perspective, it was the successful combination of technological breakthroughs and social innovations that gave Europe the world economic leadership in the nineteenth century; and it was the transition toward a regime of mass production and mass consumption that evolved jointly with a new economic role for the state in the process of capital accumulation that allowed the US to overtake the European lead economies in the early twentieth century.

History amply demonstrates that those periods of leadership do not last forever. While there are serious doubts about the argument that leadership comes and goes in a *regular* wave-like pattern where the former forerunners turn into losers and the latecomers come to the front, it has been convincingly shown that forerunners have not been able to hold their position over the long term (Arrighi and Silver 1999; Reuven y and Thompson 2001). Dominant nations in the global economy come and they usually go in irregular fashion. This seems to be different in the current situation. Unlike the avant-garde of European economies in the nineteenth century that lost their formerly superior position to the US, this dominant power renewed its ability to lead the innovative race and to safeguard its comparative advantages during the 1990s.

Even though the reasons for this resurrection are manifold, it seemed obvious at the time that it was driven by technological innovations, mainly ITCs, generated and made exploitable by the smooth working of the normative principles of a free market economy. The governments of the European Union's member states acknowledged the challenge of the revival of the US at their Lisbon Summit in 2000 and agreed on the goal to make the EU by 2010 into "the most competitive and dynamic knowledge-based economy in the world, capable of sustainable economic growth with more and better jobs and greater social cohesion" (European Union 2000).

The main instrument to make this happen would be an increase in research and development expenditures. The Barcelona Summit in 2002 confirmed this approach by explicitly targeting R&D expenditures up to 3 percent of EU-GDP in 2010 (European Union 2000). Given current expenditures, it would need an increase of about 33 percent up from 2004 to make this happen (Meister and Verspagen 2004). Even though it is a well-established fact that R&D expenditures show positive effects for economic growth, this linkage neither works automatically nor does growth get proportionally stronger with an increase in the share of R&D expenditures in GDP (Rodriguez-Pose 1999).

The *new economy* of the 1990s is the offspring of innovations that date back at least to 1971 when Intel introduced the 4004 computer chip and prepared the ground for the personal computer.[12] ICTs as the technological base of this evolving growth regime can best be understood as General Purpose Technologies (GPTs) that generate new products, new ways of producing new and old products and services as well as new ways to think about generating and using new technologies (Bresnahan and Trajtenberg 1995). Such transforming technologies neither fall from heaven nor do they appear very often in history. Steam and electricity are two of the few examples of GPTs that students of economic and technological history agree upon (Jovanovic and Rousseau 2003).

Following the work of David (1999), Crafts (2002) and others, ICTs will be conceptualized as the latest version of this kind of technology (see Erber and Hagemann and Zagler in this volume). ICTs can be characterized as an enabling technology that opens possibilities rather than provides final products. Such technologies not only need *innovational complementarities* (Bresnahan and Trajtenberg 1995: 84) in the form of adequate infrastructures, but even more so need complimentary institutional forms to come to grips with their main defining feature, namely *uncertainty*. As Lundval (1998: 407) reminded us, innovation is by definition a process where "all alternative outcomes cannot be known in advance" and carries a degree of uncertainty that cannot be clarified by consideration of previous probabilistic distributions. This area of the unknown opens up the chances for new products and processes that come with extra profits for the successful innovator. There are also increased chances for big failures. The short history of the *new economy* illustrates this two-headed monster.

From boom to bust

There are at least two versions of the tale of the *new economy*; both deal with the nexus of ICT and financial markets. One story talks about the upbeat expectations of the financial markets during the 1990s that helped to start a self-fulfilling technological/financial virtuous circle, nourished by the success stories of a few forerunners in the technological race. The eBays, Amazons and Oracles, SAPS and Microsofts of this world have not only changed the ways we think of companies and their modes of operation. It is foremost the products they and others have marketed and integrated into the daily life of average households of OECD-economies that have changed consumer as well as producer bundles of goods and services.

Even though it is obvious that the Internet and the computer have drastically altered ways of communications and economic as well as social forms of transactions, be it the way products and services are produced, or be it how they were delivered, it is less clear what the economic effects of the new products and processes look like. Neither is there any kind of clear-cut vision of how the optimal microeconomic business models and macro modes of regulation will and should look. Extrapolation from individual success stories to the macroeconomic level was, as investors had to learn the hard way, a problematic procedure. In the second half of the 1990s it seemed as if the lead sectors of technological renewal for a few developed economies passed the critical threshold, enabling them to harvest the fruits of technological change in the form of increasing rates of productivity and economic growth.

New technology firms listed at the stock markets and enjoyed enormous jumps in their values, which provided them with splendid amounts of working capital to drive their projects forward. When the equities of new economy companies started to tumble in 2000, the expectation that the achievements of the forerunners would more or less automatically trickle down to the latecomers was gravely disappointed. As a result, catching-up turned into a race-to-the-bottom where the free fall of the forerunner economies brought the latecomers along. All of a sudden, the new economy was like the emperor with no clothes and it was precisely this crisis that seemed to demonstrate the nakedness of this technology-based business model.

Even though the share of ICT investment in overall private investment was still comparatively small at the height of the ICT boom, the speed of those investments was extraordinary. In only a few years, ICT investment turned into one of the central investment categories, reaching close to 30 percent of non-residential gross fixed capital formation in the US in 2001. Even the ICT latecomers of the *olive belt* could mark increases of the ICT share in GDP of 5 to 10 percent. The build-up of this capital stock was spurred by drastic price reductions for computers and chips and increases in speed and range of user opportunities. Driven by highly positive expectations about the future profitability of these technologies, the equity prices first of "new technology firms" and then also of "old technology firms" experienced – even in historical perspective – an enormous rise, which was not covered by an increase in actual profits.[13]

This discrepancy, expressed in a stellar rise of P/E values, was the sharp point that burst the bubble in 2000.[14] This familiar business cycle story has had some peculiar twists. First, the capital accumulation process in respect to income in these new lead sectors was not profit-driven, rather a strongly wealth-driven activity. Due to the enormous rise in equities and overall asset inflation, companies used the increase in their capitalization value as collateral, as a tool to finance further investment and acquisition. The disconnection between actual and future profits and current fictional values produced the now infamous notion of *irrational exuberance*, a phrase that captures the systemic nature of the restricted rationality of the economic actors quite nicely. Second, the hype over the revolutionary effects of ICT went hand in hand with an enormous increase in income inequality. It was not just that the highly demanded knowledge worker got higher premiums for his or her skills. It was mainly the upper management levels that introduced *winner take all*-structures into the enumeration frame, a sign of the gilded income pyramid of a past which seemed to be gone forever (Phillips 2002).

The other version of the tale of the *new economy* follows a slightly different narrative by arguing that the burst of the bubble should not be understood as one more example of the regular crises so familiar in the history of capitalist growth but as a *specific* type of a crisis, which points to fundamental inconsistencies of the regime of accumulation and mode of regulation. Crises can be seen as decisive moments, like episodes in a heart patient's recovery.

Economic systems are not patients, yet crises play a similar role. This is particularly true for capitalist money economies that can intrinsically feature spans of long-term stability but reproduce and transform themselves through periodic crises. Crises act as corrective mechanisms, which punish the economy for overshooting and underachieving the functional requirements of a profit-driven system of markets and so prepare the ground for more stable periods of capital accumulation. Such corrections are not free lunches. On the contrary, economic crises come with enormous costs that are distributed highly unevenly between different classes of economic actors. Not all economic crises are born equal and one should add, not all crises are driven by the same factors. The distinction between two types of crises can help to understand the crisis of the new economy in a more comprehensive way.

From a functionalist perspective, small crises are defining elements of the regular business cycle (Juglar) that develop in regular seven to nine year intervals. Although such crises drive marginal producers out of business and by this generate unemployment as well as reduce tax incomes of the fiscal state, they do not necessarily induce fundamental changes in the economic behaviors of actors or in the economic/political structures of the overall system. Instead, they are built-in automatic correctors that bring derailed economies back on their established trajectories. In contrast, great crises not only indicate grave problems in the process of capital accumulation and profitability, they also hint at fundamental structural and institutional restrictions of the once-established institutional setting, which can only be overcome by deep-seated changes. In other words, great crises have a trajectory-changing quality.

Such crises have at least a twofold nature. First, there are those elements of great crises where the established institutional settings are exploited and exhausted and no longer provide the adequate incentives and constraints for dynamic accumulation of capital. Crises of this type do not show the same regularity as small crises and even more importantly, only develop over a long period of time, every thirty to forty years or so. The last example of such a crisis was the crisis of Fordism, which occurred in the 1970s and ended the golden age of capitalist accumulation and growth after the Second World War.

The second kind of great crisis has a related but different nature. The basic elements of this crisis are not the exploitation of an established regime of accumulation and corresponding mode of regulation but the lack of an adequate mode of regulation for a newly developing regime of accumulation. Unlike the first type of great crisis, this is a comparatively open process where adjustments and changes both in the mode of regulation as well as in the regime of accumulation can occur in an asynchronic way leading to non-complementary developments in both realms.

In the best case, this type of crisis leads to a new socio-economic technological paradigm, which is characterized by a complementarity between the mode of regulation and the regime of accumulation. Yet crises of this type do not come with such a guarantee. Great crises carry a trait of "Knightian uncertainty": actors are aware that they have to act differently according to the changing circumstances but they can neither rely on previous experiences nor are they equipped with a proactive knowledge. The search for adequate practices needs time and involves costs.

Figure 1.1 illustrates the complex relationships between technological innovations in form of GPTs, modes of regulation and productivity. Technological paradigms (TPs) induced by GPTs have the potential to generate increases in the growth rates of productivity as well as in the scope of economic activities and by this they can lift given productivity levels of an economy. Such lifts only happen if – and only if – the TP is accompanied by complementary institutions of production, consumption and regulation, indicated by a Social System of Production, Consumption and Regulation (SSPCR). Graphed as an isosceles triangle, ABC represents the best of all possible worlds. In contrast, A'B'C represents an inferior constellation due to its lack of a complementary SSPCR. This imbalance generates a comparatively lower level of productivity than in the best-of-all-world-state. Compared to the forerunner of the new TP, A still may represent a higher level of productivity and thus be an improvement in social welfare but one that is not living up to its potential.

As simple as it is, Figure 1.1 allows for some sketchy generalizations from the short history of the new economy. First, the concrete economic potential of ICTs was at no point clear for the actors. As discussed above, innovations are literally innovations because nobody knows exactly what the technological, social and economic implications of technological breakthroughs will be. Once inventions turn into innovations, their economic quality is characterized by a high degree of uncertainty. Economic actors are in a steady research and trial process that leads them well into the zone of risk and beyond. This *zone of uncertainty* is a general feature of economic activities that reach into the future. In so far as innovations hold promise of future profits plus technological rents, some actors will enter this zone of uncertainty and induce imitators to follow. What started with a nucleus of actors willing to handle the challenges of uncertainty

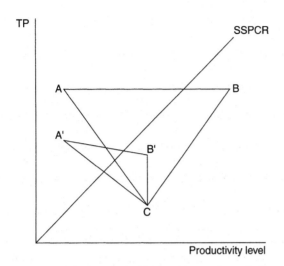

Figure 1.1 Technological innovation and regulation.

turns into a growth motor that attracts more actors from a variety of sectors.

Second, the economic exploitation of innovations is a time-consuming process. Their potential is not only unknowable in the present, but a number of costly trials must occur, many of which will fail. Given the trait of uncertainty, the observation holds that in the trial and error phase new actors dominate the landscape. It comes as no surprise that out of the sample of companies that ranked highest on the NASDAQ index during the 1990s the majority of players only came into existence after 1970. The economic success of first mover companies does not automatically translate into a macroeconomic success. The debate of the so-called *Solow Puzzle* has highlighted the time gap between the launch of innovations and its showing up in statistical indicators like labor productivity (see Erber and Hagemann and Ziegler in this volume).

As David (1999) and Crafts (2002) argued vehemently, GPTs like the electric dynamo and ICTs need time to properly adapt. Not only do companies need the time to develop appropriate business models, but new technologies also need infrastructural support in the broadest sense. Seen in this light, ICTs have not behaved differently than previous GPTs that likewise needed long periods of social learning to deliver the expected productivity rates. GPTs are best understood as moving targets, which develop into a range of new processes and products. Unlike Gordon (2003) who strongly argued that ICTs cannot live up to the "great inventions" of the past, argue that ICTs have not yet used up all of their potential. If David (1999) is right in that it took nearly half a century before the US economy understood the concept of the electric motor, ICTs will demonstrate their productivity and growth effects only in the next decades.[15] Even though time is an essential analytical category in understanding the delay between technological innovation and economic effects, it is only the social use of time that is of importance. Moving anywhere close to ABC in the graph requires a process of social learning as well as institution building.

Third, innovations can clash with given sets of institutions. The beginning of the twenty-first century has witnessed the turn from the first to the second element of a great crisis in the world of capitalist market economies. Based on the technological breakthroughs of the 1960s and 1970s, these economies have experienced strong processes of capital deepening since the second half of the 1980s due to the changing structures of investments in favor of efficiency improving capital goods, a process that accelerated in particular between 1995 and 2000. However, the promises of the technological breakthroughs were not realized immediately, at least not on the macroeconomic level.

It was only in the second half of the 1990s that significant increases in productivity and stronger economic growth could be observed and this was only true in a small sample of capitalist market economies. The hype about the new economy not only mirrored the strong beliefs and hopes in technology but also the desire for a new model of economic development that would act as the workhorse for designing the features of a post-Fordist society. It turned out that the economic upsurge was short lived, an indication that problems still existed, either in the regime of accumulation or the mode of regulation, or in the relationships between both. In this respect the burst of the dot.com bubble in 2001 has cleared the way and paved the road for more serious analyses of the so-called new economy.

Varieties of institutions

Earlier visions of a *new economy* are dead. However, the technological innovations that carried this vision are still around and make up the building blocks for a restructuring process of the capitalist world economy. Even though the forerunner economies of ICT-related activities of the 1990s still enjoy some of their advantages, it should be treated as a historical as well as an analytical open question whether the comparative technological advantages of the forerunners are a guarantee to keep those advantages dynamic and to reestablish them as technological and economic leaders. Much will depend on the depth of the ongoing restructuring processes in the various economies, in particular with respect to the institutional settings that have to be developed to enhance the benefits of the technologies brought into use many years back. The concept of *spaces of innovation*, therefore, not solely refers to new technologies but also to the overall institutional setting that makes technologies work.

In the last twenty years or so, much research has been undertaken to identify the sources of economic growth, theoretically as well as empirically. Technical change is not the only candidate that helps explain why economies grow. Established growth theories relied much more on variables like population growth or the quantitative accumulation of physical capital goods. Concepts like the New Growth Theory and Endogenous Growth Theory describe the importance of intangible investment in knowledge as driving forces of growth. As important as those efforts are, they should be understood as one more example of economists forgetting the history of their own discipline (Lipsey 2000). Far from being a new analytical concept, the main idea of recent efforts in growth theory have been around a long time thanks to the work of a variety of authors ranging from Marx and Ricardo to Schumpeter. Though it is true that, for example, the concept of innovation has been redefined since its early extensive use of Schumpeter, it is a fair statement to conclude that this concept is still in an early stage and needs much more in-depth elaboration.

Two dimensions seem of particular importance. First, the analytical as well as empirical relations between technological and social innovations have to be clarified. It may have been an enormous leap for economic theory to overcome the long-standing black box approach of technological change and to develop a more appropriate understanding of the role of technologies for economic growth. Yet, much of the work in the realm of newly established endogenous growth theory is still preoccupied with explaining the relationship between technical change and aggregate growth[16] and formally establishing the insight that long-term growth depends on innovation as well as on capital accumulation (Zeng 2004).

New approaches that allow importing the notion of "institution" and "embeddedness" into the realm of proper economics may improve our understanding. Unlike the studies which take the US as the benchmark for a growth-optimizing institutional model, the chapters by Archibugi and Coco, Amable, and Heidenreich in this volume amply demonstrate that a variety of institutional settings exist that can either lead to path-changing innovations or successfully contribute to the economic exploitation and enhancement of new technologies. Second, the economic theory of innovations needs to be connected with the spatial dimension of economic activities. Technological innovations in general and ICTs in particular are not public goods everybody can acquire for free as neoclassical economists are assuming. Thus, there is no analytical reason to assume that the global economy resembles a homogenous innovatory space. On the contrary, the global economy consists of diverse and competing spaces of innovation.

In such a perspective it comes as no surprise that a careful analysis of the spatiality of economic globalization shows that the free movement of finance, capital, goods and services has not resulted in the *death of distance* but given the notion of space an even higher relevance than before (Morgan 2004). This seems particularly true for the processes of innovation. Despite the fact that information can flow across borders faster and cheaper than ever before, knowledge still keeps its sticky character due to much of its tacit properties.[17] Geographic proximity may be essential at least for some forms of knowledge-based production.[18]

Even though the analysis of the patenting behavior of multinational companies by Patel and Pavitt (1991) and the argument that technology is an element of "non-globalization" seems to overstate the case, recent empirical findings on the spatial dimension of patenting (Verspagen and Schoenmakers 2004) still show a narrow trans-border clustering of patents. As the price to transfer one unit of information ("codified knowledge") from one actor to the other has decreased steadily since the launch of ICTs, the opposite has happened with tacit knowledge. Spatial proximity is highly important for creating and diffusing knowledge and renders tacit knowledge a comparatively expensive good. New knowledge is not only unstructured and complex but also comes with a flair of uncertainty for all actors involved. Economic spaces which have a pre-existing stock of knowledge and which are equipped with innovation-supporting institutions, therefore, attract more innovational companies than others.[19]

Making the argument that *geography matters* is one thing. To turn this hint into a theoretical approach is another. Following the lead taken by Krugman (1991), economists came forward with the concept of a *new economic geography*. The basic theory uses a general equilibrium model which includes increasing returns, transportation costs, some minimum regional production of manufactured goods and monopolistic competition. This model then allows to distinguish between the factors which lead to centripetal or, alternatively, to centrifugal spatial outcomes.[20] Unfortunately, empirical data as well as theoretical insights refer to the fact that such a dichotomy does not cover the variance of actual cases.[21] Regional spaces may be destined by geography but not absolutely. It is the history of spaces combined with its institutional capabilities that make them more or less open for new growth trajectories.[22] As Krätke and Krauss (this volume) in their case studies on new economy assets in Berlin and California show convincingly, linear models of spatial processes of innovations are not helpful in explaining concrete historical processes. Out of a broader spectrum of actors and institutions, it seems that three features seem of particular importance for innovational processes, namely regional systems of innovations (Fritsch in this volume), urban governance (Brenner in this volume) and transnational policy networks (Gibbs in this volume).

Though much has been written on the crisis of the new economy, many of the above discussed puzzles of this specific type of technological innovation are still unsolved and under investigation. Taking an institutional view on the processes of innovation, the contributions of this book undertake to analyze the degree of (non-) complementarity of the technological, economic, social, political and spatial changes which came with the launch of ICTs. In a strict comparative manner the contributions discuss the reasons for the significantly different trajectories of national economic spaces in regard to this particular kind of technological change. Furthermore, they ask how the regimes of accumulation and modes of regulation of different economic spaces deal with the processes of competitive innovation.

Although it would be an exaggeration to postulate that the chapters solve all or even most of the open questions, they will help to improve our understanding of the complex processes of innovatory activities.

The race for successful innovations between economic spaces has not ended with the first crisis of the *new economy*. On the contrary, the crisis of 2001 was not the beginning of the end of a new economy but the turning point for a capitalist accumulation and growth process, which is in urgent need of a new institutional matrix. The ongoing restructuring of the economic sectors that produce and/or use ICTs in the universe of developed capitalist market economies can pave the way for more sound economic trajectories that could generate increases in productivity and economic growth comparable to former phases of the "golden age." Such developments will not lead to a new economy in the ideological sense of a post-capitalist economy but transform the sectoral composition of the developed market economies and foster new institutional settings, which will have to reflect social compromises on the distribution of the expected gains in productivity.

Notes

1 Following the procedures of the different chapters in this book, I use a broad concept of ICT that encompasses hardware, software and communication equipment.
2 While such views were abundant during the highs of the new economy during the second half of the 1990s, the US euphoria has leveled since then. However, new economy optimism never vanished. Cooper (2001) is one of many who point out that the structure of the US economy has changed fundamentally and in some respects even irreversibly.
3 The OECD (2003b: 1) observes rightly that "throughout the 1960s and 1970s, countries with lower GDP per capita were generally growing faster than richer ones, leading to a gradual convergence in income levels. This convergence process appears to have reversed during the 1990s, at least among the largest OECD economies, as growth in the United States rose above that observed in Japan and in the major European countries." Whereas this observation is beyond dispute, the question is how this reversal can be explained. Led by OECD publications and mainstream economic analyses, the proposed recipe very much focuses on the degree of the welfare state, regulations of the labor and product markets as well as the economic role of the states. However, those analyses show serious deficiencies by neglecting the positive contributions of institutional settings (Schettkat 2001; Stockhammer 2004).
4 See OECD (2003a) for a policy-oriented review of those effects.
5 For an overview see UNCTAD 2003.
6 International comparisons of ICT-related economic activities run into several problems. One has to do with different national practices of dealing with soft-

ware products. In Germany, for example, software has been treated statistically as an intermediate product and thus does not enter the GDP calculation. In the US, in contrast, software is treated as an investment good and thus contributes to the overall investment expenditures. With the introduction of the European System of National Accounts, the European Union's economies follow the US procedure. The second important problem that makes international comparisons difficult has to do with the different statistical procedures in dealing with the quality aspect of ICTs. As ICTs not only show relative or even absolute decreases in price but also enormous improvements in efficiency, statistical offices have changed in favor of introducing hedonic price indices which include improvements in quality of ICT products (Linz and Eckert 2002; Deutsche Bundesbank 2004).

7 Figures for the indicator come from OECD (2003b) and refer to the year 2000. The distinction of the three groups is based on a maximum value of index point of 39 for the three indicators. The first group consists of economies in the range of 39 to 27 points; the second group is in the range of 26 to 13 points; and the third group ranges from 12 to 0.

8 The most prominent comparative indicators include the UNDP Technology Achievement Index and the Industrial Performance Scoreboard developed by UNIDO. Lately, Archibugi and Coco (2004) introduced a further index with an even broader scope that covers the creation of technology, the technological infrastructure and the skill formation. For the period 1990–2000, this indicator shows Sweden and Finland in the first two positions, the US at five and Denmark at nine. Despite the simplicity of my own calculations, the results closely resemble the ranking generated by the far more elaborate procedure of Archibugi and Coco in particular regarding the ranking for our second and third group of European economies.

9 Unlike Gordon (2003), I will neither argue that the productivity effects solely came up in the ICT producing sector, nor will I argue, as for example Oliner and Sichel (2000) do, that productivity effects stem mainly from the usage of ICTs. Both effects have to be seen in the light of different national regimes of growth.

10 While such a proposition seems self-evident, economic theory is still grasping with the concept of technological change and innovation. Attempts to overcome the exogenous character of technological change in the traditional Solow models are numerous but are still confronted with fundamental problems (see Aghion and Howitt 1998). The bottom line is that technological knowledge is no global public good. Even though ICTs are a driving force for the globalization of information and know-how, it still holds that those technologies do not automatically bring the "death of distance."

11 Mokyr (2003) provides an illuminating presentation on the multi-level relationship of long-term economic growth and technology.

12 These innovations drew from inventions that were generated by state programs to cope with strong competition of other economies and to prepare the ground for a continuing role as technological leader. Given the circumstances in the US, this endeavor took the form of *military enterprise* (de Medeiros 2003).

13 According to Ofek and Richardson (2002) the aggregate earnings of the Internet-related sector in the US was negative by February 2000.

14 Wheale and Amin (2003) provide an insightful analysis of the dot.com bubble from a financial behavioral perspective. Shiller (2000) calculated that p/e at the end of the 1990s were at their highest value of any period in the twentieth century.

15 A thorough policy-oriented analysis of the potential of ICTs is given by Ferguson (2004).

16 Aghion and Howitt (1998) for a survey of the literature.

17 Tacit knowledge is by definition a sketchy concept as it addresses the phenomenon that we can know more than we can tell (Polanyi 1966). In some sense, this is a residual category because it refers to the part of overall knowledge that exists but is not codified. Whereas codification, driven by ICT, makes information impersonal and tradable, tacit knowledge is person-embodied and context dependent. Nightingale (2003) provides some arguments in favor of a more careful use of the concept of codification and tacit knowledge.

18 See, for example, Morgan (2004). Distinguishing between those two types of knowledge also helps to understand the globalization of ICT activities. Globalization mainly concentrates on all those processes that deal with codified knowledge (Mann 2003).

19 This hypothesis is empirically verified in the German case (Dohse and Schertler 2003).

20 More on those "modeling tricks" in Krugman (1999). Acs and Varga (2002) give a brief overview on how the concept of a new economic geography can be combined with the concept of endogenous (new) growth theory. A helpful annotated bibliography on regional development theories is given by Dawkins (2003).

21 As the chapters of this book show, ICT-led growth regimes still come with a variance of institutional settings. See also Boyer (2004).

22 See David's (1999) critical stance toward Krugman's efforts to develop a general theory of space.

Bibliography

Abramovitz, M. (1986) "Catching up, Forging Ahead, and Falling Behind," *Journal of Economic History* 46(2): 385–406.

Acs, Z. and Varga, A. (2002) "Geography, Endogenous Growth, and Innovation," *International Regional Science Review* 25(1): 132–148.

Aghion, P. and Howitt, P.W. (1998) *Endogenous Growth Theory*, Cambridge: MIT Press.

Archibugi, D. and Coco, A. (2004) "A New Indicator of Technological Capabilities for Developed and Developing Countries (ArCo)," *World Development* 32(4): 629–654.

Arrighi, G. and Silver, B. (1999) *Chaos and Governance in the Modern World System*, Minneapolis: University of Minnesota Press.

Boyer, Robert (2004) "New Growth Regimes, but Still Institutional Diversity," *Socio-Economic Review* 2(1): 1–32.

Bresnahan, T.F. and Trajtenberg, M. (1995) "General Purpose Technologies "Engines of Growth?," *Journal of Econometrics* 65(1): 83–108.

Cooper, R.N. (2001) "What's New in the New Economy?," Paper Presented at PAFTAD, Canberra, Australia, August 20–22.

Crafts, N. (2002) "The Solow Productivity Paradox in Historical Perspective," CEP Discussion Paper No. 3142, London: Centre for Economic Performance.

Daveri, F. and Silva, O. (2004) "Not Only Nokia: What Finland Tells Us About New Economy Growth," *Economic Policy* 19(38): 117–163.

David, P.A. (1999) "Krugman's Economic Geography of Development: Negs, Pogs, and Naked Models in Space," *International Regional Science Review* 22(2): 162–172.

Dawkins, C.J. (2003) "Regional Development Theory: Conceptual Foundations,

Classic Works, and Recent Developments," *Journal of Planning Literature* 18(2): 131–172.

de Madeiros, C. (2003) "The Post-War American Technological Development as a Military Enterprise," *Contributions to Political Economy* 22(1): 41–62.

Deutsche Bundesbank (2004) "Zur Bedeutung der Informations- und Kommunikationstechnologie," *Monatsbericht April*, 47–57, Frankfurt: Deutsche Bundesbank.

Dohse, D. and Schertler, A. (2003) "Explaining the Regional Distribution of New Economy Firms – a Count Data Analysis," Working Paper No. 1193, Kiel: Kiel Institute for World Economics.

European Union (2000) "Lisbon European Council: Presidency Conclusions," Brussels: European Union. Available online at http://europa.eu.int/ISPO/docs/services/docs/2000/jan-march/doc_00_8_en.html. (May 15, 2004).

Ferguson Jr., R.W. (2004) "Lessons from Past Productivity Booms," *Remarks at the Meeting of the American Economic Association*, San Diego, January 4. Available online at http:// www.federalreserve.gov/boarddocs/speeches/2004/200401042/default.htm (May 16, 2004).

Gordon, R.J. (2003) "Why Was Europe Left at the Station When America's Productivity Locomotive Departed?," Paper Presented at the DEMPATEM Conference, Seville, October 18.

—— (2004) "Five Puzzles in the Behavior of Productivity, Investment, and Innovation." Available online at http://faculty-web.at.northwestern.edu/economics/gordon/FivePuzzles.pdf (May 11, 2004).

Henwood, D. (2003) *After the New Economy*, New York: The New Press.

Jovanovic, B. and Rousseau, P.L. (2003) "General Purpose Technologies," unpublished manuscript. Available online at http:www.econ.nyu.edu/user/jovanovi/GPT.pdf (May 13, 2004).

Krugman, P. (1991) *Geography and Trade*, Cambridge: MIT Press.

—— (1999) "The Role of Geography in Development," *International Regional Science Review* 22(2): 142–161.

Linz, S. and Eckert, G. (2002) "Zur Einführung Hedonischer Methoden in die Preisstatistik," *Wirtschaft und Statistik* 10: 857–863.

Lipsey, R.G. (2000) "New Growth Theories and Economic Policy for the Knowledge Economy," in Rubenson, K. and Schuetze, H.G. (eds) *Transition to the Knowledge Society: Policies and Strategies for Individual Participation and Learning*, Vancouver: Institute for European Studies, University of British Columbia.

Lundval, B.A. (1998) "Why Study National Systems and National Styles of Innovation," *Technology Analysis & Strategic Management* 19(4): 407–421.

Mann, C.L. (2003) "Globalization of It Services and White Collar Jobs: The Next Wave of Productivity Growth," *Policy Brief 03/11*, Washington, DC: Institute for International Economics.

Meister, C. and Verspagen, B. (2004) "European Productivity Gaps: Is R&D the Solution?," *Merit-Infonomics Research Memorandum Series*, 005.

Mokyr, J. (2003) "Long-Term Economic Growth and the History of Technology," *Draft Section for the Handbook of Economic Growth*, edited by Philippe Aghion and Steven Durlauf. Available online at http:// www.faculty.econ.northwestern.edu/faculty/mokyr/Durlauf.PDF (May 15, 2004).

Morgan, K. (2004) "The Exaggerated Death of Geography: Learning, Proximity and Territorial Innovation Systems," *Journal of Economic Geography* 4(1): 3–21.

Nightingale, P. (2003) "If Nelson and Winter Are Only Half Right About Tacit Knowledge, Which Half? An Aearlan Critique of Codification," *Industrial Corporate Change* 12(2): 149–182.

OECD (2003a) *The Sources of Economic Growth in the OECD*, Paris: OECD.

—— (2003b) *ICT and Economic Growth: Evidence from OECD Countries, Industries and Firms*, Paris: OECD.

—— (2004) *The Economic Impact of ICT: Measurement, Evidence and Implications*, Paris: OECD.

Ofek, E. and Richardson, M. (2002) "The Valuation and Market Rationality of Interest Stock Prices," *Oxford Review of Economic Policy* 18(3): 265–287.

Oliner, S. and Sichel, D. (2002) "The Resurgence of Growth in the 1990s: Is Information Technology the Story?," *Journal of Economic Perspectives* 14(4): 3–22.

Patel, P. and Pavitt, K. (1991) "Large Firms in the Production of World's Technology: An Important Case of 'Non-Globalisation,'" *Journal of International Business Studies* 22(2): 1–21.

Phillips, K. (2002) *Wealth and Democracy: A Political History of the American Rich*, New York: Broadway Books.

Polanyi, M. (1966) *The Tacit Dimension*, Garden City: Doubleday.

Reuveny, R. and Thompson, W.R. (2001) "Leading Sectors, Lead Economies, and Economic Growth," *Review of International Economy* 8(4): 689–719.

Rodriguez-Pose, A. (1999) "Innovation Prone and Innovation Averse Societies: Economic Performance in Europe," *Growth and Change* 30(1): 75–105.

Schettkat, R. (2001) "Sind Arbeitsmarktintegrität die Ursache der Wirtschaftsschwäche in Deutschland? Der niederländische und deutsche Sozialstaat im Vergleich," *WSI Mitteilungen* 11: 674–684.

Shiller, R.J. (2000) *Irrational Exuberance*, Princeton: Princeton University Press.

Stockhammer, E. (2004) "The Rise of European Unemployment: A Synopsis," Working Paper No. 76, Amherst: Political Economy Research Institute.

United Nations Commission on Trade and Development (UNCTAD) (2003) "E-Commerce and Development," *Report 2003*, Geneva: UNCTAD.

van Ark, B., Inklaar, R. and McGuckin, R. (2003) "The Employment Effects of the 'New Economy': A Comparison of the European Union and the United States," *National Institute Economic Review* 86–98.

Verspagen, B. and Schoenmakers, W. (2004) "The Spatial Dimension of Patenting by Multinational Firms in Europe," *Journal of Economic Geography* 4(1): 23–42.

Wheale, P.R. and Amin, L.H. (2003) "Bursting the Dot.Com 'Bubble': A Case Study in Investment Behaviour," *Technology Analysis and Strategic Management* 15(1): 117–136.

Zeng, J. (2004) "Reexamining the Interactions between Innovation and Capital Accumulation," *Journal of Macroeconomics* (forthcoming).

2 The *new economy* in a growth crisis*

Georg Erber and Harald Hagemann

Introduction

Until the end of 2000 there seemed to be a broad consensus in the economy that the increasingly intensive use of modern information and communication technologies (ICTs) had brought about a sustainable acceleration of growth and productivity. This was certainly the case in the US, which was the undisputed leader of this development. The economic upswing that the US had been experiencing since the beginning of the 1990s differed significantly from previous ones. Thus, at the Lisbon Summit in March 2000, following the US example, EU leaders decided to set their target at a 3 percent minimum annual real GNP growth rate over the next decade.

Since the beginning of 2001, however, a more sober view has come up with regard to such development prognoses.[1] Currently it seems quite likely that Germany will end the first half of this decade with an average annual GDP growth rate of 1 percent, well below the already low average growth rate of 1.56 percent for the 1990s. Hopes for the dawning of a continuous period of non-cyclical economic growth based on new technologies – a "golden age" of the information society (see Schwartz *et al.* 1999) – have obviously vanished. However, issues remain to be clarified regarding the changes taking place in long-term economic growth and the new types of cyclical effects the ICTs may have on the economy as a whole. Thus, there is an urgent need for research that investigates these questions and the explanations postulated so far. This will produce a clearer picture of the growth and cyclical effects of ICTs on the economy. Future research should especially focus on changes in endogenous growth cycles that are rooted in the new technologies.

The ICT industry's current crisis

The European Information Technology Observatory (EITO) recently issued a forecast for the market development of ICTs (EITO, Update 2002). According to this report, EITO expects 5.7 percent growth of the

ICT markets worldwide in 2004, while there was a 4.5 percent growth in 2003 (see Table 2.1). For 2000, however, the annual growth rate was still 12.7 percent. Both the US, which led the new-economy boom, and Japan are currently performing better than Europe. It is expected that these growth differences will continue in the coming year. However, in the US, with regard to ICT expenditure growth, ICT spending is falling behind the rest of the world including Japan and Europe. Compared with the forecasts published in spring 2002, the latest data published by EITO for the IT-industry have been significantly adjusted year after year to meet negative trends. This reflects the delay of a significant recovery in the OECD-countries. After the bust of the UMTS-bubble in the telecommunication industry, Europe experienced a particularly rapid decline from double-digit growth. However, the slow growth of the IT-industries is even more pronounced. To some extent, this might be a statistical artifact because no revised data for the telecommunication industries have been published yet.

The data currently available also enable us to predict a more severe growth slowdown for information technologies than for communication technologies. The latter's significantly faster growth until 2000 can be

Table 2.1 Annual growth rates of the information and communication technologies, 2000–2004

	USA	Europe (including Eastern Europe)	Japan	Other countries	World
Information and communication technologies					
2000	11.1	13.3	7.4	17.8	12.7
2001	−1.4	3.2	7.1	6.6	2.8
2002	−2.7	0.7	3.2	6.0	1.2
2003	1.1	2.9	4.7	10.4	4.5
2004	2.6	4.4	4.9	11.0	5.7
Information technologies					
2000	11.0	12.0	8.0	14.6	11.4
2001	−4.5	1.6	3.8	2.8	−0.7
2002	−6.3	−1.2	−0.9	0.4	−3.1
2003	−0.6	1.6	4.0	11.0	2.5
2004	1.1	4.0	5.1	14.3	4.7
Communication technologies					
2000	11.1	14.7	6.7	19.2	14.1
2001	3.9	4.8	10.0	8.2	6.3
2002	2.8	2.6	6.8	8.4	5.1
2003	3.5	4.2	5.3	10.2	6.2
2004	4.7	4.9	4.7	9.6	6.5

Sources: EITO (2001), EITO Update (October 2002) include only new estimates for IT in 2003 and 2004 plus own calculations.

attributed to the massive economic boom in the area of mobile phones in Europe, the US and Japan. In terms of world market volumes, the two areas possessed similar market shares in 2001: 1.133 billion euro for information technologies and 1.159 billion euro for communication technologies (for 2004 the numbers are 1.060 billion euro for information technologies and 1.318 billion euro for communication technologies). As in 2002 and 2003, the ratio shifted away from information technologies and in favor of communication technologies.

With regard to the various regions' world market shares, the US is the unchallenged world leader in information technology; in 2001 its market share was 42.5 percent. Europe follows at a distant second with 29.4 percent. In communication technologies, however, Europe (29.1 percent) is ahead of the US (25.9 percent). The other countries are just ahead of Europe with a 33.1 percent market share. It is likely that the differing focal points between Europe and the US revealed by these data will continue to exist in the future (see Table 2.2). In particular, the rapid upgrading of mobile phone networks in Europe to the UMTS standard can lead to large differences in market structures between Europe and the US. In light of recent developments, it remains highly uncertain to what extent the investment risks associated with this development will result in a sustainable competitive advantage for Europe.

At the same time, numerous jobs in German ICT industries are moving away from the production of hardware – and increasingly software – toward ICT services. This confirms observations of a shifting trend in world market shares. This also demonstrates the increasing human capital intensification of the information society itself: a decrease in the demand for labor and resources required for the direct production of ICT equipment goods.

Table 2.2 Forecasts for 2004 on the world market for information and communication technology

	Information technology	Communication technology	Information and communication technology
Regional world market shares in %			
USA	40.5	25.6	24.1
Europe[a]	31.9	28.9	27.1
Japan	13.0	13.2	12.4
Other countries	19.4	38.8	36.5
In billion €			
World market volume	1,060	1,318	2,378

Sources: EITO (2001) and EITO Update (October 2002) plus own calculations.

Note
a including Eastern Europe.

According to the German Federal Statistical Office, in 2001 there were 83,000 jobs in communication hardware (10.1 percent of the total ICT volume) and 108,000 in IT hardware (13.2 percent of the total ICT volume). The large majority of jobs were in the areas of telecommunication services (247,000 or 30.1 percent of the total ICT volume) and software and IT services (382,000 or 46.6 percent of the total ICT volume).[2] However, the slump in the ICT industry will significantly reduce the employment in Germany: in 2002, 28,800 jobs were lost in the ICT-industries. In 2002, the number of jobs in ICT-industries rose by 10.1 percent to 820,000. However, by the end of 2002, this number had declined to 791,000. In 2002, Deutsche Telekom, which accounts for 90 percent of all revenues and is still Germany's biggest communication service provider, announced to cut down its employment by about 50,000 jobs until 2005.

Since 2000, to these developments, mobile phone manufacturers (Nokia, Ericsson, Siemens, Alcatel) considered relocation from Europe to Asia, in particular to the PR of China, which is expected to be one of the world's largest growth areas over the next couple of years. This relocation of production sites from Europe to China led to substantial job losses in Europe since 2001. Even if the mobile phone market in Europe recovers, this will not change companies' strategic decisions. Thus, the jobs lost during the recession will not be replaced in the future.

Similarly, in 2002 the expectations of a solid recovery in the global semiconductor industry were erased. However, there were expectations for a strong recovery in 2003,[3] with annual growth rates of 19.8 percent and 21.7 percent in 2004. However, this short-term boom will settle down to a long-term annual growth of about 8 to 10 percent.

Moore's Law

According to many assessments, an important determinant of the growth effects induced by ICTs is the long-term constant increase in computer processing power. Over the last decades, this indicator has doubled approximately every 18 months.[4] The following analysis applies Moore's Law – in a slightly modified form (see Figure 2.1) – in combination with the data published by Kurzweil (2000).

A logarithmic linear regression of the relationship between computer performance – measured in MIPS (million instructions per second) – and the costs required for this level of performance in US dollars at 1998 prices produces a value of approximately 31 percent annually for the period of almost one century. Moore's Law would call for 58 percent. Thus, the fall in economic costs is not as extreme as the increase in physical processing performance.

If Moore's Law were to remain valid for the coming decades, computer performance would increase approximately one-hundred-fold by 2010 and more than ten-thousand-fold (in exact terms, by a factor of 10.231) by 2020

CPS per $1,000 US$

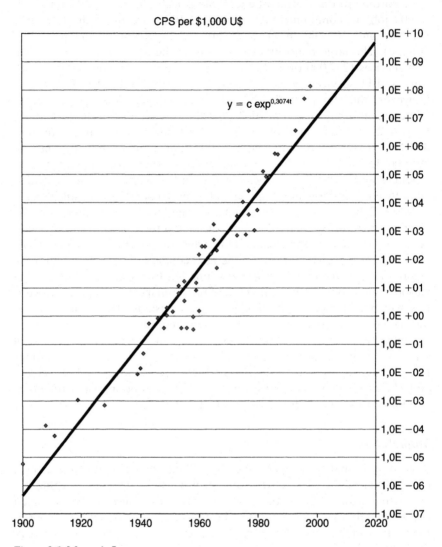

Figure 2.1 Moore's Law.

compared to current computer processing power, for example, that of a Pentium IV processor. Even in the second half of the 1990s, the US trend in cost reductions accelerated rapidly: it approximately doubled. Thus, this shows the rapid increase in future technological potential in information processing. However, the fundamental question with regard to economic effects still remains to be answered: is the supply side of a continual increase in information processing performance adequate to induce a sustainable rise in growth and productivity?

ICT-induced acceleration of economic growth in the 1990s

Since the middle of the 1990s, the question of what ICTs have contributed to macroeconomic expansion and productivity growth has been the subject of heated debate among leading economists in the USA. In his presidential address to the 113th meeting of the American Economic Association, Dale W. Jorgenson summed up the current state of research on this question (see Jorgensen 2001). First among the findings he presented is the idea that the dramatic acceleration of macroeconomic expansion and productivity growth in the US can be attributed mainly to the new ICTs. Second, as shown in Table 2.3, the long-term trend of a radical decline in computer prices has accelerated significantly since 1995. This has been accompanied by a dramatic increase in computer performance: from a decline of 15.77 percent on a yearly average in the first half of the 1990s to 32.09 percent in the second half. According to Jorgenson (2001), this can be traced back to a shift from a three-year to a two-year product cycle in the computer semiconductor industry. The motto "faster, better, cheaper" has thus become the trademark of the new economy.

Three channels of impact

The radical decline in prices[5] and the simultaneous improvement of performance have led to a major increase of investment in computers, software and telecommunication equipment, as well as a rising demand for information services. In 1999 alone, US businesses invested as much money in ICTs as they did in the entire decade of the 1970s. In 2000, this investment dynamic was even more profound and the result thereof was a dramatic increase in businesses' ICT-capital intensity. This has also played a central role in increased labor productivity since 1995. In this regard, three channels of ICTs' impact on the economy can be distinguished:

- *The first channel of impact* is direct and consists of the effects generated by rapid technical progress itself within the ICT-capital goods producing sector. Oliner and Sichel (2000) state that the growth of total factor productivity[6] in the US computer sector increased from 11.3 percent in the first half of the 1990s to 16.6 percent in the second half. Meanwhile total factor productivity growth of the semiconductor sector even doubled, rising from 22.3 percent to 45 percent in the same period. This demonstrates the outstanding position of the semiconductor sector among the ICT sectors with regard to productivity trends. Despite the relatively small dimensions of the ICT sector – even in the US, the sector only made a total contribution to value added activities of approximately 8.3 percent in 2000 – it boosted macroeconomic development and productivity growth significantly. The previously mentioned studies produced similar results when

Table 2.3 Rate of change of the GDP in the USA and for components separated according to inputs and outputs

	1990–1995 (1)		1995–1999 (2)		Difference (3) = (2) – (1)	
	Price	Quantity	Price	Quantity	Price	Quantity
Average annual percentage rates on growth						
Outputs						
Gross domestic product	1.99	2.36	1.62	4.08	-0.37	1.72
Investments in ICT	-4.42	12.15	-9.74	20.75	-5.32	8.60
Computers	-15.77	21.71	-32.09	38.87	-16.32	17.16
Software	-1.62	11.86	-2.43	20.80	-0.81	8.94
Communications equipment	-1.77	7.01	-2.90	11.42	-1.13	4.41
Information technology services	-2.95	12.19	-11.86	18.24	-8.91	6.05
Investments in other capital goods	2.15	1.22	2.20	4.21	0.05	2.99
Consumer expenditures for other products	2.35	2.06	2.31	2.79	-0.04	0.73
Inputs						
Aggregate income	2.23	2.13	2.36	3.33	0.13	1.20
Capital income for ICT services	-2.70	11.51	-10.46	19.41	-7.76	7.90
Computer capital services	-11.71	20.27	-24.81	36.36	-13.10	16.09
Software capital services	-1.83	12.67	-2.04	16.30	-0.21	3.63
Capital services for communications equipment	2.18	5.45	-5.90	8.07	-8.08	2.62
Capital income for other capital goods	1.53	1.72	2.48	2.94	0.95	1.22
Labor services	3.02	1.70	3.39	2.18	0.37	0.48

Source: Jorgenson (2001), own calculations.

calculating this contribution for the US: an increase in labor productivity of 0.2–0.3 percent. The main explanations for this first channel of impact are the positive effects which are generated by increasing returns to scale that characterize the production of ICT goods.

- The most important studies[7] state that a further 0.3–0.5 percent increase in macroeconomic labor productivity in the latter half of the 1990s did result from the increasing accumulation and use of ICT goods and services (see Erber *et al.* 2001: 217). These effects of capital intensification upon macroeconomic labor productivity constitute *the second channel of impact* of ICTs on economic and productivity growth of individual national economies.

- ICTs' positive spillover effects comprise *the third channel of impact*: they lead to "disembodied" increases in efficiency – that is, independent of investment – in the sense of "learning by doing" in the end-user sectors or accelerate product innovations in other areas of the economy (indirectly induced efficiency increases). The broad use of the rapidly growing potential for information processing and communication stimulates an ICT-specific innovation process throughout the entire economy.

These indirect effects are especially emphasized by the proponents of the new economy. They are, however, inherently difficult to measure empirically. Additionally, there are numerous methodological problems regarding their adequate measurement. Thus, the calculations of indirect effects that have been presented in the literature so far are highly contested and constitute the main reason for the divergent results of different studies. Only when the last two channels of impact produce major macroeconomic productivity effects can a sustainable surge in productivity and growth be expected.

ICTs as "general purpose technologies"

For the reasons presented, ICTs must possess the character of "general purpose technologies" (GPTs) (see Helpman 1998), that is, they must be applicable on a broad scale within the entire economy. Information technology certainly fulfills this criterion on the whole. However, the availability of ever-increasing computer processing power also requires that it is used in an equally growing number of products and production processes in order to achieve a corresponding growth in effective demand. The diffusion of ICTs in all areas of the economy thus constitutes one of the central preconditions for technological potentials to exercise a comprehensive impact on economic growth and productivity (see van Ark 2001). The broader the macroeconomic diffusion in new products and processes, the greater the macroeconomic impact in terms of efficiency gains. ICTs will only live up to their character as general purpose technologies if they take shape in "recombinant product and productivity growth"[8] – i.e. a productivity increase resulting from a manifold increase in consumer utility – through the complex value chains of industry and service sectors in the economy. For this to occur, however, further criteria must be met.

Thus, with regard to growth dynamics, if there are limits to the effective demand for products and services made available by ICT industries – neglected in standard growth theory – these limits will prevent computer processing power from automatically being absorbed, whatever its current price is. To use Say's terminology, "supply does not always create its own demand." It has been demonstrated as well that one-dimensional techno-logical progress, such as continuous increase of microprocessors' speed, could face a demand barrier due to a law of diminishing demand for higher performance. In his path-breaking book Christensen (1997) demonstrated through numerous industry case studies that innovators, persistently aiming to increase certain performance patterns of their prod-ucts (incremental innovators), face an innovator's dilemma (an off-spring of the well known prisoner's dilemma). Innovators following a different technological trajectory of disruptive innovations can even undermine markets of technologically superior producers if their customers are increasingly willing to substitute low-price-low-performance goods with high-price-high-performance goods. A technological trajectory's final boundary is always determined by testing if there are customers willing to pay enough for a certain technological product to cover its cost of produc-tion. Engineers often tend to develop high-performance technologies and products which face an insufficient demand due to their high price. Hence they are not successful on the market. Therefore one should be careful to accept simple rules like Moore's Law as a long-term forecasting device. It does not guarantee an accurate prediction of future market conditions. Technology-push innovations might not always succeed if potential cus-tomers are unwilling to pay the price and therefore spend their money elsewhere.

When relevant product or process innovations lacked in the past, the semiconductor and computer sectors repeatedly experienced major crises. The cyclical nature of the semiconductor sector is therefore fundamentally determined by fluctuations in demand. Without the orientation of the sup-pliers of ICT goods and services to the needs of their customers, the risk of a growing mismatch between supply and demand will constitute a signific-ant barrier to accelerated growth at the industry level as well as at the economy-wide level.

Demand side constraints

Currently, there is a worldwide weakness in demand for semiconductors and PCs, and in the area of telecommunication. For the first time, this has led to a significant slump in sales in these important ICT sectors in 2001.[9] On the one hand, these signs of a tendency toward market saturation stem from the fact that the current standard PC is already capable of processing multimedia digital data – that is, audio and video. Until recently these were among the most computationally-intensive processes involved in information processing and were driving demand to substitute less powerful by more powerful computers. Technological obsolescence dominated the demand for computers compared to physical depreciation of the computer equipment. Today, however, a modern PC can be sold to individual households and companies at prices once paid for significantly less powerful computers. Since the key driver of PC demand in the past has been the wish to obtain high-performance multimedia front-end terminals (PCs or others), the convergence of the performance of this equipment to this boundary leads to a switch back to a demand behavior governed by physical depreciation rather than by technological obsolescence. Thus, concerning effective demand, a further increase in PC performance then easily arrives at its limits. If producers of such equipment still assume that effective demand is dominated by a high willingness of customers to substitute old equipment against new high-performance equipment at a rate common in the past, they will have to learn this lesson from the market place.

On the other hand, there is a lack of corresponding increase in the demand for additional memory capacity for the CPUs (central processing units). Without storage of multimedia content of audio, photo or video data ordinary customers have a decreasing demand for more and more storage capacity. Nowadays, user data stored on high capacity disk drives are just a tiny fraction of the overall capacity compared to the huge area covered by extremely large operating systems and application software.[10] This has led to a deep plunge in the prices of products in these segments of the IT industry. Because of less extreme price reductions for other components, standard PC system prices have remained at approximately 1,000 euro for a commercial-quality computer without monitor, despite increasing performance. Thus, there is no evidence of a market expansion effect due to falling PC prices, as simpler and cheaper PCs are seldom offered for sale. There is currently also a fundamental lack of adequately innovative applications for the consumer market – with the exception of computer games – which would require even more computing power than the currently available standard (2 GHz processors). And even in this case, the workload of computing is increasingly transferred to customized high-speed graphic processors.

To overcome the IT sector's current crisis, linear performance improvement in processor capacity and a further cost decrease are not sufficient. In addition, new memory-intensive applications that stimulate additional demand among broad categories of buyers must be developed. Whether or not this kind of success will be achieved through rapid stimulation remains to be seen with demand in the coming months. A new generation of color-laser printers, multimedia phones with color displays or PDAs, DVD-recorders, blue-laser-disc-technology, digital-cameras and digital-video recorders, IP6-protocol-based network equipment, etc. might create a sufficient turnaround in consumer demand to facilitate a new growth-cycle in ICT-industries in the coming years. Furthermore, for a long-term growth trend to take place, it will be important that ICT-service innovations continue to emerge in the area of e-commerce and e-business, such as local-based services and new convenient one-shop services.

Key drivers of market development

With the availability of increasing high-end computer performance capacities, additional need to reduce implicit user costs arises. These costs emerge for users if they have to spend large amounts of time or money on learning materials, training or technical maintenance before actually being able to use the product. Thus, the bare hardware and software costs often only represent a small part of the total costs of using the computer system.

Thus, it was not only the development of higher computer processing performance or large and fast computer memory chips that was crucial for the success of the PC, but also the creation of an applications platform that enabled people who do not possess special abilities in abstract analytical thought to use the PC. The same is true for the Internet; the use of which would not have spread so rapidly without the creation of browsers that can be operated intuitively or the World Wide Web's standards for presentation of website contents. If PCs are to be employed successfully in schools providing general education and in households which possess only a basic level of education – and if they are to meet the needs of these people – then the costs of learning to use the new technology should not be too high. The usability of information and communication technologies is thus one of the key factors in market development and in opening up new customer groups and fields of application. As a result, effective demand is determined by the availability of simple user interfaces that enable an intuitive use of ICTs. Thus, in addition to those purely technical improvements in computer performance that constitute the key motor for long-term economic growth, other factors also play a role; in particular the usability or convenience of the product.

The end-user's need for maintenance services will probably also be reduced in the future through a more comprehensive range of services offered by "application service providers" (ASPs).[11] ASPs present interesting new market opportunities for ICT services. However, these will first have to be met with an adequate level of customer acceptance.

Product-skill complementarity

Product-skill complementarity is understood as the fact that the final design of the product itself demands a respective skill-level on the side of the users to unlock its potential usefulness for them.[12] Just as an automobile, which can only generate a utility as a means of transportation for an owner of a driver's license, a PC user must possess abilities and skills that enable him or her to achieve desired goals with the computer. With the increasing diffusion of modern ICTs in the economy and society, the related services offered to acquire the necessary skills to use these products have increasingly become one of the key motors of a long-term increase in demand for such products. This is particularly true for education and training services.

If all the possibilities for designing ICT products with a simple user interface have been exhausted, then the characteristics of that ICT product have established the structural conditions for a potential user. As the costs associated with the hardware and software are just a diminishing fraction of the overall system costs, demand for ICT goods can only rise if overall system costs decrease or at least remain constant. Otherwise, demand expansion will only be moderate or will not occur at all because the decreasing costs for hardware and software are exceedingly overcompensated by increasing costs for training and maintenance services.

The higher a population's level of education – especially concerning the use of PCs – the more marketable ICT products that require such knowledge and skills will be later. People who possess basic skills in computer operation can then put them to use personally and at no cost, or offer them as common capabilities to employers. Literacy in ICT is already becoming an integral part of general literacy (basic reading, writing, arithmetic skills) and employers no longer pay an extra premium in the form of higher wages for these kinds of skills. As general education is usually not financed privately and is considered as the standard educational level, skills in the use of PCs do not usually entitle one to higher pay. The creation of a general level of ICT competency in the population thus serves companies in various areas: it reduces their labor costs and also develops new markets for products that require such skills and taps into new customer groups. By providing cost-effective offers for multimedia education through the framework of e-learning, it is possible to significantly reduce costs in this sector as well.

Capital-skill complementarity

With the increasing differentiation of possible ICT applications in enterprises, the training costs involved in maintaining a pool of skilled specialists within the enterprise – commensurate with the productive utility – will equally rise due to capital-skill complementarity (see Griliches 1969). In particular rapid technological progress has the effect of shortening the life cycles of ICT products. At the same time, the product-specific knowledge connected to these products depreciates. For example, when a user switches to a new word-processing program, he or she must relearn to use the specific new product, which means that a more rapid depreciation of educational investments as well as of physical ICT products themselves takes place. Simultaneously, these losses in value must be compensated for by constantly increasing investments in education and training (see US Department of Commerce 1999). A system change that necessitates extensive retraining and instruction of employees can thus, due to the related costs, lead to a demand retention on the side of enterprises.

The rapidly growing employment possibilities in the field of education and training for ICT-specific industries demonstrate that the provision of an adequate supply of qualified workers on the labor market constitutes a growing problem for the economy with regard to the successful exploitation of the technological potentials of ICT. The lack of highly qualified workers in this field has long been lamented as a significant obstacle to economic growth (see EITO 2001; BITKOM 2001). Where domestic education and training capacities are not flexible enough in the short term or even in the long term to meet the growing demand for qualified specialists, international competition for these workers increases. The German federal government responded to this problem by launching a "greencard" initiative and an immigration law, which together are designed to increase the supply of labor in this segment.

Increasing mismatch

Due to user and employee competencies, the use of the growth potential generated by purely technological development is thus increasingly limited by the demand-side absorption possibilities for information and communication technologies. Thus, users' product-specific knowledge and abilities are decisive in restricting future ICT-driven growth both on the labor market as well as in the private sphere. These limits have increased dramatically in recent years due to the growing complexity of IT systems in enterprises as well as in the private sphere of individual households. Mistakes in system operation, downtime due to incorrect installation of new computer systems or system breakdowns due to computer viruses often result in disappointment on the part of enterprises or consumers with regard to expected benefits of these new products and technologies. This leads, in turn, to a weakness in demand.

The current growth crisis in the area of ICTs can thus be seen as the result of an increasing mismatch between purely technological potentials on the one hand and the complementary human resources required to make use of them on the other. At present, the central problem lies in society's inability to apply available technological potentials to achieve sustainable improvements in social welfare, as product-skill complementarities and capital-skill complementarities cannot keep pace with technological development. Thus, now more than ever, resources must be diverted into education and training in order to strengthen forces of endogenous economic growth (see Murphy *et al.* 1998; Romer 2000).

However, the supply side of the state educational system as well as the general and vocational educational systems, lack the necessary flexibility to quickly react to these labor market demands with an expansion of supply. With regard to the skill shortage, the narrow wage spread also provides too little incentives for individuals to expend efforts to learn on their own or obtain training (see Kohnz and Erber 2000). This lies at the root of the much-lamented backlog of ICT applications, which can easily develop into a cost-intensive bad investment when hardware systems are purchased without planning for the necessary human resources needed to operate them.

To sum up, ICTs can only stimulate long-term economic growth when major mismatches in product-skill and capital-skill complementarities are avoided; that is, when structural imbalances do not occur. If structural rigidities are not eliminated quickly, this raises the specter of falling back to a lower growth path.

Cyclical effects of ICTs

In recent years the discussion on the new economy has focused on the question of the long-term acceleration of growth in the US. Initially, this seemed to make sense in light of the fact that the US had not experienced any significant macroeconomic slumps in the course of the 1990s. However, the current recession in many OECD countries raises the question whether there is a need for more careful analysis, not only of the long-term effects of ICTs but also of their cyclical macroeconomic effects.

On the basis of "real business cycle theories" current theory has found that, along with monetary factors, exogenous productivity shocks are the main source of short-term fluctuations (see Lucke 1998). As a result of adjustment processes, the economy transforms these shocks into business-cycle movements.

These approaches supplant older theories (Schumpeter 1939), which were based on the overlapping of various business cycles:

- an inventory cycle (Kitchin),
- an investment in equipment goods cycle (Juglar),
- an investment in construction goods cycle (Kuznets),
- the long wave cycles caused by basic technological innovations (Kondratieff).

For a long time, the theoretical basis of general business cycle discussions was the pattern that is produced when the fixed periodicities attributed to each of these individual cycles are superimposed on one another.

However, concurrent with the neoclassical emphasis on the efficiency of an economy with flexible markets, this endogenous view of business trends lost popularity among macroeconomists. In the same way that endogenous growth theory generally did not correspond to the notions of the economic fraternity of this period – whose interest was reawakened only by the work of Romer, Barro, Grossman, Helpman, Aghion and Howitt – the question of an endogenous cyclical trend based on the new technologies has been largely neglected in the current economic debate. In light of the current business trend, this could prove to be a serious flaw and could be used to gain a better understanding of the nature of the modern information society's cyclical growth.

As several recent studies on this topic have shown, growth dynamics changes considerably when a non-neutral, that is, an investment-specific technological change is taken as a basis (see Greenwood *et al.* 1997). In the framework of a model with endogenous growth, the specific annual investment vintages, together with the structure of the capital stock, can lead to the emergence of endogenous cycles. Oscillations in investment in ICT goods thus have the effect of generating cycles, which in turn trigger an "echo effect" (see Boucekkine *et al.* 1997) due to replacement needs resulting from the previous investment cycle.

Regarding the current development in the world economy, approaches such as these have interesting implications. First, because of the ICT investment boom in the second half of the 1990s, the current slump can be interpreted as a new type of ICT investment cycle. Along with the disproportionately large economies of scale (when compared to the previous year), the non-recurring replacement pressure exerted by the threat of the Y2K bug and the strong incentive it provided to make early ICT investments could have triggered this boom. The latter would explain the drastic reduction in ICT investments after the turn of the millennium, as market saturation has occurred since then, at least temporarily. However, if one postulates a boom in ICT investment goods and uses the period of depreciation as a base, then – using a vintage capital model as a theoretical approach – one would be able to calculate a strong echo effect in replacement needs.

Likewise, the question of a changed pattern of market fluctuations still requires further research. Thus, at its core, the classical (Juglar) business cycle is based on a reinvestment need or echo effect. With the sharply increasing share of ICT-capital goods in total equipment investments or in the physical capital stock thereof, there is an increase in the share of investment that implies a need for reinvestment after three to five years – instead of after seven to eleven years – due to their shorter technological and economic lifetime. The echo effect of ICT-capital goods exhibits a temporal period due to rapid technological obsolescence that corresponds most closely to the inventory cycle à la Kitchin and less to the classical time frame of the Juglar cycle. This dramatic increase in the depreciation requirements for ICT-capital goods counteracts the tendency toward capital-saving technical progress. This is connected to Moore's Law and therefore constitutes one of the essential arguments in the explanation of Solow's productivity paradox.

To empirically test the explanation of the new economy's current crisis that has been put forward here only in summary form would require sufficiently reliable data, which currently are nowhere available. Nevertheless, a number of extremely interesting research perspectives emerge out of this study. The question of which endogenous cyclical patterns a market economy exhibits ultimately deserves as much attention as the analysis of long-term development which has been the focus of growth theory for a long time.

Differences in growth performance between Germany and the US

Unlike in the US, Germany's economy barely shows any sign of the new economy in the macroeconomic data on growth, productivity and employment trends in the 1990s. The contribution of the ICT-capital stock to overall growth of GDP was just 0.05 percent in the first half of the 1990s and doubled to only 0.11 percent in the second half. This has led to the media exaggeratedly portraying the US's return to a "golden age" of growth while Germany's economy plods along in a "melancholy state." Even a high growth of the ICT-capital stock of 7.35 percent and 11.65 percent in the first and second half of the 1990s (see Table 2.4) did not have a similarly strong impact on aggregate growth as it did in the US.[13] To some extent, this is due to the fact that Germany has not built up the same amount of ICT-capital stock in the previous decade. Therefore, its overall share of total capital just rose from 2.5 percent to 5 percent in the 1990s – much below the level in the US.

A further reason for this difference in performance between the US and Germany is due to a dramatic decline in the productivity of ICT-capital investment in Germany. German companies seem to be constrained by organizational rigidities and value chains that limit the effective use of ICTs. The capital-skill complementarity between ICT-equipment and the workforce also hampers an efficient use of ICT compared to the United States. This has triggered a debate on increasing immigration of high-skilled foreigners via greencards to Germany.[14] Furthermore, a smaller sector of producers of ICT equipment, software and services diminishes the impact of ICT compared to the US. This is particularly the case as the embodiments of ICT into traditional manufacturing products like machinery and electrical equipment or automobiles are not well calculated in the National Accounting Systems which favor the highly visible information technology investments in office computers but less so the embedded ICT in traditional products. Looking at input-output-table data

Table 2.4 Decomposition of the German GDP 1992–2000

	1992–1995	*1996–2000*	*1992–2000*
Real GDP growth[a]	1.29	1.78	1.56
Percentage annual growth rates			
Contribution of TFP growth based on			
working hours	0.89	0.85	0.87
Contribution of changes in working hours	−0.69	−0.01	−0.31
or			
Contribution of TFP growth based on employees	0.64	0.43	0.52
Contribution of changes in number of employees	−0.44	0.42	0.04
plus			
Contribution of real capital stock growth	1.10	0.93	1.01
Residential real estate capital stock	0.53	0.48	0.51
ICT-capital stock	0.05	0.11	0.08
Non-ICT-capital stock	0.52	0.34	0.42
Average for...			
Labor income share[b]	0.62	0.60	0.61
Average annual growth rates...			
Working hours	−1.11	−0.01	−0.50
Employees	−0.71	0.70	0.07
Labor productivity per working hour	2.40	1.79	2.06
Labor productivity per employee	2.00	1.08	1.49
Capital stock[c]	2.90	2.36	2.60
Residential real estate capital stock	3.10	3.05	3.07
ICT-capital stock	7.35	11.65	9.74
Non-ICT-capital stock	2.47	1.58	1.97
Capital productivity	−1.61	−0.58	−1.04
Capital productivity of residential real estate capital stock	−1.81	−1.27	−1.51
ICT-capital stock productivity	−6.06	−9.87	−8.18
Non-ICT-capital stock productivity	−1.18	0.20	−0.42
Capital intensity per working hour	4.01	2.37	3.10
Capital intensity per employee	3.61	1.66	2.52
ICT-capital intensity per working hour	8.46	11.66	10.24
ICT-capital intensity per employee	8.05	10.95	9.66
Non-ICT-capital intensity per working hour	3.58	1.59	2.48
Non-ICT-capital intensity per employee	3.17	0.88	1.90

Notes

a   In constant prices (1995 = 100). Deviations between aggregate and the sum of components is due to rounding errors.

b   Labor income share = ratio of labor income to GDP.

c   Capital stock including residential real estate.

for Germany, it becomes clear that nominal growth in gross production values in the computer industry is mainly due to a tripling of imports and a stagnant domestic production level. Thus, growth of this industry took place elsewhere in the globalized economy, such as the US, Japanese or Asian NICs and in European production locations such as Ireland.

The fact that the long economic upswing in the US led to both an acceleration of productivity growth and a sharp increase in employment is particularly striking. The result was an unemployment rate of 4 percent – distinctly below the level (6 percent) long considered as "natural" or the "non-accelerating inflation rate of unemployment" (NAIRU). The surge in the labor productivity growth rate caused such a striking reduction in the inflation pressures that American monetary policy was able to follow an expansionary course without endangering its objective of monetary stability.

In contrast, after the short boom of 1990/91 that was the immediate result of reunification, Germany's economy suffered a deep recession in 1992/93 and recovered only very slowly thereafter. However, until today, economic growth rates remain significantly below that of the other EU member states. Additionally, the difference between labor productivity growth per employee and per working hour denotes that a decreasing or stagnant employment pattern was highly unfavorable to facilitate a high productivity growth rate. The restructuring of the German economy, in particular of the East German part, could not be accomplished by a straightforward increase in labor productivity. Incapability in utilizing the costly ICT-capital stock by flexible working hours, with the exception of some large scale plants like semiconductor producers or a tiny group of start-up companies, further decreased the efficiency by lower operating hours for ICT-capital stock compared to other countries.

A waste of economic resources in building up overcapacities in the residential real estate market and weak privatized former state companies, which did not manage a transition to highly effective and international competitive enterprises, slowed down the economic transition of the East German states. Subsidies by the German federal and state governments which made the payment of a high level of wages in the East possible – e.g. the unit labor costs are still about 20 percent higher in the Eastern states than in the Western states with no sign of closing this gap in the near future – have decreased investment incentives in many areas of the East German economy since then. Investments could only be attracted at high social costs, that is by subsidizing investments to compensate for the higher wage costs associated with the East German productivity–wage gap. Many of these investment subsidy programs were cut down in the late 1990s because of their distorting effects and increasing budget problems. As a result, the investment boom of the first half of the 1990s came to an end.

Furthermore, the financing of the above productivity wage-level in East Germany was and still is accompanied by an increase of the social security payments for West German workers. Rising wage costs in Germany caused by high social transfers to the East put extra pressure on the West German labor market. This increased the incentive for German and foreign investors to relocate the demand for low-skilled labor abroad to other locations like Asia, in particular to the PR of China, or more nearby to the Central and Eastern European states, such as the Czech Republic, Hungary and Poland, where wages for low-skilled labor are just a fraction of those in West Germany. This lowered the investment and employment incentives in Germany in general and also contributed to the unbundling of the national value chains and changed the allocation structure from an efficiency-oriented toward a more social-justice based one.

A short surge of foreign direct investment into Germany associated with the deregulation of the telecommunication industry and the auctioning of the UMTS licenses in 1998 until 2000 could not be maintained after the high expectations linked to these developments ended up being overoptimistic. Higher expected returns on investment in the US, in particular in the new economy industries, encouraged high foreign direct investments to turn to the US. Megamergers like those of Deutsche Bank/Bankers Trust, Daimler-Benz/Chrysler, Deutsche Telekom/Voicestream and numerous investments into companies of the NASDAQ led to a significant shift of investment flows.

Although the annual labor productivity growth rate of Germany remained above that of the US until 1998, it would be false to assume that the stronger economic dynamics in Germany had been the result of higher speed of diffusion of new technologies. For decades, the catching-up process vis-à-vis the US was characterized by efforts to close the productivity gap accompanied by very limited long-term employment gains (see Erber *et al.* 1998). However, in the 1990s this resulted mainly from intensified employment reductions in less-productive sectors and the significantly lower capacity of the German labor market to absorb workers with lower qualifications.

As a result, Germany's strong lead was gradually reduced throughout the 1990s until it disappeared altogether in 1998. Ever since, Germany has not been able to catch up with the US. The macroeconomic consequences of German reunification provide significant explanations for this development. The acute need for infrastructure investment in the new *Bundesländer* of former East Germany limited the possibilities for investment in new technologies compared to other OECD countries. These developments were further intensified by a flawed tax policy, which led to excessive expansion of the construction industry and an associated massive misallocation of capital. Additionally, German monetary policy was more restrictive compared to that of the US, which prevented stronger demand growth and therefore higher productivity growth that – in accordance with Verdoorn's Law – goes hand in hand with economic growth. Thus, Germany's hopes of duplicating the US development of the late 1990s are thoroughly understandable. However, the cyclical downswing that began as early as the end of 2000, has silenced naive hopes that with the new economy, the US has seen the end of the business cycle or that at least any further recessions will be shorter or milder.

After re-unification, German investment activities had a rather different focus than in the US. This was the case because of the way in which the integration of East Germany was implemented caused inefficient allocation of resources. Additionally, it was partly due to wrong subsidies in the construction sector, a predisposition with investment into traditional industries, such as steel plants and basic chemical plants and significant waste due to corruption in the distribution process of these subsidies as well as wages that were higher than productivity. Furthermore, many infrastructure projects of local governments encouraged gold plating of infrastructure in areas where it was not needed, or where it only had the capability to create short-term employment effects. Because these misallocations continued over the entire decade, the traditional pattern of high productivity-driven growth was lowered in Germany.

As incentives for workers and investors were relocated away from the restructuring of the economy toward new high growth areas, investments did not generate a sufficiently high return. The newly created group of small- and medium-sized companies in East Germany also suffered from undercapitalization and a lack of experience to operate and sell their products in West German or even international markets, thus not creating a significant customer base. When Germany ran into a slowdown or mild recession, the West German economy caught a cold while the East German economy easily got pneumonia. This still makes the German economy vulnerable for the predictable future. It emerged during the 1990s as a laggard in growth performance among EU countries and it could become a sick man of Europe if major corrections continue to emphasize on social redistribution rather than efficiency.

Summary

In summary, with regard to macroeconomic growth and business cycle effects, the ICT research landscape is dotted with "uncharted territories" that render it more difficult to make exact assessments that are quantitatively reliable and to derive predictions for future developments. Further research needs to focus on achieving the following aims. First, it should attempt to close the gap in the data by creating a dependable statistical basis on the specific investment behavior regarding ICT products and the analysis of human capital creation, especially concerning ICT-specific qualifications. Second, it should develop new concepts for the theory of growth cycles that make it possible to specify respective hypotheses and to empirically test a theory of endogenous growth cycles against the background of technology-specific diffusion, by relying, for example, on the basis of the work of Murphy *et al.* (1998).

The initial question of this section, whether the new economy is currently in a crisis, can be answered by stating that on the one hand, the cyclical character of ICTs has become particularly clear in the current phase of the business cycle. As a result, we are indeed experiencing a growth crisis of the new economy. However, even in the midst of the crisis, the economic growth of the ICT markets still remains at 4.0 percent, which is significantly higher than the worldwide average of 2.6 percent. For 2003 and 2004, the comparison of growth forecasts between the US and Germany yields a continuing positive difference of 2.5 percent and 3 percent for the "new" economy in the US against 0.6 percent and 1.0 percent for the "old" economy in Germany (see DIW 2003: 2). Consequently, there is a continuous trend toward an information and network society.

Notes

* We thank Markus Schreyer and Stephan Seiter for valuable comments on an earlier draft.
1 See the results of the current "Six Institutes Forecast" of Germany's economic research institutes in DIW 2002.
2 See BITKOM's publication on the Internet on jobs in information technology and communication (in German), 2000. Available online at http://www. BITKOM.org.
3 See 2002–2005 Forecast: SIA Projects Double-Digit Growth for Global Semiconductor Sales, Press Release, Semiconductor Industry Association, San José, November 6, 2002.
4 Moore's Law refers to "the observation made in 1965 by Gordon Moore, co-founder of Intel, that the number of transistors per square inch on integrated circuits had doubled every year since the integrated circuit was invented. Moore predicted that this trend would continue for the foreseeable future. In subsequent years, the pace slowed down a bit, but data density has doubled approximately every 18 months. This is the current definition of Moore's Law, which Moore himself has blessed. Most experts, including Moore himself, expect Moore's Law to hold for at least another two decades" (webopedia 1998).
5 However, the rapid decline of semiconductor prices may be attributable not only to cost reductions based on technological efficiency increases in production but is also a result of increased competition between industry leaders like Intel and new market entrants. Price wars in the semiconductor market may have played a role in the acceleration of the price decrease observed in the second half of the 1990s. Aizcorbe (2002) provides evidence that the mark-up price for microprocessors of Intel has declined significantly from 1993 to 1999 as a market leader in this field. Usually such price wars are not sustainable in the long term and therefore cannot be expected to contribute to future productivity growth.
6 Total factor productivity, along with its share of costs, is the weighted sum of the partial factor productivities, for example labor and capital productivity. To measure the influence of investment in ICT equipment goods, ICT-specific goods are separated from other equipment goods.
7 See Council of Economic Advisors 2000 and 2001; Gordon 2000; Jorgenson and Stiroh 2000; Oliner and Sichel 2000; Whelan 2000.
8 See Evans *et al.* 1998. The modular character of numerous ICT products

enables them to be recombined into new products with new characteristics ad infinitum. Thus, depending on what it is equipped with, a PC can be used for a variety of things: playing computer games, taking measurements, producing CAD drawings, word processing, making music, accessing the Internet or making videos. The possible product combinations thus exceed the imagination.

9 For the most recent estimates, see EITO Update 2002.

10 As anecdotal evidence one should realize that on the standard PC bought from a supermarket chain like Aldi in Germany with Windows XP and a couple of application software packages pre-installed one has about 80,000 files stored on the hard disk without any personal data files store on it. If they are not extremely large and need high computing capacities because of complex calculations and high volume of these calculations, text or numeric data files are hardly capable to exceed the needs of ordinary customers at the same speed as in the past.

11 ASPs provide comprehensive services in the remote maintenance of hardware and software, offering services that are highly time-consuming for users such as data backups, software updates, etc. at a reasonable price. Because of the bundling of services at computing centers and the availability of qualified specialists there, the end-user can avoid a process that would otherwise be cost intensive. By offering special software packages at "pay-per-use" fees, companies can tap into new customer segments that would otherwise never purchase the licenses to these products due to the high price. Nevertheless, it remains to be seen whether or not the expectations for ASPs will be fulfilled on the market. At present, the ASP market is still in its infancy.

12 As we know from production theory, a Leontief-type limitational consumption function as the dual form on the consumption side compared to the supply side with its limitational production function just increases the utility of a user for a particular type of equipment as a durable consumption good or its respective services only when the user has the necessary capabilities to unlock its services.

13 Calculations are based on the most recent national data for Germany published by the national statistical office in August 2002 and the capital stock data for the break down into different types of capital stock are based on van Ark *et al.* (2002).

14 However, the current recession in the ICT and other industries in Germany reversed this tendency so that many of the new migrant ICT-workers were fired first when the companies shed labor during the recession.

Bibliography

Aizcorbe, A. (2002) *Why Are Semiconductor Prices Falling So Fast? Industry Estimates and Implication for Productivity Measurement*, Washington, DC: Federal Reserve Board.

BITKOM (2001) *Europäischer Markt Für Informationstechnik Und Telekommunikation Wächst Um 6.8%*, EITO. Available online at http://www.eito.com/Press-rel/press-rel-4.html (December 4, 2003).

Boucekkine, R., Germain, M. and Licandro, O. (1997) "Replacement Echoes in the Vintage Capital Growth Model," *Journal of Economic Theory*, 74(2): 333–348.

Christensen, C.M. (1997) *The Innovator's Dilemma*, Boston: Harvard Business School Press.

Council of Economic Advisors (2000) *Annual Report*, Washington, DC: Council of Economic Advisors.

—— (2001) *Annual Report*, Washington, DC: Council of Economic Advisors.

DIW (2002) "Die Lage der Weltwirtschaft und der deutschen Wirtschaft im Herbst 2002," *DIW-Wochenbericht*, 43.

—— (2003) "Grundlinien der Wirtschaftsentwicklung 2003/2004," *DIW-Wochenbericht*, 1–2.

Erber, G., Hagemann, H. and Seiter, S. (1998) *Zukunftsperspektiven Deutschlands im Internationalen Wettbewerb: Industriepolitische Implikationen der neuen Wachstumstheorie*, Heidelberg: Physica.

Erber, G., Hagemann, H., Schreyer, M. and Seiter, S. (2001) "Produktivitätswachstum in der 'New Economy:' Übergangsphänomen oder Strukturbruch?," in Heise, A. (ed.) *USA – Modellfall der New Economy?*, Marburg: Metropolis.

European Information Technology Observatory (EITO) (2001) "ICT Skills in Western Europe," *European Information Technology Observatory 2001*, Frankfurt: EITO.

—— (2002) "Update 2002," *European Information Technology Observatory*, Frankfurt: EITO.

Evans, G.W., Honkapohja, S. and Romer, P. (1998) "Growth Cycles," *American Economic Review* 88(3): 495–515.

Gordon, R.J. (2000) "Does the 'New Economy' Measure up to the Great Inventions of the Past?," *Journal of Economic Perspectives* 14(4): 49–74.

Greenwood, J., Hercowitz, Z. and Krusell, P. (1997) "Long-Run Implications of Investment-Specific Technological Change," *American Economic Review* 87(3): 342–362.

Griliches, Z. (1969) "Capital-Skill Complementarity," *Review of Economics and Statistics* 51(4): 465–468.

Helpman, E. (1998) *General Purpose Technologies and Economic Growth*, Cambridge, MA: MIT Press.

Jorgenson, D.W. (2001) "Information Technology and the U.S. Economy," *American Economic Review* 91(1): 1–31.

Jorgenson, D.W. and Stiroh, K. (2000) "Raising the Speed Limit: U.S. Economic Growth in the Information Age," *Brookings Papers on Economic Activity* 1: 125–211.

Kohnz, S. and Erber, G. (2000) *Lohnspreizung und Arbeitslosigkeit: Theoretische Erklärungsansätze und Stand empirischer Forschung*, Berlin: DIW.

Kurzweil, R. (2000) *The Age of Spiritual Machines: When Computers Exceed Human Intelligence*, London: Penguin.

Lucke, B. (1998) *Theorie und Empirie realer Konjunkturzyklen*, Heidelberg, Berlin, New York: Springer.

Murphy, K.M., Riddell, W.C. and Romer, P.M. (1998) *Wages, Skill, and Technology in the United States and Canada*, Cambridge, MA: National Bureau of Economic Research.

Oliner, S.D. and Sichel, D.E. (2000) "The Resurgence of Growth in the Late 1990s: Is Information Technology the Story?," *Journal of Economic Perspectives* 14(4): 3–22.

Romer, P.M. (2000) *Should the Government Subsidize Supply or Demand in the Market for Scientists and Engineers?*, Cambridge, MA: National Bureau of Economic Research.

Schumpeter, J.A. (1939) *Business Cycles. A Theoretical, Historical and Statistical Analysis of the Capitalist Process*, New York and London: McGraw-Hill.

Schwartz, B.P., Leyden, P. and Hyatt, J. (1999) *The Long Boom: A Vision for the Coming Age of Prosperity*, Reading, MA: Perseus Books.

US Department of Commerce (1999) *The Digital Workforce: Building Infotech Skills at the Speed of Innovation*, Washington, DC: Office of Technology Policy.

van Ark, B. (2001) *The Renewal of the Old Economy: An International Comparative Perspective*, Paris: OECD.

van Ark, B., Melka, J., Mulder, N., Timmer, M. and Ypma, G. (2002) *ICT Investment and Growth Accounts for the European Union, 1980–2000*, Groningen/Paris: Groningen Growth and Development Centre and CEPII.

Whelan, K. (2000) *Computers, Obsolescence, and Productivity*, Washington, DC: Federal Reserve Board.

3 Innovations, economic growth and productivity in the *new economy**

Martin Zagler

The stylized facts about the *new economy*

The information, communication and biotechnology sectors (ICBT sectors) of the economy have undergone rapid technological change recently. These technological innovations have had a significant impact, not only on the dynamics of these sectors, but potentially on the economy as a whole. This is due to the specific characteristics of the products in these sectors. ICBT products require little or no physical resources to increase the quantity supplied, they are in that sense non-rival in consumption. They exhibit little or no transaction costs – best seen with software sales over the Internet – and they exhibit "superstar dynamics," that is the inventor of a new product receives a (at least temporary) monopoly over the sale. Finally, it takes time and effort to invent new products in ICBT while the innovation process is uncertain, irreversible and exhibits an important role for the exchange of existing knowledge (Quah 1998).

Despite the relatively small size of the ICBT sectors – the share of the information and communication technology sector was only 8 percent of GDP in 1999 (Shapiro *et al.* 2000) – it has been argued that the impact on the economy as a whole has been so severe that a set of novel empirical regularities could not be explained by conventional economic theory any more (Greenspan 1998). These stylized facts include phenomena such as initially low productivity growth rates despite advances in technology and high rates of economic growth, a low inflation rate despite high rates of capacity utilization (including a low rate of unemployment), high volatility in stock prices and vast international differences of the development of an information and communication technology sector.

In the recent past, the ICBT sectors have been blessed with enormous technological advances. These range from the invention of the Internet to the decoding of the human genome. Evidently, these technological advances should foster total factor productivity. Total factor productivity is the change in output of a particular sector or the economy, which cannot be attributed to changes in factor inputs such as capital or labor. Assume that output Y_t is produced following a conventional constant return to scale production function,

$$Y_t = A_t F(K_t, X_t, L_t) \tag{1}$$

with physical capital K_t, ICBT capital X_t and labor L_t. Then labor productivity equals,

$$y_t = Y_t/L_t = A_t F(k_t, x_t, 1) \tag{2}$$

Taking time derivatives, we find that labor productivity increases due to capital deepening both in physical and ICBT capital and changes in total factor productivity,

$$\hat{y}_t = \hat{A}_t + \frac{k_t F_1(k_t, x_t, 1)}{F(k_t, x_t, 1)}\hat{k}_t + \frac{k_t F_1(k_t, x_t, 1)}{F(k_t, x_t, 1)}\hat{x}_t = \hat{A}_t + \alpha\hat{k}_t + \beta\hat{x}_t, \tag{3}$$

where α is the physical capital elasticity of output and β is the ICBT capital elasticity of output. These growth accounting exercises are fairly conventional (see Maddison 1987, for the survey). The critical issue has always been to determine the change in the real capital stock over time. Whilst we can identify the nominal value of ICBT capital, it is difficult to identify its real value. This is due to permanent changes in the quality of particular ICBT products and the continuous introduction of novel ICBT products, which renders the task of identifying changes in the price of ICBT products difficult. Using different price indices, different authors come up with different results.

Table 3.1 provides an overview of the results from four studies for the

Table 3.1 Growth accounting studies

	1972–1995	*1990–1995*	*1991–1995 (NFB)*	*1991–1995 (PNFB)*
	Gordon	Jorgenson Stiroh	Oliner/ Sichel	Rabitsch
Growth of labor productivity	0.66	1.37	1.53	1.58
Capital deepening	–	0.64	0.62	0.54
Information technology capital	–	–	0.51	0.34
Software	–	–	0.23	0.14
Communication equipment	–	–	0.05	0.05
Other capital	–	–	0.11	0.20
Human capital	–	0.37	0.44	0.24
Total factor productivity	0.02	0.36	0.48	0.79

Source: Rabitsch 2001.

period before 1995. The different measures of labor productivity are merely due to different time periods and sector coverage. We then obtain contributions to labor productivity due to the deepening of physical, ICBT and human capital and find that in all studies, they account for a large proportion of changes in labor productivity. Indeed, a large proportion of total capital deepening is due to the implementation of ICBT. Conversely, technological change in the ICBT sector has little impact on total factor productivity. In the words of Robert Solow (1987), "You can see the computer age everywhere but in the productivity statistics."

The fact that prices for ICBT products has major implications for the above growth accounting exercise has led several authors to develop hedonistic price indices for ICBT products. In order to solve the previously introduced Solow productivity paradox, Jorgenson and Stiroh (2000) undertake several quality adjustments themselves in order to obtain a revised deflation series for ICBT products. Recently, following the seminal study of Boskin *et al.* (1996) on the bias in the consumer price index, the Bureau of Economic Analysis (BEA) has revised the official US price index to include hedonistic elements. Whilst Oliner and Sichel (2000) have to resort to their own estimates of the final numbers that are based on the expressed intentions of the BEA, Rabitsch (2001) presents the first estimates using the final data for price deflation in ICBT products to assess the changes in total factor productivity due to new developments in ICBT. In order to ensure comparability, Table 3.2 presents its results using revised price indices for the recent past. Compared to Table 3.1, Table 3.2 finds dramatic differences both in the amount of capital deepening and in the change of total factor productivity. First, capital deepening in ICBT remains a dominant element in the explanation of labor productivity.

Table 3.2 Growth accounting studies – revised versions

	1995–1999	*1995–1998*	*1996–1999 (NFB)*	*1996–1999 (PNFB)*
	Gordon	Jorgenson Stiroh	Oliner/ Sichel	Rabitsch
Growth of labor productivity	2.19	2.37	2.57	2.48
Capital deepening	–	1.13	1.1	0.86
Information technology capital	–	–	0.96	0.86
Computers; Hardware	–	–	0.59	0.5
Software	–	–	0.27	0.28
Communication equipment	–	–	0.1	0.08
Other capital	–	–	0.14	0
Human capital	–	0.25	0.31	0.21
Total factor productivity	1.25	0.99	1.16	1.4

Source: Rabitsch 2001.

Second, we now also find a significant impact of changes in total factor productivity, which contributes at least one percentage point to changes in labor productivity.

The productivity paradox is not the only novel empirical regularity associated with the new economy. The second biggest issue is certainly the impact of ICBT on macroeconomic variables. Comparing the 1990s to previous expansions, we find a very different picture. This is illustrated in Figures 3.1a–c. Whilst growth rates previously declined after the first six

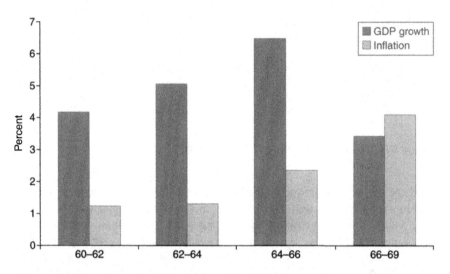

Figure 3.1a Growth and inflation, USA 1961–1969.

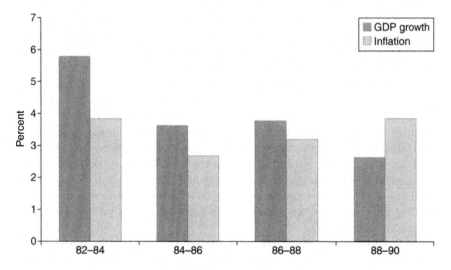

Figure 3.1b Growth and inflation, USA 1982–1990.

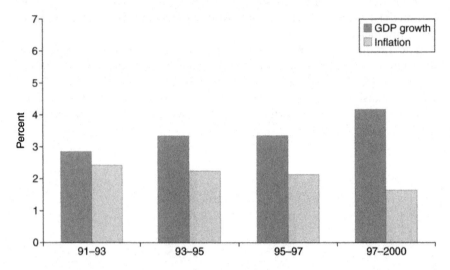

Figure 3.1c Growth and inflation, USA 1991–2000.

years of the expansion and typically vanished after eight or nine years, the
recent expansion has seen continuously increasing growth rates through all
nine years. In 2001, growth was still above one percentage point growth.
Even more surprising, we used to find inflation rates overtaking GDP
growth rates after the first six years of the expansion. This is no longer the
case. The recent expansion has experienced ever decreasing rates of inflation. The argument behind these figures was – and still is – that there is
something fundamentally different in the last expansion when compared
to previous expansions and that this is due to the nature of the new
economy. The empirical puzzle is how we can explain high and lasting
growth rates along with inert prices and whether this is due to ICBT
innovations.

The question which immediately follows is whether this phenomenon is
peculiar to the United States, or whether these phenomena can be
observed elsewhere in the world, particularly in Europe? Figures 3.2a–c
identify three European expansions. We find that European expansions
typically lag behind US expansions. The length of the first expansion, from
1960 to 1973, can be attributed to convergence after the war. Both in the
US and in Europe, inflation overtook growth after six years. The second
expansion exposes a familiar pattern: GDP growth rates would start to
decline after six years, whereas inflation rates again overtook growth rates
after a six-year period.

In the last expansion we can only identify seven years due to data limits
– a different image is presented. First, growth rates accelerate from year to
year, reaching their highest level at the end of the recorded period.

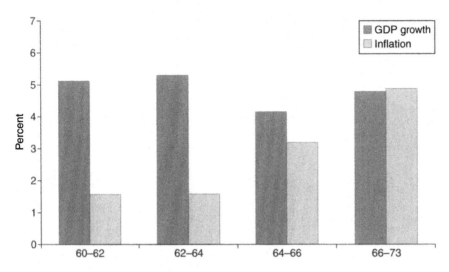

Figure 3.2a Growth and inflation, EU15 1960–1973.

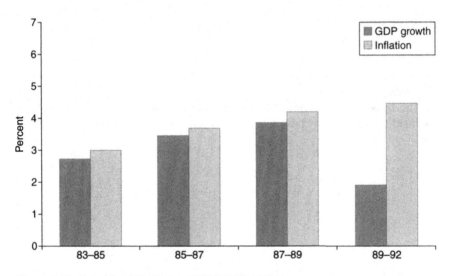

Figure 3.2b Growth and inflation, EU15 1983–1992.

Second, inflation rates again decline during the expansion. Given the relatively small growth rates of the last European expansion – in particular compared to the US – we find inflation rates that are initially above GDP growth rates, but then end well below. In that respect, the same novel pattern that has emerged in US macroeconomic time series can also be identified in Europe. However, this pattern is not homogenous across Europe. Whilst the UK follows the US and the general European pattern

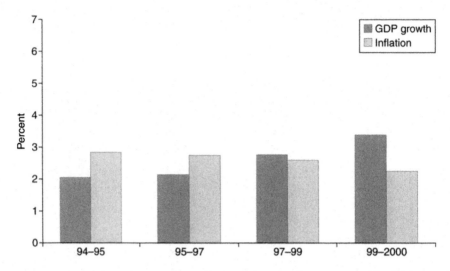

Figure 3.2c Growth and inflation, EU15 1994–2000 (sources: OECD National Accounts, own calculations).

in the last expansion, Austria, for instance, does not. This is shown in Figures 3.3 and 3.4.

In that respect, the new economy has installed itself in some, but not all, economies. The question that remains is what prevents economies from developing a "new economy."

The last stylized phenomenon of the new economy are stock markets. In the medium range, they have been more volatile than they were in the second

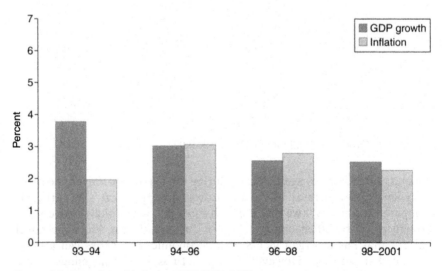

Figure 3.3 Growth and inflation, UK 1993–2001.

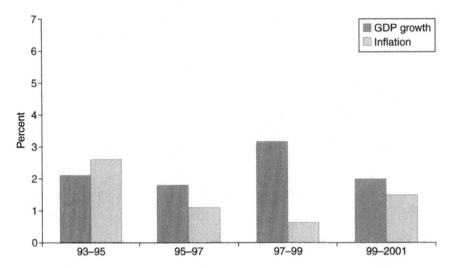

Figure 3.4 Growth and inflation, Austria 1993–2001 (sources: OECD National Accounts, own calculations).

half of the last century. From December 1997 to March 2000, stock markets roared. The New York Stock Exchange experienced a 26.6 percent increase. This development spread internationally, with London gaining 37 percent, Amsterdam 45.4 percent and Frankfurt even 77.7 percent. Most remarkably, however, was the increase of the technology-prone NASDAQ – it almost tripled its stock market capitalization and exhibited an annual increase of 76.6 percent. From March 2000 onwards, stock prices plummeted, with Amsterdam dropping 6 percent, Frankfurt 13.4 percent, London 9 percent – only New York slightly improved at 1.7 percent. Most startling was the performance of the technology values on the NASDAQ, which almost halved its value, dropping by 42.8 percent in only nine months (Helmenstein and Zagler 2001).

The chapter addresses these three stylized facts: the productivity puzzle, the seemingly unexplainable macroeconomic performance and the stock market boom which simultaneously accompanied the expansion of the ICBT sectors. The following section briefly sketches a model that specifically focuses on the product characteristics of the ICBT sector. The other sections will provide an explanation of these empirical phenomena.

A simple model

Let us assume that firms produce output using labor, physical capital and ICBT capital according to the technology given in equation (1), which we simplify to a Cobb–Douglas specification,

$$Y_t = A_t K_t^\beta X_t^\alpha L_t^{1-\alpha-\beta} \tag{1'}$$

According to Table 3.1 and Table 3.2, the deepening of non-ICBT capital has not been a major issue over the period of interest. We therefore assume that the capital to labor ratio is constant and equal to k, further simplifying technology to,

$$Y_t = X_t^\alpha (B_t L_t)^{1-\alpha} = X_t^\alpha Z_t^{1-\alpha} \qquad (1'')$$

where B_t collects all exogenous variables, $B_t = A_t^{1/(1-\alpha)} k_t^{\beta/(1-\alpha)}$. It turns out to be useful to think of this production function (equation (2)) to contain two separate technologies, a traditional technology $Z_t = B_t L_t$, which uses labor and physical capital and a new technology X_t, which uses ICBT capital.[1] Then we can identify the optimal transfer price p_t, which the firm would be willing to pay for an additional unit of ICBT capital by its marginal product,

$$\partial Y_t / \partial X_t = \alpha X_t^{\alpha-1} (B_t L_t)^{1-\alpha} = \alpha Y_t / X_t = p_t \qquad (4)$$

Similarly, we can identify the optimal transfer price for the old technology q_t,

$$\partial Y_t / \partial Z_t = (1-\alpha) X_t^\alpha Z_t^{-\alpha} = (1-\alpha) Y_t / Z_t = q_t \qquad (5)$$

As the total factor productivity B_t is exogenous, all revenues from within the old technology go to the factor labor. As one unit of labor produces $Z_t / L_t = B_t$ units of the old technology production factor, the wage paid to labor is equal to the transfer price times productivity, $w_t = B_t q_t$.

We find that the ratio of nominal spending for ICBT capital to nominal spending for other physical capital is constant and depends only on α,

$$\frac{p_t X_t}{q_t Z_t} = \frac{\alpha}{1-\alpha} \qquad (6)$$

Whilst this appears appropriate for a given state of ICBT technology, firms will increase their nominal spending for ICBT if new applications arrive. These are valuable on their own but also enhance the value of all existing ICBT applications. We will capture this feature by assuming that α depends positively on the number of available ICBT applications n, $\alpha = \alpha(n)$. Different ICBT applications are certainly no perfect substitutes. In order to further simplify matters, we will assume that the elasticity of output with respect to aggregate ICBT capital is identical to the elasticity of output with respect to a particular ICBT capital good i,

$$X_t^\alpha = \sum_{i=1}^{n} x_{i,t}^\alpha \qquad (7)$$

The optimal transfer price $p_{i,t}$, which the firm would be willing to pay for an additional unit of a particular ICBT application again equals its marginal product,

$$\partial Y_t / \partial x_{i,t} = \alpha x_{i,t}^{\alpha-1} Z_t^{1-\alpha} = p_{i,t} \qquad (4')$$

Providers of ICBT are innovators, who will be the single provider (directly or via licenses) for ICBT applications demanded by final goods producers (Bresnahan and Trajtenberg 1995). Assuming that these ICBT providers can turn one unit of the final product into one unit of the ICBT application[2] $x_{i,t} = y_{i,t}$, they maximize profits by setting marginal revenues equal to marginal costs $\alpha p_{i,t} = 1$. The mark up turns out to equal $1/\alpha$,

$$p_{i,t} = \frac{1}{\alpha} \qquad (8)$$

The mark up declines as the nominal share of the ICBT sector increases. This profit squeeze is due to the fact that competition within the ICBT sector gets fiercer as new applications partially drive out older applications.

Given that all ICBT firms will ask an identical price, the demand will be identical for all ICBT firms and equal to,

$$x_{i,t} = \alpha^{\frac{2}{1-\alpha}} Z_t \qquad (9)$$

As technology in the ICBT sector (equation (7)) exhibits constant returns to scale, we can identify a price index for ICBT applications p_t without referring to purchasing shares. Dividing equation (4') by equation (4), taking everything to the power of $\alpha/(\alpha - 1)$, summing over all i and eliminating quantities from equation (7), we find that the price index for ICBT applications equals,

$$p_t = \left[\sum_{i=1}^{n} p_{i,t}^{\frac{\alpha}{\alpha-1}} \right]^{\frac{\alpha-1}{\alpha}} = \frac{1}{\alpha} n^{\frac{\alpha-1}{\alpha}} \qquad (10)$$

where we have made use of mark-up pricing (equation (7)) to eliminate the summation.

The productivity paradox revisited

Productivity differs between sectors. First, productivity in the old technology Z_t equals output per worker, which equals $Z_t/L_t = B_t$. Note that the productivity of the old technology increases continuously at the rate of total factor productivity. However, as the share of the old technology in production $(1 - \alpha)$ declines continuously, we should expect a continuous decrease in total factor productivity.

In a particular ICBT firm, one unit of the final product produces one unit of an ICBT application, hence productivity equals one by definition, $x_{i,t}/y_{i,t} = 1$. However, the ICBT sector as a whole does exhibit productivity gains due to increases in variety. We obtain a measure of productivity of the ICBT technology straightforward by dividing output as defined in equation (7) by all ICBT inputs that is the sum of all $y_{i,t}$ final product inputs in the ICBT sector. In order to better understand the empirical results, we will pursue a different track. First, note that aggregate nominal spending for ICBT applications $p_t X_t$ must equal the sum over all expenditures for all particular applications $p_{i,t} x_{i,t}$. Making use of the mark-up equation (8) and substituting final product inputs for ICBT application outputs, after some rearrangement, we obtain,

$$X_t / \left[\sum_{i=1}^{n} y_{i,t} \right] = \frac{1}{\alpha p_t} = n^{\frac{1-\alpha}{\alpha}} \tag{11}$$

Productivity in the ICBT sector is growing proportionally to the rate of innovation. The reason is that the expenditure based price index for ICBT inputs (equation (10)) corrects for productivity gains at the sectoral level. If, by contrast, the ICBT price index would be simply a weighted average of all particular ICBT input prices $p_{i,t}$, the aggregate price index would equal $1/\alpha$ and we would observe no productivity gains in the ICBT sector. This was common practice until the revision of prices by the BEA. After the revision, we should expect the productivity increase to show up in the capital stock, which remains the dominant source of increases in labor productivity according to Tables 3.1 and 3.2. There is evidence that BEA adjustments of quality are incomplete (Pakko 2002). This implies that an even greater share of labor productivity growth should be attributed to ICBT capital.

Economic growth

Equation (11) allows us to interpret new technology as a product of the inputs into the new technology $(x_{i,t})$ and productivity growth in the new technology, which depends on the number of ICBT innovations n. Substituting this into the production function (1″), we can rewrite per capita output as a function of raw inputs and technological change,

$$y_t = Y_t/L_t = B_t^{1-\alpha}(X_t/L_t)^{\alpha} = \left(\sum_{i=1}^{n} y_{i,t}/L_t \right)^{\alpha} (nB_t)^{1-\alpha} \tag{2'}$$

We can now separate growth in output into an extensive component – the growth in factor inputs – and an intensive component – the change in technology. There is a natural limit to reinvest output into the new technology. It does not make any sense to reinvest all output $y_{i,t}$ into the production process, as nothing would be left for consumption. Noting from equation (4) that the nominal spending share for ICBT capital equals α and eliminating ICBT factor inputs from equation (11), we find that the share of ICBT inputs in production equals α^2,

$$\left[\sum_{i=1}^{n} y_{i,t}\right] = \alpha^2 Y_t \tag{11'}$$

Given that the price for the factor inputs $y_{i,t}$ is equal to the price of output Y_t, which are both normalized to unity, this implies that the nominal share of raw inputs is α^2, whereas the share for ICBT capital X_t was α. The difference, $\alpha(1-\alpha)$, is the profit share for monopoly suppliers of ICBT inputs, which they use to finance costs of innovation. Substituting (equation (11')) into labor productivity (equation (2')), we find,

$$y_t = \left(\sum_{i=1}^{n} y_{i,t}/L_t\right)^{\alpha} (nB_t)^{1-\alpha} = (\alpha^2 Y_t/L_t)^{\alpha}(nB_t)^{1-\alpha} = (\alpha^2 y_t)^{\alpha}(nB_t)^{1-\alpha} = \alpha^{\frac{2\alpha}{1-\alpha}}nB_t \tag{2''}$$

Ignoring the impact of structural change (changes in α), we find that per capita output growth equals the sum of growth is exogenous technical change B_t and the rate of innovation n. Note once again that we will measure the latter effect if – and only if – we correctly adjust ICBT prices for productivity changes.

If the ICBT sector is bigger, then we should be able to devote more resources to the innovation of novel ICBT applications (Zagler 2002). Hence, an emerging new economy may actually exhibit higher growth rates of potential output, thus easing the inflationary pressure from monetary expansions. But there is another important aspect that can explain why, during the last expansion, prices have not been accelerating despite higher growth rates, as there is an intrinsic inertia in ICBT prices. In order to understand this, we have to turn to pricing mechanisms of our simple model.

Prices and inflation

Final product providers pay implicit transfer prices to the old and new technology. Unit costs will equal the sum of costs for the old technology and for the new technology, divided by output,

$$\frac{C_t}{Y_t} = p_t\frac{X_t}{Y_t} + q_t\frac{Z_t}{Y_t} = p_t\left(\frac{X_t}{Z_t}\right)^{1-\alpha} + q_t\left(\frac{X_t}{Z_t}\right)^{-\alpha} \tag{12}$$

where we have made use of technology (equation (1'')) to express unit costs as a function relative to real sector shares. We can use nominal sector shares (equation (6)) to eliminate all quantities,

$$\frac{C_t}{Y_t} = p_t\left(\frac{\alpha}{1-\alpha}\frac{q_t}{p_t}\right)^{1-\alpha} + q_t\left(\frac{\alpha}{1-\alpha}\frac{q_t}{p_t}\right)^{-\alpha} = \alpha^{-\alpha}(1-\alpha)^{\alpha-1}p_t^\alpha q_t^{1-\alpha} \equiv cP_t \qquad (12')$$

which we can separate into a unit cost component c depending solely on α and an implicit expenditure based producer price index P_t, which is a Cobb-Douglas weighted index of the two transfer prices p_t and q_t. Pressure for changing producer prices will depend on changes in unit costs or equivalently changes in the producer price index P_t,[3]

$$\hat{P} = \alpha\hat{p}_t + (1-\alpha)\hat{q}_t = \alpha\left(\frac{\alpha-1}{\alpha}\right) + (1-\alpha)(\hat{w}_t - \hat{B}_t) = (1-\alpha)(\hat{w}_t - \hat{B}_t - \hat{n}) \qquad (13)$$

We find that increasing productivity-adjusted wages are a first source for increasing pressure to adjust prices upwards. As the size of the new technology increases, this cost-push element of inflation declines. This is the first bias in the inflation rate and already leads to a decline of the inflationary pressure. Over the past decade, this has been exploited by monetary policy in the US. If ICBT transfer prices are simple weighted averages of individual ICBT prices, the ICBT price index would be constant and the story would stop here. However, if individual ICBT prices are corrected downward to adjust for the added benefit for one application from the adoption of another,[4] it turns out that inflationary pressure further declines. Evidently, the faster new applications get adopted, that is the faster the rate of innovation, the more inert prices will be.

The regional divide

In the previous chapter, we assumed that when firms make their pricing decisions, they consider the state of the ICB technologies as given. The result is certainly a good approximation in the short term. In the long term, however, firms can realize cost advantages by adopting new ICBT technologies at a greater extent. In the long term, perfect competition drives unit costs to the price of the final product, which we have normalized to unity, a result which we can obtain by substituting equation (6) into equation (12). But this implies that unit costs cP_t as defined in equation (12') will equal unity, or

$$p_t^\alpha q_t^{1-\alpha} = \alpha^\alpha(1-\alpha)^{1-\alpha} \qquad (12'')$$

This gives us an expression for relative prices, which we can use to identify relative real shares of the old to the new technology,

$$\frac{X_t}{Z_t} = \frac{\alpha}{1-\alpha}\frac{q_t}{p_t} = \frac{\alpha}{1-\alpha}\frac{1-\alpha}{\alpha}\left(\frac{p_t}{\alpha}\right)^{\frac{1}{\alpha-1}} = \alpha^{\frac{2}{1-\alpha}}n^{\frac{1}{\alpha}} \qquad (6')$$

An increase in the number of innovations will exhibit an unambiguously positive impact on the nominal share of the ICBT sector, α. Hence the first term will always be increasing over time. A sufficient condition for an increasing relative real share of the new technology would be the second term increased over time, which, taking logs and derivatives, will be the case if, and only if,

$$\epsilon \ln n < 1 \qquad\qquad (6'')$$

where ϵ is the elasticity of the ICBT sector share with respect to ICBT innovation. A large sector share will typically imply a small elasticity, as there will be no more room for an expansion of the ICBT sector. Hence an excessively large number of ICBT applications will help an economy to overcome this technological threshold. In this respect, only technology prone countries will manage to develop ICBT production techniques, whilst others will stay behind. This explains the regional divide in the use of ICB technologies and the emergence of the new economy in some parts of the world, but not in others.

Stock market volatility[5]

Over the medium term, stock markets have been more volatile over the last few years than they were in the second half of the last century. The adoption of new technologies is one reason for the considerably higher volatility. We will analyze this difference within the model framework by investigating the different reactions of firms predominantly using the old technology (with α close to zero) and firms predominantly using the new technology (with α close to unity) to a sudden small λ-fold increase of intermediate inputs, driven, for instance, by an increase in productivity in the respective sector.

With the old technology, an increase in supply, $dy_t/y_t = \lambda$, will not change profits, as perfect competition ensures zero profits. In an efficient stock market, the price of a stock reflects the discounted stream of future profits. Hence stock prices should not react to the productivity shock. In order to sell the additional output, firms will have to cut prices by a proportional amount, $dP_t/P_t = \lambda$. Unless productivity gains permanently render every unit of labor more efficient, this will lead to losses and eventually a withdrawal of the original increase in supply.

With the new technology, an increase in the supply of each ICBT application, $dx_{i,t}/x_{i,t} = \lambda$, will force every ICBT provider to cut prices. Given a price elasticity of demand equal to $1/(1-\alpha)$, firms will cut prices by $(1-\alpha)\lambda$. As profits in the provision of ICBT applications are proportional to revenues, this will lead to an increase in profits by $\alpha\lambda$. Profits will therefore increase less than proportionally, but given a discount rate of r, the price of the company stock will increase more than proportionally if $\alpha > r$, or if the share of ICBT use in production exceeds the real interest rate. Hence it comes as no surprise that the stock market boom set in only after the ICBT share was exceeding roughly 6 percent. By itself, this can explain the information technology stock market boom.

As is evident, an increase in quantity of all ICBT applications will induce a proportional increase in aggregate factor supply (equation (7)), $dX_t/X_t = dx_{i,t}/x_{i,t} = \lambda$ and a decrease in every price will lead to a proportional decline in the price index (equation (10)), $dp_t/p_t = dp_{i,t}/p_{i,t} = -(1 - \alpha)\lambda$. An increase in profits increases firms' incentives to engage in innovation. Free entry ensures that the number of firms in the service sector will drive discounted running profits down to their previous level, which is just enough to finance the cost of innovation.

There are three possible ways in which this process comes to an end. First, the initial effect – in our example an increase in productivity – is reversed. Second, the expansion in quantity raises the demand for labor. If the service sector is large enough, this will raise wages, inducing an increase in prices. Not surprisingly, on the doomsday of the information technology stock market boom, warehouse workers at the Internet book seller Amazon were threatening to strike for higher wages. Third, once the first new innovators succeed to enter the product market, they will start to have an impact on aggregate prices and quantities. Aggregate ICBT provision will increase, whilst the ICBT price index (equation (10)) will fall. This implies that the increase in quantity of every ICBT provider falls and the bubble begins to implode.

Conclusions

The aim of this chapter was to explain several distinguished stylized facts of the new economy. We found that these facts are low rates of total factor productivity despite high rates of innovation in information-, communication- and biotechnologies (ICBT), but high rates of capital deepening due to investment in ICBT, an inflation inertia despite high rates of economic growth and full capacity utilization, regional differences in the emergence of macroeconomic phenomena associated with the new economy and an increasing volatility in stock markets.

A simple model of production, which embeds both an old technology and a new technology in a single production function, can mimic these facts surprisingly well. If ICBT innovations increase productivity only through their impact on existing or parallel innovations, we should expect the productivity gains to show up in the capital deepening term in a conventional growth accounting equation and not in total factor productivity, and even then only if one correctly estimates the impact of innovations on ICBT prices.

Additionally, inflation rates are biased downwards for two reasons. First, the declining share of the old technology in production makes cost-push elements from wage increases above productivity less and less important in determining the pressure on firms to adjust prices upwards. Second, as new ICBT innovations render existing ICBT innovations more productive, actual prices of ICBT applications have to be adjusted downward with an increase in the number of ICBT applications, or adjusted for the innovation rate in ICBT.

Despite the fact that in principal every firm has access to the new technology, not all firms will tend to adopt it. If there is a low share of ICB technologies in place and if there is a low number of ICBT applications available – examples are political restrictions to use the Internet, technical limits for mobile phones, or legal restrictions to experiment with genetic modifications – then firms will continue to use the old technology, even if a shift to new technologies has already taken place in other parts of the world.

Finally, the new technology intrinsically generates profits for ICBT providers in order to finance the cost of innovation. Given that future profits are uncertain, even rational changes in profit expectations can lead to more than proportional changes in stock prices, resulting in an increasing volatility of stock markets.

Notes

* I would like to thank Steve Ambler, Andrea Ichino, Marcel Jensen, Alfred Taudes, Hank Thomassen, Brigitte Unger and two anonymous referees for fruitful comments and discussions.
1 As an example, you may think of a farmer producing corn. The farmer can either use traditional technology only, which uses land, a tractor and manual labor to produce corn. Or the farmer can add biotechnology to the production technology, which would, for instance, genetically manipulate the corn in order to best fit the conditions of the soil and climate to maximize output.
2 Sticking to our example of the corn farmer, once corn has been genetically modified, the technology for producing the crops for next year is to put aside part of the harvest, hence one unit of output produces next year's input.
3 We consider firms to be myopic with respect to shifts in technology, ignoring that an increasing number of ICBT innovations induces an increasing application of ICBT technology. In that respect, firms consider nominal expenditure for ICBT α as given.
4 Imagine someone inventing a new and faster processor or IT platform with identical production costs as the previous model. If nobody invents an application that makes use of this processor or platform and can only run on the new model, the sale price of the new model cannot exceed the sale price of the old model. Once an application that only runs on the new model gets invented, the firm can ask for a higher price, but this is matched by higher productivity of the new model. Subtracting the innovation rate from ICBT prices is therefore a good proxy to capture the productivity adjusted increase in ICBT prices. I am indebted to Alfred Taudes for turning my attention to this point.
5 The exposition of this chapter draws on Zagler (2002).

Bibliography

Boskin, M., Dulberger, E., Gordon, R., Grilichies, Z. and Jorgenson, D. (1996) *Toward a More Accurate Measure of the Cost of Living*, Final Report to the Senate Finance Committee from the Advisory Commission to Study the Consumer Price Index.

Bresnahan, T. and Trajtenberg, M. (1995) "General Purpose Technologies: 'Engines of Growth'," *Journal of Econometrics* 65(1): 83–108.

Gordon, R.J. (2000) "Does the New Economy Measure Up to the Great Inventions of the Past?," *Journal of Economic Perspectives* 14(4): 49–74.

Greenspan, A. (1998) *Question: Is There a New Economy?*, Remarks by Chairman Alan Greenspan at the Haas Annual Business Faculty Research Dialogue, University of California Available online at http://www.federalreserve.gov/boarddocs/speeches/1998/19980904.htm (accessed November 2, 2003).

Helmenstein, C. and Zagler, M. (2001) "Economic Performance: Between a New Economy Boom or Bust?" *Wirtschaftspolitische Blätter* 48(2–3): 228–237.

Jorgenson, D.W. and Stiroh, K. (2000) "Raising the Speed Limit: U.S. Economic Growth in the Information Age," *Brookings Papers on Economic Activity* 1: 125–211.

Maddison, A. (1987) "Growth and Slowdown in Advanced Capitalist Economies: Techniques of Quantitative Assessment," *Journal of Economic Literature* 25(2): 649–698.

Oliner, S.D. and Sichel, D.E. (2000) "The Resurgence of Growth in the Late 1990s: Is Information Technology the Story?," *Journal of Economic Perspectives* 14(4): 3–22.

Pakko, M.R. (2002) "The High-Tech Investment Boom and Economic Growth in the 1990s: Accounting for Quality," *Federal Reserve Bank of St. Louis Review* 84(2): 3–18.

Quah, D. (1998) "A Weightless Economy," *The Unesco Courier* December: 18–20.

Rabitsch, K. (2001) "The New Economy: A Comprehensive Challenge of a Claimed Paradigm on the Basis of the US Economy in the 1990s," Thesis, Wirtschaftsuniversität Wien.

Shapiro, R., Lee Price, R. and Mayer, J. (2000) *Digital Economy 2000*, Washington, DC: US Department of Commerce.

Solow, R. (1987) "Review of Manufacturing Matters," *New York Times Book Review* July 12: 36.

Zagler, M. (2002) "Services, Innovation, and the New Economy," *Structural Change and Economic Dynamics* 13(3): 337–355.

Part II
Institutional matrixes

4 Is there an institutional base of the *new economy*?

Bruno Amable

Introduction

The phenomenon of the *new economy* possesses many interrelated aspects that affect the micro, meso and macro levels. The basic idea behind the concept is that "something new" is happening in the fields of technology, internal organization of firms, macroeconomic policy, pattern of public intervention and economic geography (see Amable *et al.* 2002). A widespread thesis assumes that: (i) the new economy defines a new long-term growth trajectory based on a few "generic" technologies – mainly information and communication technologies (ICTs) but also biotechnologies – and more generally the "weightless" economy[1]; (ii) associated with this new trajectory are an array of institutions that are capable of stimulating the technical change and structural changes which are needed to launch the technological trajectory that the new economy has defined; (iii) lastly, as would seem to be indicated on the one hand by the United States' advance in the new ICT-related fields and on the other hand by its superior macroeconomic performances during the 1990s, one has to adopt American institutional characteristics in order to be successful. The example of the United Kingdom allegedly represents the confirmation of this thesis, as well as the proof that it is possible to overcome Euro-sclerosis. In sum, changes in modern capitalism are supposedly leading the developed countries toward an "Anglo-Saxon" model, replete with deregulated financial markets, "flexible" labor markets, technologically dynamic and newly created firms, greater competition in the product markets, etc. All in all, a situation that is relatively distant from the trajectory followed by the Continental European economies in the aftermath of the Second World War.

Underlying such a thesis is the idea that certain ideal institutional infrastructures correspond to a set of given technological and economic constraints. Since the new economy seems to have redefined the bases for growth and competitiveness, it is recommended that countries should adopt the institutions that appear to warrant the best possible adaptation to the requirements of the new economy. Thus, there is a need for institutional change in areas such as labor markets, finance, scientific systems and education. Since the weightless economy seems to be based on ICT and since ICT favors relocation and reorganization of the value chain, institutions that promote change and flexibility are best suited to the full exploitation of the benefits of the new technologies.

An extreme version of this thesis is that there exists one best way to achieve the most satisfying economic performance regardless of the historical period, the dominant technological paradigm or the international regime. The new economy thesis referred to above does not require such a starting point. On the one hand, the institutional features of Continental European countries might have been instrumental in achieving a high degree of economic stability and growth in the post-war period, but they might no longer be suited to the new growth trajectory for a variety of reasons. On the other hand, the institutions of the Anglo-Saxon economies appear to favor entrepreneurship and investment in ITC and hence the emergence of the "new" economy. Therefore, if there is an ideal economic model at the present time, it would appear to be the US system.

This statement questions the existence of institutional diversity among developed economies. Diversity is a fact that can be easily observed, but the interpretation of this diversity is a matter of debate. Should diversity be interpreted as heterogeneity of countries with respect to the process of adaptation to the ideal model? However, several researchers argue that diversity should not be understood in such a way (see Hall and Soskice 2001). In fact, diversity reflects the fact that there is no single one-best-way for a modern capitalist economy. Moreover, several varieties of capitalism may coexist. Each one of these may possess its own strong and weak points, reflected among other things in its pattern of trade specialization[2] or its innovation system.[3]

The purpose of this contribution is to briefly analyze the diversity of capitalism and attempt to assess whether one particular type of capitalism is particularly suited for the new economy trajectory. The first section of the chapter analyses the diversity of capitalism with the help of the concept of institutional complementarity. The second section proposes a typology of modern capitalism based on identified complementarities. The third section suggests an empirical analysis and a typology of countries with respect to the production and diffusion of ICT and compares the results with the "varieties of capitalism." The fourth section offers some tests of ICTs' effects on economic growth. The fifth section provides a conclusion.

Institutional complementarity

Globalization and institutional diversity

The current debate about transformations affecting contemporary economies is often centered on globalization and the consequences of new ICTs. As a result of the deregulation of international trade and increasing competition on the product markets, globalization brings about an intensification of international economic relationships. The liberalization of financial activities facilitates international investment flows and tends to generalize the principles of market-based corporate governance worldwide. These include the provision of attractive incentives to high-ranking executives and the necessity of takeovers in order to achieve an efficient market for corporate governance. Capital has become more mobile, leading to an extension of the sphere within which private companies can act. As a result, the possibility for public intervention in the economy decreases. Firms have centered their strategies on the global market rather than national or "regional" spheres. This has increased the firms' outside options and more generally their bargaining position vis-à-vis labor and the state. A consequence of this trend is increased competition between national territories that define their competitiveness in terms of their "factor endowment," infrastructure, but also (and above all) local economic institutions. These regulations affect the functioning of factor markets (labor and capital) as well as the efficiency of the educational and training systems. The implications of this increased competition can be understood intuitively. If countries do not wish to fall behind in terms of their international competitiveness, countries experiencing economic difficulties need to align themselves with current best practices. But how can a country recognize these best practices? A rapid comparison of growth and unemployment performance over the 1990s would lead to the conclusion that the institutions of the USA and more generally "Anglo-Saxon" economies come very close to best practices. The USA was able to explore the new growth trajectory commonly understood as the *new economy*.

The notion of a new economy is composite (see OECD 2000). The effect of this intensification of technical progress has been to raise productivity gains wherever they had been stagnating (in the United States). Technical progress has been concentrated in certain technologies and sectors, especially those involved in information and communication technologies. Innovation and technological dynamism played a greater role in the definition of competitiveness, both for firms and for countries as a whole. If ICTs define a new technological paradigm, it is tremendously important to adopt and perhaps produce these technologies in order to benefit from the productivity advances that they will make possible. Besides, technological dynamism at the onset of a technological cycle is seen as being dependent on small innovative firms. In order to develop efficiently, these firms need a favorable environment that includes flexible labor markets, facilitation of company forming and splitting, the availability of qualified personnel and easy access to venture capital. Market-based institutions, which are supposed to favor flexibility and entrepreneurship, play an important part in this story.

As a result of the combination of globalization and the new economy, one might expect to observe a disappearance of national institutional specificities. Such specificities are the main preoccupation of a more or less homogenous school of thought that focuses on the varieties of capitalism. This diversity is not seen as something that is accidental or temporary, but rather as the consequence of mechanisms that can be grouped under the generic title of institutional complementarities (see Aoki and Dore 1994; Aoki 2000, 2001; Amable 2000; Amable *et al.* 2000a). In this view, economies basically diverge in terms of the institutions that characterize them, depending on the particular aspect of the economy that is being studied. Thus, the labor market can be more or less regulated too, wage bargaining more or less centralized and the financial systems more or less reliant upon the banks or on the freedoms they have extended to the financial markets. In general, education is organized quite differently from one country to the next, with more or less close ties to the industrial sector, varying levels of university independence and different intensity of competition between private companies.

Institutions' influence on the economy should not be considered independently from one another. Rather, they exert a joint influence. Institutions affecting one area of the economy (e.g. the labor market) will have consequences beyond that particular area, if only because of general equilibrium effects. A rather simple example is that of wage bargaining: the outcome depends on each party's outside options. These outside options are in turn dependent on the institutions affecting other areas than the labor market. These include the alternative job for the worker, which may depend on its skill level and hence on the institutions concerning the education and training system. Meanwhile, the alternative option for the firm may depend on its relocation possibilities, i.e. on the regulatory environment or the liquidity of the financial market.

Amable *et al.* (2002) provide several definitions for institutional complementarity:

- The differential definition requires continuity and is derived from the standard definition of complementarity in economics. The marginal efficiency of a certain institution is positively related to the presence/intensity of another institution in another area. For instance, if there is a complementarity between deregulated labor markets and deregulated product markets, less regulation in the labor market increases the marginal gain to deregulation in product markets.
- The same logic as above applies to the case of comparative perform-

ance. However, a comparison between several situations is made. Adhering to product and labor markets, which may be regulated or not, there are four possibilities. Which is the best institutional combination? One considers discrete changes in the institutional environment instead of an institutional continuum. The conclusion may differ from that obtained with the differential method.[4]

- In the case of the dynamic definition, the presence of one institutional form in one area leads to the adoption of an institutional form in another area. The foundations of the institutional dynamics are left unspecified.

- The principle of conformity to a general logic maintains that institutions are said to be complementary when they have the same operating principles. Thus, the liberal or the coordinated logic leads to the adoption of deregulated or coordinated market features respectively.

The first three definitions are very clearly related to one another. They make implicit reference to a "performance" criterion, which is necessary for appreciating complementarity. One may also rely on local criteria such as the level of unemployment for labor markets, the level of investment or the cost of capital for the financial system and the rate of innovation for the innovation system. However, the logic of institutional complementarity seems to imply the consideration of an aggregate indicator: welfare, GDP level or growth rate. Of course, this is not a matter of statistics, it rather concerns the way in which specific institutional forms are chosen. Agents with conflicting objectives will have different criteria for appreciating the performance of institutions: wages for workers or profits for firms. Several questions arise from such an assumption. How are each agent's criteria related to a global performance index? Do agents internalize the interrelations between criteria? Workers may be aware that future employment depends on investment and hence on profits. This internalization is itself dependent upon institutions. Whether agents' time horizons are long term or short term may depend on the capacity of institutions to stabilize the forecasting perspectives.

The fourth definition is a little more problematic. The institutional complementarity approach considers economic models or systems as a set of complementary institutions. Whether one can sum up this pattern of complementarities into one general logic is debatable. For instance, if we define Anglo-Saxon economies through a set of complementary institutional forms such as a deregulated labor market and a markets-based financial system, can we then identify a general principle which would ensure that the whole liberal market economies (LME)[5] model is coherent and viable? This remains an open question.

The challenge to the institutional complementarity approach is accountable for the existence of diverse institutional configurations (economic models). Their stability and viability is long term but not eternal as changes need to be possible. These changes may result from different factors (see Amable *et al.* 2002):

- A changing environment: technology is often mentioned in this respect. The existence of technological regimes suggest that inherent technological requirements may make industries perform differently in countries with distinct institutional systems. However, technology may evolve over time. Consequently, a change in the technological requirements of well-established industries may put a country's institutional system under stress, eventually leading to a break-up of the historic compromise that underlies the system. Moreover, technologies may benefit differently from distinct institutional systems during their evolution from nascent to mature stages. Hence, an exogenous dynamic pattern of technological evolution may, from time to time, put pressure on any institutional setting. For instance, the new technological regime centered on ICTs is supposed to have endangered the compromise between labor and capital on which economies, different from the Anglo-Saxon model, relied.
- Unintended consequences: agents may take decisions that have unintended affects on the institutional structure. This can be caused by the presence of externalities, or because the consequences of their decisions are effective well beyond their time horizon. For instance, workers eager to obtain the highest income from their savings may favor the emergence of financial markets, which may destabilize a bank-based financial system, which was important in the system of institutional complementarities. If this bank-based system was complementary with a stable employment relation (see Amable *et al.* 2000b), its weakening may worsen the relative position of workers.
- Conscious attempts at institutional design: institutions are the result of deliberate decisions. In times of crisis, agents may have their own motives for altering the institutional structure. Whether change actually takes place depends on the polity. The current debates over the necessity of "reform" in Continental Europe refer to these kinds of attempts to orient economies toward a more market-based system.

Diverse types of capitalism

Many studies on the diversity of capitalism have been published (see Jackson 2002). These studies either focus on specific countries or analyze more general categories such as liberal market economies versus coordinated market economies. In a theoretical analysis and an exercise in international comparisons, Amable *et al.* (1997) highlight four main types of capitalism or Social Systems of Innovation and Production (SSIP):

- the market-based SSIP, encompassing the USA, the UK, Australia and Canada;
- the social-democratic SSIP in the Scandinavian countries;
- the meso-corporatist SSIP in Japan;
- the "European" SSIP of France, Germany, Italy and the Netherlands.

Rather than more or less stylized descriptions of the main characteristics of a given country, SSIP should be seen as ideal-types. Table 4.1 provides a summary of the main characteristics of each SSIP.

The classification of SSIP into four groups resulted from a difficulty in classifying European countries. A homogeneous European group, which lumped together France and Germany with Italy and possibly other southern European countries raised some questions about the precise definition of European SSIP. Limiting oneself to the realm of innovation, Italy and other Mediterranean countries seemed very different from Continental Europe, most notably in terms of R&D intensity and the importance of high-tech industries. Amable and Petit (2001) offer new analyses, which provide for a refined typology of SSIP. Extending the empirical analysis to 21 countries[6] and updating it to include the end of the 1990s, they distinguish between six SSIP:

- market-based SSIP;
- social-democratic SSIP and meso-corporatist SSIP, with Korea joining Japan;
- the "European integration" (or "public") SSIP. This includes the countries that already belonged to this SSIP (France, Germany, the Netherlands). However, Italy is now categorized as a "Mediterranean" variant while Belgium and Ireland are now included in this category;
- an "Alpine" variant of the preceding SSIP now comprises Austria and Switzerland;
- the "Mediterranean" variant of the European SSIP is made up of Spain, Italy, Greece and Portugal.

Besides the differentiation between the European SSIP into three variants, the main results reported in Amable and Petit (2001) were that there did not seem to be any general pattern of convergence toward the market-based SSIP. Rather, there had been an advance of some market mechanisms in specific areas (mostly the financial system), while globalization affected SSIP in a differentiated manner. The market-based and "Mediterranean" SSIP were not affected as a group of countries by the empirical analyses of data that related to the new pattern of internationalization.[7] Other groupings of countries were reshuffled, indicating a process of recomposition within the SSIP.

Table 4.1 Four types of social systems of innovation and production

	Market-based	Meso-corporatist	European	Social-democratic
Science	Competitive research system (individuals and institutions)	Firm-integrated research system	Public research system	Public research system
Technology	High-technology activities are a strong point; technological dynamism	Important product innovation but relative unimportance of science-based discoveries	Importance of public-funded large technological projects	Fast diffusion of technological innovations
Competence and skills	Highly polarized labor force (high skills/low skills)	Homogeneous labor force w.r.t. skills. Constant upgrading within the corporation	Relatively homogeneous labor force but shortages of high skills	Homogeneous highly-skilled work force
Labor markets	Decentralization of wage bargaining, individualized wage and labor market segmentation	Coordinated wage bargaining and dualism: employment stability for the large firm, flexibility for small firms	Strong institutionalization of employment rules, working hours and social protection	Centralization of wage bargaining

Competition	Promotion of competition; importance of anti-trust issues	Competition between large corporations	Moderate competition	Strong external competition pressure
Finance	Market-based system	Stable long-term relationships between banks and corporations	Bank-based systems	Bank-based financial system
Products	Important product innovation in high-tech industries	Adaptation of products and processes in the catching-up phase, fast product innovation after	Moderate pace of innovation	High rate of innovation
Innovation	Innovation in high-tech sectors and science-based industries	Innovation in industries where skill accumulation matters	Both "mission"-type innovation and incremental, quality innovation in mid-tech industries	High-tech and skill-based industries
Industrial specialization	Information technology, aerospace, pharmaceuticals, finance, etc.	Automobile, machines, electronics, robotics	Aerospace, mechanics, automobile	Electronics, health- or environment-related industries

Diversity of capitalism

The previous characterizations of SSIP were based on institutional variables as well as variables reflecting the economic structure. For instance, these include scientific, technological and industrial specialization. As a close connection between institutions and economic structures was assumed, this argument seems logical (Amable 2000). Furthermore, data on economic and technological structures are readily available whereas variables on institutional elements related to these elements are much more difficult to find.

The analysis proposed in Amable (2003) distinguishes, as much as possible, institutional from economic variables. Five institutional areas are identified: product market competition, the labor market, the financial sector, social protection and the education sector. Based on previous results and other contributions to the literature (Aoki 2001; Hall and Soskice 2001), five different varieties of capitalism are distinguished:

- market-based, or liberal market economies or the Anglo-Saxon model: the USA, the UK, Australia and Canada;
- social-democratic economies: Sweden, Finland and Denmark;
- Asian capitalism: Japan and Korea;
- Continental European capitalism: France, Germany, Belgium, Austria, Ireland and Norway.
- south European capitalism: Italy, Spain, Portugal and Greece.

The institutional characteristics of these five varieties of capitalism are briefly summarized in Table 4.2.

The existence and relative stability of differentiated models of capitalism is based on complementarities between the institutional features specific to each type of capitalism. The complete description of the institutional complementarities is outlined in Amable (2003).

It is worth emphasizing the difference between this representation of the diversity of capitalism and the "variety of capitalism" approach of Hall and Soskice (2001). Hall and Soskice distinguish between two basic types of capitalism: liberal market economies (LME) and coordinated market economies (CME). The coordination dimension is crucial for understanding the pattern of differentiation among countries. In LME, actors primarily coordinate among each other through market signals whereas non-market relationships dominate in CME. Thus, countries can be arrayed along a continuum reflecting the extent of non-market coordination. This dimension is present in many areas of the economy such as processes of wage bargaining and the financial system.

Due to its one-dimensionality, Hall and Soskice's partition of countries cannot distinguish more than two models of capitalism. Also, even if the distinction between some blatant LME such as the USA or the UK and some typical CME such as Sweden or Germany is clear, the position of some other countries is more ambiguous. For instance, Hall and Soskice (2001) cannot clearly identify France and Italy as either CME or LME. Being intermediate cases, they are also assumed to be less competitive than any of the pure types and thus condemned to join one or the other club sooner or later.

It is possible to consider more than two types of capitalism, if one allows for more than one dimension for differentiation. The institutional complementarities between the various institutional forms of Table 4.2 allow these kinds of dimensions. In order to check the empirical relevance of the 5-type partition, Amable (2003) performs an empirical analysis, using variables that characterize the institutional areas taken into account previously. A cluster analysis broadly confirms the existence of five to six types of capitalism, depending on whether one distinguishes Switzerland and the Netherlands as a separate group apart from the rest of Continental Europe. The cluster analysis' results are presented in Figure 4.1: the two dimensions describe the most fundamental oppositions between the different models.

A first basic dimension is the regulation of markets. The one end of the spectrum shows deregulated markets, the other represents few obstacles to competition and regulated markets and limited competition. This dimension does not so much oppose LME and CME as found in Hall and Soskice (2001), but rather LME (or market-based economies, or "North Atlantic" capitalism) to south European capitalism. The second dimension is that of social protection and separates social-democratic countries from Asian capitalism. With regard to the competition and regulation of markets, continental capitalism might be considered as an intermediate form between market-based capitalism and South-European capitalism. Continental capitalism also possesses some of the social-democratic model's features, particularly a less extensive social protection system, as is shown in Figure 4.1 (p. 76).

ICT and the diversity of capitalism

The spread of the *new economy* can, in part, be assessed through the relative importance of ICTs in production and consumption. As mentioned earlier, the *new economy* in general and ICTs in particular are often associated with market-based capitalism. How accurate is this judgement? In order to answer this question, there is a need for an empirical analysis of the ICT sector. The sample of countries is the same that was used for the analysis of the diversity of capitalism. The OECD's database on ICTs provides various statistical indicators on the production and diffusion of ICTs. These indicators are available for most OECD countries. A cluster analysis of these indicators checks whether ICTs exhibit the typology of varieties of capitalism introduced in the previous section.

Table 4.2 Five types of capitalism

	Market-based capitalism	Social-democratic economies	Asian capitalism	Continental European capitalism	South European capitalism
Product markets	Deregulated markets Coordination through price signals Openness to foreign competition and investment	Regulated markets Coordination through "non price" signals Importance of quality competition Openness to foreign competition and investment	High involvement of the state in coordination Price and quality competition High protection against foreign firms and investment Importance of large firms	Regulated markets Openness to foreign competition and investment	Regulated markets Importance of price competition Moderate protection against foreign trade or investment Importance of small firms
Labor market	Weak employment protection Decentralization of wage bargaining	High employment protection Corporatist industrial relations Centralized wage bargaining	Dualism: employment protection within the large corporation; flexibility in small businesses Coordinated wage bargaining Firm-level unions	Substantial employment Coordinated wage bargaining	High employment protection (large firms) Centralization of wage bargaining

Financial sector	Low ownership concentration High share of institutional investors Active market for corporate control Well-developed venture capital	High ownership concentration No market for corporate control High degree of banking concentration	High ownership concentration Involvement of banks in corporate governance No market for corporate control High banking concentration	High ownership concentration Limited market for corporate control High banking concentration	High ownership concentration Bank-based corporate governance No market for corporate control
Social protection	Very limited social protection Emphasis on poverty alleviation (social safety net)	High level of social protection Universalist model	Low social protection Expenditures directed toward poverty alleviation	High degree of social protection Conservative model	Moderate level of social protection Conservative model
Education	Low public expenditures Competitive universities Relatively weak secondary education Weak vocational training	High level of public expenditures Strong primary and secondary education Importance of vocational training	Low level of public expenditures Emphasis on secondary education Training within large firms	High level of public expenditures Emphasis on secondary education Developed vocational training	Low public expenditures Weak vocational training

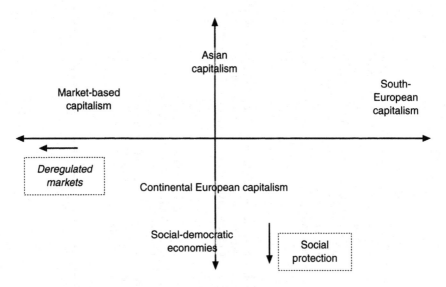

Figure 4.1 The five types of capitalism in two dimensions.

The results of the cluster analysis can be briefly summarized: Figure 4.2 presents the projection of countries on the first two factorial axes of the principal components analysis. These axes explain over 45 percent of the variance. The first axis represents the extent of diffusion of ICTs, investment in ICTs and the importance of ICT-related innovation. The second axis is more related to the production and export of ICT goods (share of ICTs in manufacturing, share of ICTs in total exports etc.). Therefore, countries located in the southeast quadrant are characterized by a high diffusion and production of ICTs, whereas countries in the northwest quadrant lag behind in terms of both diffusion and production of ICTs.

Are these results compatible with the typology of capitalism presented in the previous section? A comparison between Figure 4.1 and Figure 4.2 would hint at the possibility of a certain correlation between the first axes of each analysis. The ranking of countries according to the extent of deregulation of markets (i.e. the interpretation of the first axis in Figure 4.1) seems very similar to the ranking in terms of ICT diffusion as measured in Figure 4.2. This is confirmed when one incorporates the projection of each country on the first factorial axis of the analysis represented in Figure 4.1 as an illustrative variable[8] in the cluster analysis for ICTs. This variable is indeed correlated to the first axis of the ICT analysis (Figure 4.2) with a coefficient of 80 percent. This seems to confirm the common wisdom about ICTs, the new economy and market-based capitalism: the three appear to be related to each other.

But even if this correlation appears to confirm the connection between

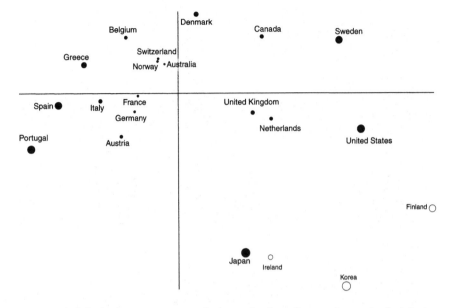

Figure 4.2 Principal components analysis; projection of countries on the first factorial plane.

the market-based model of capitalism, it does not sum up all the information provided by the cluster analysis. The clusters and their characteristics
are presented in Table 4.3; four clusters can be identified. The first one can
be subdivided into two groups of countries. The first group comprises
France, Germany, Italy, Greece and Australia; it is characterized by a
relatively weak production of ICTs. However, the second group (Belgium,
Switzerland, Norway and Denmark) is similarly characterized by a lower
than average diffusion of ICT-related consumption goods. Within the
cluster comprised of Portugal, Spain and Austria, the diffusion of ICTs is
relatively low. However, the diffusion is more rapid than in other countries, thus indicating that these countries are catching up. The two other
clusters are characterized by a higher than average presence of ICTs in the
economy. In the Netherlands, the UK, Japan, Ireland and Korea this is
more the case with respect to production and exports while diffusion and
use of ICTs plays a more prominent role in the USA, Sweden, Canada and
Finland. This last group is, to some extent, characterized by a slowing
down of the diffusion process. When compared to the other countries, this
reflects some saturation effects.

The clustering presented in Table 4.3 only partly confirms the close relation between the market-based model and the new economy, at least when
measured by ICT diffusion. On the one hand, Australia, although a market-
based economy, does not exhibit a clear superiority either in terms of

Table 4.3 Cluster analysis

	France, Germany, Italy, Greece, Australia	Belgium, Switzerland, Norway, Denmark	Portugal, Spain, Austria	The Netherlands, UK, Japan, Ireland, Korea	USA, Sweden, Canada, Finland
Indicators significantly lower than average	Share of ICT value added in business sector value added	Share of ICT consumption in GDP	Share of computer and related services in market services employment Fixed access paths to Internet per 100 inhabitants		Average annual growth rate of access paths to Internet 1995–1999 Average price for 20 hours Internet access
Indicators significantly larger than average			Average annual growth rate of access paths to Internet 1995–1999 Average price for 20 hours Internet access 1995–2000	Share of ICT manufacturing trade in total trade Share of ICT sector exports in total merchandise exports ICT export specialization index ICT import propensity index ICT patents as a percentage of total national patents filed at the EPO	Number of Internet hosts per 1,000 inhabitants Number of DSL cable modem lines and other broadband per 100 inhabitants Software investment as percentage of non-residential gross fixed capital formation Share of ICT investment in non-residential investment Share of telecommunication services in market services employment

| Indicators significantly lower than average | Share of ICT sector exports in total merchandise exports ICT export specialization index Share of ICT consumption in GDP | ICT sector trade balance | Share of ICT manufacturing in total R&D expenditure of the manufacturing sector Internet subscribers per 100 inhabitants Web sites per 1,000 inhabitants ICT import propensity index |

diffusion or production of ICTs. Ireland and the Netherlands on the other hand, are two countries that are close to the Continental European model, belong to the same cluster as the UK, Japan and Korea. Finally, Sweden and Finland, which represent the social-democratic model, are in the same cluster as the US. Therefore, if countries are market-based economies, this may indeed facilitate them to explore the technological trajectory of the new economy, however, it does not seem to be a necessary condition.

The differentiation of economic performance

The analysis now turns to the impact of ITCs on macroeconomic performance. The new economy is held to lead to renewal of economic growth because the nature of technical change has been modified. ITC industries play a double role in this perspective. They enjoy the highest level of technical progress, with productivity gains that are significantly above those in other sectors. They also feature a very high rate of product innovation. Besides, their diffusion throughout the whole economy enables other sectors to improve their own productivity and to modify their offer in a way that encourages innovation. As such, information technologies play a role in their production as well as in their diffusion.

As a result, we can expect that countries that have experienced a rapid diffusion of ICTs, or who have been involved in a significant production of ICTs, will be ahead of other countries, at least during the ascending phase of a long-term cycle. It will be easier to understand this ascending phase insofar as its institutional conditions facilitate innovative dynamism. In particular, these conditions relate to the flexibility of the labor market and above all to the dynamism of the financial markets: the availability of venture capital, the possibility that corporate executives can be motivated through the attribution of stock options, the liquidity of the financial markets, etc. Market-based finance can be synthesized in one single indicator – the price index of listed securities. In this view, the stock markets' dynamism can be crystallized as the changes in this indicator.

Another argument is closer to traditional macroeconomics and stresses that the developed countries did not all experience the same macroeconomic conditions over the course of the decade – if only because of the diversity of the macroeconomic policies that were being pursued (monetary policies in particular). The European recession of the early 1990s is not in fact unrelated to the restrictive monetary policies that were being carried out in light of the upcoming economic and monetary union.

Is it possible to explain international variations in macroeconomic performance on the basis of the aforementioned elements? The influence of ICT-related variables on growth was tested for a sample of the following ten OECD countries over the period 1991–2000: Canada, Denmark, Finland, France, Germany, Italy, Japan, the Netherlands, the UK and the USA. The test considered two separate ICT variables: the proportion of

Table 4.4 Regression results

	Growth rate of GDP	Growth rate of GDP per hour
Share of ICT producing sectors in GDP (logs, lagged)	0.074**	0.066**
Share of ICT using sectors in GDP (logs, lagged)	−0.043	−0.018
Real rate of interest	−0.002*	−
Lagged level of productivity per hour		−0.009***
	Fixed effects	Fixed effects

Note
Significance levels: *10%, **5%, ***1%.

total GDP accounted for by the ICT-producing sectors and the same figures for sectors employing ICTs. Data on ICT producing and using sectors is drawn from the ICT database of the Groningen Growth and Development Center (University of Groningen, the Netherlands). The ICT-using sectors' proportion of total GDP replaces a variable that relates to the diffusion of such technologies as it is difficult to obtain capital goods diffusion variables for an entire economy over a period of several years. Additionally, these kinds of variables are not particularly reliable. The real rate of interest is introduced in order to control macroeconomic policy. The test considers two macroeconomic performance indicators: the rate of growth of GDP and the rate of growth of GDP per hour.

The findings are summarized in Table 4.4. One single ICT variable is significantly associated with growth rates: the proportion accounted for by the ICT producing sectors. The utilization of these technologies, as far as it can be measured by the employed variable, does not seem to have had any significant influence; in fact, the estimated coefficient is negative. Restrictive monetary policy, recognized with the level of the real rate of interest, seems to have played a negative role over the period; at least for the GDP growth rate regression. The negative coefficient of the lagged productivity level variable indicates a catch-up effect.

Conclusion

The diversity of modern capitalism seems to be a durable fact, not because of the existence of rigidity in the process of adapting to the "one-best-way," but because there are systemic reasons for countries to adopt different institutional structures. Just as the post-war growth regime was characterized by the diversity of capitalism, there is no reason to think that the new economy regime, if it is stable, will generate more institutional convergence. The superiority of the market-based model to other models of capitalism during the 1990s is not that evident. A satisfying growth performance was attributable to "sound" macroeconomic policies (particularly monetary policy) and the ability to produce technologies related to the new paradigm, i.e. ICTs. In this respect, the adequation of market-based capitalism and ICTs is not perfect: not all market-based economies are particularly competitive with respect to ICT production while some European countries, whose economies are very distant from the market-based model, seem to be performing well. Thus, there is no strong evidence in favor of the impossibility for a non-liberal market economy to engage in the new technological trajectory.

As a result, there is room to argue for a diversity of trajectories developing toward a "knowledge-based economy." Diversity, however, does not mean absence of change. The different models will change by adapting to the new technological regime and new patterns of internationalization. In fact, some types of capitalism are likely to be more affected than others: the Continental European model is certainly under more stress than the market-based model. Some transformations are under way in the fields of product markets competition, labor markets and financial systems, which question the somewhat fragile stability of this model. But this stability is not a simple question of relative economic efficiency; more fundamentally, it is a matter of the stability of the socio-political compromises that underlie the institutions of the European model.

Notes

1 The weightless economy is generally understood as comprising four main elements: (i) information and communications technology (ICT), the Internet; intellectual assets; (ii) electronic libraries and databases; (iii) biotechnology; (iv) carbon-based libraries and databases, pharmaceuticals.
2 See the chapter on institutional comparative advantage in Hall and Soskice (2001).
3 See the analysis of social systems of innovation and production in Amable *et al.* (1997).
4 If certain conditions are met, negotiations between social partners in a given labor market can create the sort of stable compromises that could help the workforce to receive a high level of training. In addition, physical investment is facilitated by the existence of close relationships between banks and firms. In this scenario, the existence of durable relationships and proximity between banks and firms enhances the implementation of long-term investment projects. In return this facilitates the establishment of stable compromises in the labor market. Conversely, a flexible labor market, one that facilitates employee mobility, is seen here as complementing a financial system that facilitates the reversibility of commitments and the liquidation of investments. This means that the range of potential complementarities can be extended to cover areas such as innovation, professional training systems, etc.
5 Hall and Soskice define LMEs as being unified by market principles. Meanwhile, coordinated market economies (CME) such as Germany are unified by a principle of "strategic coordination."
6 The United States, Japan, the United Kingdom, Canada, Australia, Italy, Spain, Portugal, Greece, France, Belgium, Denmark, Norway, Sweden, Finland, Germany, Austria, Switzerland, the Netherlands, Ireland and Korea. The empir-

ical data related to scientific and technological fields, economic structure, the educational system and the labor market. As such, this is an extended conception of the innovation system.

7 The data included figures on foreign direct investment, international trade and the evolution of the financial systems.

8 Illustrative variables do not contribute to the definition of the factorial axes.

Bibliography

Amable, B. (2000) "Institutional Complementarity and Diversity of Social Systems of Innovation and Production," *Review of International Political Economy* 7(4): 645–687.

—— (2003) *The Diversity of Modern Capitalism*, Oxford: Oxford University Press.

Amable, B. and Petit, P. (2001) *The Diversity of Social Systems of Innovation and Production During the 1990s*, Document de Travail CEPREMAP no. 15.

Amable, B., Askenazy, P., Goldstein, A. and O'Connor, D. (1997) *Les systèmes d'innovation à l'ère de la globalisation*, Paris: Economica.

—— (2000a) "Institutional Complementarities: An Overview of the Main Issues," Presented at the seminar on Institutional Complementarity and the Dynamics of Economic Systems, Paris, April 5–6.

—— (2000b) *Institutional Complementarity: Labour Markets and Finance*, Paris: CEPREMAP.

—— (co-ordinated by Cohen, D.) (2002) "Internet: The Elusive Quest of a Frictionless Economy," Report presented at Fondazione R. Benedetti "Gli aumenti di produttività e la disuguaglianza digitale nella nuova economia," Catania, June 15.

Aoki, M. (2000) *Information, Corporate Governance, and Institutional Diversity*, Oxford: Oxford University Press.

—— (2001) *Towards a Comparative Institutional Analysis*, Cambridge, MA: MIT Press.

Aoki, M. and Dore, R.P. (eds) (1994) *The Japanese Firm: The Sources of Competitive Strength*, Oxford and New York: Oxford University Press.

Beffa, J.L., Boyer, R. and Touffut, J.-Ph. (1999) *Les Relations Salariales En France*, Notes de la Fondation Saint Simon no. 107.

Boyer, R. (2001) "La 'Nouvelle economie' Au future antérieur: histoire, théories, géographie," Document de Travail CEPREMAP no. 13.

Edwards, J. and Schanz, J. (2001a) "Faster, Higher, Stronger: An International Comparison of Structural Policies," Lehman Brothers Structural Economics Research Papers no. 3.

—— (2001b) "Lehman's Structural Database. Sources and Methods," Lehman Brothers Structural Economics Research Papers no. 4,

Freeman, C. and Soete, L. (1997) *The Economics of Industrial Innovation*, Cambridge, MA: MIT University Press.

Freeman, R. (2000) "Single-Peaked Vs. Diversified Capitalism: The Relation between Economic Institutions and Outcomes," NBER Working Paper.

Hall, P. and Soskice, D. (eds) (2001) *Varieties of Capitalism: The Institutional Foundations of Comparative Advantage*, Oxford: Oxford University Press.

Jackson, G. (2002) *Varieties of Capitalism: A Review*, Draft Rieti.

OECD (2000) *A New Economy? The Changing Role of Innovation and Information Technology in Growth*, Paris: OECD.

5 Europe in the innovation race

Daniele Archibugi and Alberto Coco

Introduction

The aim of this chapter is to comparatively discuss the future trajectory of the so-called *new economy* in Europe, North America and East Asia. The idea that there is a "new" economy is certainly fascinating and it is not surprising that it has taken so much ground in the business world, the political community and the press. John Maynard Keynes knew very well that expectations play a fundamental role in fostering the business cycle. The hope that we might be experiencing the development of something as intriguing as a new economy has helped some corporations to support their stock market performance, some politicians to be elected or re-elected and the press to increase their sales.

The academic community is certainly not immune from these tendencies, although its function is to critically examine ideas that might have spread out too quickly. The scientific community should remember that new terms that are boldly introduced are often forgotten rather quickly and are replaced by others that seem more appealing. A certain extent of skepticism does not imply that one does not share the assumption that there is nothing new under the sun: now and then something new does occurs in economic and social life. Major changes have taken place in the last decade and some key components can be singled out. In particular:

1   The exploitation of knowledge has become more and more systematic, with an increasing propensity of business companies now searching for profit and growth opportunities in the exploitation of know-how.
2   The transfer in space of commodities, financial resources, expertise and information has become much easier. While the technical feasibility has increased exponentially, the economic costs have been dramatically reduced.
3   The number of players able to enter into old and new fields has also increased, leading to an accelerated pace of economic competition.

Perhaps if one combines these three aspects, they can be labeled a new economy. Students of technological change, however, have preferred to use other terms such as knowledge-based economy, which emphasizes the role played by know-how and competences in the economic sphere. We prefer to use the term "globalizing learning economy" (Lundvall and Borrás 1998; Archibugi and Lundvall 2001) since this seems to better capture the key role played by human learning in the economic and social landscape. The term globalizing (rather than global or even globalized) should help to remind us that the vast majority of the population of the world still does not have access to know-how that has already become obsolete in other parts of the globe (UNDP 2001).

There is a widespread belief that economic growth, employment and welfare in the old continent will be more and more associated to its capability to generate, acquire and diffuse new knowledge. It is therefore not surprising that there is a major policy concern within governments, business and trade unions about the ways to promote scientific and techno-logical activities, to foster innovation in firms and to upgrade the competencies of human resources.

In order to develop a proper innovation strategy, Europe has to face the fact that it is composed of a number of states that do retain a substantial autonomy. What the old continent is gaining in terms of variety and diversity, it is losing in terms of lack of cohesion and central policy decision-making. Not surprisingly, Europe can better be described as an agglomeration of different innovation systems. While some regions of the EU are strongly integrated in knowledge transmission, others continue to be peripheral and are excluded by the major technology transfer flows. Therefore, one of the core issues that should be addressed both at the national and at the European policy level is how to integrate the different local and national components into a single innovative system comparable to the systems in the US and Japan.[1]

The transformations toward a knowledge-based economy regard Europe as being engaged in a major institutional change. European integration has been driven by a variety of common policies such as the creation of a custom union, a common agricultural policy and, more recently, even a single currency. In spite of the efforts undertaken with the various multi-annual Framework Programs since the early 1980s, European integration is not yet driven by science and technology policy. Not more than 4.6 percent of the European Commission's total budget is devoted to Research and Technological Development (RTD) – this accounts for less than 6 percent of the total amount spent by EU governments for RTD (Sharp 2001). In spite of the growing amount of resources that the EU has dedicated to RTD, this is still a minor part of the budget.

However, it is significant that European governments continue to indicate very ambitious targets for the "old continent." At the Lisbon Summit in March 2000, the European Council declared its willingness to make the European Research Area the world's largest knowledge economy. At the Barcelona Summit in March 2002 the goal was formulated that Europe should reach a R&D/GDP ratio equal to 3 percent by 2010.[2] How realistic are these targets? Additionally, how is Europe performing in the technological race now?

In the next section we present a broad set of data describing the technological status of Europe, as regards both investments – by means of the expenditure on R&D – and performance in innovative activities – by means of other well-known technological indicators. We compare Europe with the US and Japan and we highlight the recent evolution. Particular attention is devoted to ICTs since these are more strictly linked to the concept of new economy. In a following section we analyze the phenomenon of scientific and technological collaborations as we assume they reveal a lot about the "attractiveness" of the various regions of the world. Finally, in the last section we discuss the strategies Europe is applying to achieve a more prominent role in the globalizing learning economy.

A new European technology gap?

Like the US and Japan, Europe is a leading player in the generation of scientific and technological competencies. The combined R&D budget of the EU member countries is almost two thirds that of the US and more than one and an half that of Japan. In terms of scientific articles, the output of the EU is slightly higher than that of the US. But this strongly reflects the size of the EU, which has a population much larger than the US and Japan (see Table 5.1).

If we look at the intensities, there are increasing signals that Europe is losing ground in the most dynamic and technologically advanced part of the economy. The concern about an increasing technological gap is certainly not new: as early as the 1960s we heard about "the American chal-

Table 5.1 Some indicators of size in the Triad, latest available year

	USA	EU	Japan
Population	283,962,304	378,938,762	127,100,000
GDP in million current international US$ PPP	9,906,927	9,247,774	3,444,549
Gross domestic R&D expenditure in million current US$ PPP	282,292	174,695	98,560
Scientific and technical articles	163,526	174,245	47,826
Internet users	95,354,000	89,861,072	47,080,000

Sources: OECD (2001) for gross R&D expenditure; Worldbank (2000) for the other indicators.

Note
PPP GDP is gross domestic product converted to international dollars using purchasing power parity rates. An international dollar has the same purchasing power over GDP as the US dollar has in the United States. Population and GDP refer to 2001, scientific articles to 1999, GERD and Internet users to 2000.

lenge" (Servan-Schreiber 1968) and similar concerns were reiterated in the 1980s and in the 1990s (see, for example, Patel and Pavitt 1987; Archibugi and Pianta 1992).

Surely, Europe is not the only region to be concerned about losing its leadership. Similar concerns were echoed in the US (Kennedy 1987; Pianta 1988; Nelson 1990) and if we had sufficient insight into Japan's discourse, we would certainly find comparable statements. But by simply saying that the neighbor's grass is always greener, we cannot dismiss the issue about European economies' poor performance in key aspects of knowledge-based production.

Table 5.2 reports some data about the R&D intensity (Gross R&D expenditure, GERD, as a percentage of GDP). The EU's intensity is equal to 1.93 percent, substantially lower than that of the US (2.69) and Japan (2.98). In the second half of the 1990s Japan grew more than the US, while the EU's

Table 5.2 Gross R&D expenditure as a percentage of GDP by country, 2000 and 1995

	GERD (% of GDP) in 2000	*GERD (% of GDP) in 1995*	*Mean annual rate of growth from 1995 to 2000 (%)*
The USA	2.69	2.49	1.53
Japan	2.98	2.72	1.83
The EU	1.93	1.90	0.32
Austria	1.80	1.56	2.96
Belgium	1.96	1.66	3.42
Denmark	2.08	1.80	2.91
Finland	3.37	2.29	8.06
France	2.15	2.31	−1.46
Germany	2.48	2.25	1.93
Greece	0.68	0.45	8.71
Ireland	1.21	1.28	−1.17
Italy	1.04	0.99	. 1.00
The Netherlands	2.02	2.10	−0.76
Portugal	0.76	0.57	5.87
Spain	0.94	0.81	2.99
Sweden	3.78	3.38	2.24
The UK	1.86	1.95	−0.97
Canada	1.83	1.70	2.50
Norway	1.70	1.69	0.30
Switzerland	2.73	na	–
The EU:			
Coefficient of variation	0.48	0.46	–
Max/min	5.56	7.51	–

Sources: EC (2002), data taken from Eurostat and OECD for USA and Japan.

Note
Data for Greece, Ireland, Italy, Belgium, The Netherlands, Denmark, Sweden, Canada, Norway, Switzerland refer to 1999; Japan data refers to 1996–2000.

growth remained stagnant. Within the EU, a clear regional divide between the North and the South emerged. The country with the highest intensity, Sweden, has a value that is almost six times higher than that of Greece.

A similar pattern emerges in terms of business R&D (BERD) as a percentage of the Domestic Product of Industry (DPI), reported in Table 5.3. In this case, the difference between the first and the last EU country is even higher: Sweden has a BERD intensity 17 times higher than Portugal. The dispersion among European countries has further increased. It will be difficult to find other aspects of economic and social life where the differences between European countries are so profound.

Table 5.4 shows the number of patents granted per million people for various countries at the US Patent and Trademark Office (USPTO). The high ratio for the US reflects the fact that inventors and firms are seeking patents in their domestic market. But Japan and the EU are on an equal footing since for both of them the American market is crucial. The figures show that Japan has a ratio that is almost four times higher than the EU's average. Not even the European countries with the highest propensity to

Table 5.3 Business R&D expenditure as a percentage of DPI by country, 1999 and 1995

	BERD (% of DPI) in 1999	*BERD (% of DPI) in 1995*	*Mean annual rate of growth from 1995 to 1999 (%)*
The USA	2.09	1.51	8.40
Japan	2.27	2.06	2.43
The EU	1.49	1.23	4.81
Austria	0.96	0.83	3.55
Belgium	1.68	1.35	5.66
Denmark	2.03	1.26	12.69
Finland	3.17	1.67	17.36
France	1.61	1.39	3.81
Germany	2.10	1.70	5.44
Greece	0.28	0.19	10.52
Ireland	0.98	0.69	9.30
Italy	0.53	0.51	0.98
The Netherlands	1.40	1.10	6.24
Portugal	0.26	0.17	11.92
Spain	0.53	0.37	9.29
Sweden	4.27	3.39	5.94
The UK	1.27	1.17	1.99
The EU:			
Coefficient of variation	0.73	0.71	–
Max/min	16.42	19.94	–

Sources: EC (2002), data taken from Eurostat and OECD for USA and Japan.

Note
Denmark and Finland have last data for 2000.

Table 5.4 Patents granted at the USPTO by country, 2000–2001 and 1996–1997

	Mean annual granted patents at USPTO per million people 2000–2001	Mean annual granted patents at USPTO per million people 1996–1997	Mean annual rate of growth from 1996–1997 to 2000–2001 (%)
The USA	305	228	7.6
Japan	254	184	8.5
The EU	69	46	10.7
Austria	67	46	10.2
Belgium	69	49	8.7
Denmark	86	54	12.0
Finland	130	87	10.5
France	67	49	7.7
Germany	131	84	11.6
Greece	2	1	9.8
Ireland	35	21	14.1
Italy	30	21	8.7
Luxembourg	70	48	10.1
The Netherlands	81	52	11.8
Portugal	1	1	12.0
Spain	7	4	12.6
Sweden	187	97	17.8
The UK	64	44	10.0
Canada	114	77	10.1
Norway	57	32	15.4
Switzerland	191	155	5.2
The EU:			
Coefficient of variation	0.73	0.67	–
Max/min	236.44	193.22	–

Sources: Authors' on US Patent and Trademark Office data.

patent, that is, Switzerland and Sweden, have the same intensity as Japan. It is reasonable to assume that all European countries have a similar propensity to seek patents in the US. On the grounds of this assumption, the data can measure intra-European variations: the ratio between the highest (Sweden) and the lowest (Portugal) country is higher than 200 to 1. The coefficient of variation has also increased in four years (on the variations in the European Systems of Innovations, see Chesnais *et al.* 2000; Cantwell and Iammarino 2001).

Patents granted in the US are complemented by patent applications at the European Patent Office (EPO) (Table 5.5). Even in the European market, Japan has a patent propensity above the average of the EU (respectively, 146 and 127 patents per million people) and the US is also close to the EU average (104 patents per million people). The data also show a remarkable increase in the number of patents granted – both at the USPTO and at the EPO.

Table 5.5 Patents applied at the EPO by country, 2000–2001 and 1996–1997

	Mean annual applied patents at EPO per million people 2000–2001	Mean annual applied patents at EPO per million people 1996–1997	Mean annual rate of growth from 1996–1997 to 2000–2001 (%)
The USA	104	73	9.5
Japan	146	96	10.9
The EU	127	84	10.8
Austria	100	73	8.3
Belgium	113	80	9.0
Denmark	143	90	12.2
Finland	270	138	18.2
France	115	84	8.2
Germany	252	158	12.4
Greece	5	2	20.1
Ireland	61	27	22.6
Italy	57	42	7.8
Luxembourg	322	178	16.0
The Netherlands	307	199	11.4
Portugal	4	2	25.0
Spain	14	8	13.3
Sweden	273	147	16.8
The UK	77	62	5.5
Canada	43	22	19.0
Norway	71	46	11.1
Switzerland	512	353	9.8
The EU:			
Coefficient of variation	0.78	0.73	–
Max/min	79.43	107.21	–

Source: Authors' elaboration on European Patent Office data.

While patents reflect the inventive and innovative activities that are proprietary in nature and mainly developed for commercial purposes, the scientific literature informs mainly on the activities of the academic community. Table 5.6 reports the number of scientific and technical articles published in the sample of journals monitored by the Science Citation Index of the Institute for Scientific Information. This is the only S&T indicator where the total dimension of the EU can be compared to the US. In terms of intensity, the EU average is below the US (respectively, 464 and 595 articles per million people), yet above Japan (375 articles per million people). It is often said that the Science Citation Index is biased in favor of the English-speaking academic community and this is probably true. It is important to point out that many of the top-ranking countries are not-English speaking. Within the EU, the ratio between the highest (Sweden) and the lowest (Portugal) country is 7 to 1. It is confirmed that the dispersion in indicators of academic activities (mainly funded with public

Table 5.6 Scientific and technical articles by country, 1998–1999 and 1994–1995

	Number of scientific publications in 1998–1999 per million people	*Number of scientific publications in 1994–1995 per million people*	*Mean annual rate of growth from 1994–1995 to 1998–1999 (%)*
The USA	595	681	−3.3
Japan	375	338	2.6
The EU	464	439	1.4
Austria	446	375	4.4
Belgium	478	442	2.0
Denmark	773	765	0.3
Finland	758	709	1.7
France	468	450	1.0
Germany	459	420	2.3
Greece	217	175	5.5
Ireland	336	290	3.8
Italy	297	270	2.4
Luxembourg	69	67	0.8
The Netherlands	673	702	−1.0
Portugal	135	85	12.2
Spain	303	245	5.4
Sweden	943	917	0.7
The UK	665	685	−0.7
Canada	644	751	−3.8
Norway	585	586	0.0
Switzerland	976	947	0.8
The EU:			
Coefficient of variation	0.52	0.58	–
Max/min	7.00	10.80	–

Sources: Authors' elaboration from NSF (2000), data from Institute for Scientific Information.

Note
In order to avoid double counting, article counts are based on fractional assignments; for example, an article with two authors from different countries is counted as one-half article to each country. Luxembourg has been excluded from the calculus of the minimum value for the EU.

money) is substantially lower than for technological activities (mainly funded by business companies). Over time, a limited convergence has occurred.

What does this battery of indicators tell us? First, the evidence has allowed a quantified presentation of how Europe is lagging behind the other two major areas. In total R&D investment, Europe's divergence is increasing. This is a particularly worrying signal since R&D is one of the main inputs for the generation of knowledge and thus an engine of economic growth. Second, the gap is more evident in the business-related indicators than in those informed by the public dimension of knowledge.

The indicators of technological activities, such as business R&D and patents, do not provide any sign of Europe catching up. Third, there are huge differences between European countries. In almost all the indicators taken into account, small- and medium-sized countries, such as Switzerland, Sweden, Norway, Finland, the Netherlands and Denmark, show a performance that is on par with or even higher than the US and Japan. However Switzerland and Norway are not members of the EU and the others are too small to be able to lift up the EU average.

Challenges for Europe in ICT

Now we briefly focus the attention on ICTs, which is the sector most closely associated to the definition of new economy. Here, Europe, despite being historically laggard in comparison to the US and Japan (see Gambardella and Malerba 1999; Fagerberg *et al.* 1999; Vivarelli and Pianta 2000; Stubbs 1997), is showing a slow process of catching up. Table 5.7 shows that the US and Japan invest 8.0 percent and 9.0 percent of their

Table 5.7 ICT expenditure on GDP, 2000–2001 and 1996–1997

	ICT expenditure (% of GDP) 2000–2001	ICT expenditure (% of GDP) 1996–1997	Mean annual rate of growth from 1996–1997 to 2000–2001 (%)
The USA	8.0	7.7	1.0
Japan	9.0	6.9	6.9
The EU	7.8	5.7	8.1
Austria	7.2	5.0	9.8
Belgium	8.1	6.0	7.8
Denmark	9.3	6.6	8.8
Finland	7.8	6.0	6.8
France	8.9	6.3	9.2
Germany	7.9	5.4	10.0
Greece	6.1	4.0	11.1
Ireland	6.5	5.6	3.6
Italy	5.7	4.2	7.9
The Netherlands	9.4	6.8	8.3
Portugal	6.8	4.9	8.8
Spain	5.1	4.0	6.6
Sweden	10.9	7.7	9.0
The UK	9.4	7.7	5.1
Canada	8.6	7.4	3.9
Norway	7.1	5.7	5.5
Switzerland	10.3	7.6	7.8
The EU:			
Coefficient of variation	0.20	0.21	–
Max/min	2.13	1.95	–

Source: Worldbank (2000), data from ITU.

GDP in ICT while the EU invests 7.8 percent. But in the second half of 1990s, the EU invested more than its counterparts (annual growth rate of 8.1 percent, against 6.9 in Japan and 1 percent in the US), by reducing the gap. Despite the partial recovery of the EU as a whole, internal dispersion does not seem to converge. On the contrary, the distance between the country with the highest ICT expenditure intensity (Sweden) and that with the lowest one (Spain) has widened (Daveri 2002).

Considering the composition of the ICT sector, the 1980s saw the dramatic rise of Japan and other East Asian economies in hardware technologies (for an overview, see Freeman 1987a; Mathews 2000). Meanwhile, in the 1990s the US managed to recover its traditional economic leadership in knowledge-intensive industries by exploiting and disseminating ICT in the service sector. Within the triad, Japan and the other East Asian economies continue to have a prominent position in the generation of hardware, while the US has a dominant position in the production of software. Europe does not perform particularly well in either sector. It should, however, be noted that Europe has recently augmented the expenditure in the software area. This follows a general tendency toward the so-called "weightlessness," that is the increase of soft components' share in ICT (Daveri 2002; EITO 2001).

After linking indicators to technological creation, we will now link indicators to the diffusion of technology, in particular Internet penetration. In fact, ICT is important not only for the highest gain in productivity it directly performs, but also because, thanks to its diffusion, it enables other sectors to increase their productivity – in other words, it entails positive externalities. Besides, while both R&D and patent-based indicators capture the technological activities developed in the manufacturing industry, Internet penetration is an indicator that provides information on both the manufacturing and the service components of the economy. Table 5.8 shows that Internet penetration in the US and Japan is much higher than in the EU. Although the EU is catching up, it is still at levels below that of the US and Japan. It should be noted that the Scandinavian countries have a higher penetration than the US. The ratio between the country with the highest (Sweden) and the lowest (Greece) penetration is nearly 5 to 1. Not surprisingly, the trend shows a marked convergence among EU countries.

Summing up, with regard to ICTs, Europe is lagging behind the US and Japan. However, the gap is narrowing. This represents a positive signal as ICT is the sector that – after some years of initial investment – is supposed to experience the highest gain in productivity both for itself and the other sectors of the economy.

Table 5.8 Internet users (% of population) by country, 2000 and 1996

	Internet penetration 2000	Internet penetration 1996	Mean annual rate of growth from 1996 to 2000
The USA	33.8	11.2	32
Japan	37.1	4.4	71
The EU	23.8	2.9	70
Austria	25.9	2.5	80
Belgium	22.6	3.0	66
Denmark	36.5	5.7	59
Finland	37.2	16.8	22
France	14.4	1.4	80
Germany	29.2	3.1	76
Greece	9.4	1.4	60
Ireland	20.7	2.2	75
Italy	22.9	1.0	118
Luxembourg	22.8	5.5	42
The Netherlands	24.5	5.8	43
Portugal	25.0	2.3	81
Spain	13.6	1.3	79
Sweden	45.6	9.0	50
The UK	30.2	4.1	65
Canada	41.2	6.7	57
Norway	49.0	18.3	28
Switzerland	29.7	4.6	60
The EU:			
Coefficient of variation	0.36	0.91	–
Max/min	4.84	16.46	–

Source: Worldbank (2000), data from ITU.

International technological and scientific cooperations

In the last decade, a new source of knowledge has become progressively more important: technological collaborations among firms. While the academic community has always had a tendency to share its knowledge with other partners, it was assumed that corporations were much more reluctant to share their know-how with potential competitors. But the need to split the costs and risks of technological development, along with the need to acquire the expertise of other partners, has acted as a strong motivation to undertake strategic technology agreements. Strategic technology agreements are defined as: (1) a partnership that involves a two-way relationship, (2) tend to be contractual in nature with no or little equity involvement by the participants and (3) they are strategic in the sense that they are long-term planned activities (Mytelka 2001: 129).

Strategic technology agreements are not only a source of knowledge; they also inform us on where companies seek expertise. Some evidence on the available statistics on inter-firm technological collaboration is illus-trated in Table 5.9, based on the database developed by John Hagedoorn and his colleagues (see Hagedoorn 1996). As much as 60 percent of the total strategic technology alliances recorded are international in scope. This form of generating technological knowledge has considerably increased its significance. As a result, the number of recorded agreements has nearly tripled between 1980 and 1982, and 1998 and 2000.

The largest and most increasing portion of alliances takes place within the US: 45.8 percent of all the strategic technological alliances recorded between 1998 and 2000 occurred among American firms only; from 1980–1982 it was only 24.6 percent (NSF 2002). Moreover, US firms have strong ties on both the Atlantic and the Pacific shores: from 1998 to 2000, US companies have participated in as much as 84.7 percent of the recorded technology alliances. On the contrary, the share of intra-Euro-pean strategic technological alliances has substantially declined: they accounted for 18.2 percent from 1980 to 1982 and less than 10 percent from 1998 to 2000. They have even decreased in absolute terms in the last decade (from 74 percent in 1989–1991 to 53 percent in 1998–2000).

European policymakers should be concerned with the strong propensity of European firms to seek American, rather than European, partnerships. Policies carried out at the European level, especially at the European Commission's level, to foster cooperation in R&D and innovation in the continent have not been able to reverse the propensity of European firms to engage in partnerships with American firms. The first possible explana-tion would be that the absolute amount of resources devoted to science and technology is much greater in US firms – firms engage in technology alliances with partners who have the adequate expertise. The shift of alliances to the US can thus be seen as the result of the amount of US companies' investment in knowledge. In order to account for this phenom-enon, we divided the number of European alliances undertaken by the total amount of European, US and Japanese business enterprises' R&D expenditure (BERD). This provides an indicator of the propensity of European companies toward collaboration in each of these regions. The results are reported in Table 5.10.

Although the attractiveness of the US economy emerges to be a bit smaller in relative terms, the results in Table 5.10 confirm that European companies have a greater propensity for American partnership. There are 1.07 European–US partnerships for each billion US dollar BERD, while the equivalent figure for intra-European partnership is just 0.62. More-over, the European business community has considerably changed its propensity for partnership over the last ten years: for the periods from 1980 to 1982 and from 1989 to 1991, European companies had a larger propensity for European rather than American partners. The figures were, respectively, 0.80 and 0.61 agreements for each billion US dollar BERD from 1980 to 1982 and 1.03 and 0.86 from 1989 to 1991. The lower part of

Table 5.9 Distribution of strategic technology alliances between and within economic blocs, 1980–2000

Year	Total	Interregional alliances							Subtotal	Intraregional alliances							Subtotal
		Eur–Jap		*Eur–USA*		*Jap–USA*				*Europe*		*Japan*		*USA*			
		Number	*(%)*	*Number*	*(%)*	*Number*	*(%)*			*Number*	*(%)*	*Number*	*(%)*	*Number*	*(%)*		
1980–1982	203	16	7.9	48	23.6	43	21.2		107	37	18.2	9	4.4	50	24.6		96
1989–1991	404	25	6.2	101	25.0	57	14.1		183	74	18.3	7	1.7	140	34.7		221
1998–2000	542	19	3.5	173	31.9	38	7.0		230	53	9.8	11	2.0	248	45.8		312

Source: Our elaboration from NSF (2002).

Table 5.10 Propensities for strategic technical partnerships, 1980–2000

Propensity of European firms for European, US and Japanese technological partners

Period	Number of agreements involving European firms by BERD of the region (in billion US$ at constant dollars PPP)		
	Europe	USA	Japan
1980–1982	0.80	0.61	0.71
1989–1991	1.03	0.86	0.50
1998–2000	0.62	1.07	0.32

Propensity of US firms for European, US and Japanese technological partners

Period	Number of agreements involving US firms by BERD of the region (in billion US$ at constant dollars PPP)		
	Europe	USA	Japan
1980–1982	1.03	0.64	1.90
1989–1991	1.41	1.20	1.15
1998–2000	2.03	1.54	0.65

Sources: Authors' elaboration from NSF (2002), data from MERIT database and from OECD (2001).

Note
Methodology: The number of strategic technological agreements recorded by the MERIT database have been divided by the Business Expenditure on R&D of the region expressed in constant 1992 purchasing power parity US billion dollar. It reads for example that in 1980–1982 there have been 0.8 strategic technology agreements involving European firms for each US dollar billion of European BERD.

Table 5.10 reports the propensity of American companies to undertake alliances. US companies are now keener to undertake joint ventures with European partners and this is a result of the overall increase of their engagement in collaborations. However, Table 5.10 illustrates a great propensity for internal partnerships, which has grown about three times in the last 20 years. If the new economy is represented – among other things – by strategic technology partnership, the evidence suggests that this strongly leans out toward the US rather than toward Europe or Japan.

Partnerships and collaborations promoted by public research institutions and universities equally play a crucial role in the international dissemination of knowledge. They can take a variety of forms: joint research centers, exchange of students and of academic staff or sharing of scientific information. One of the ways to measure it is by looking at internationally co-authored scientific papers. A dramatic increase in the internationally co-authored papers – facilitated by the diffusion of the Internet and e-mail

– is evident in all countries (Table 5.11). From 1986 to 1999, the percentage of internationally co-authored papers has nearly doubled and this represents a clear signal of globalization in the generation of knowledge. On an individual level, European countries are keener to collaborate than the US and Japan. Given the smaller size of each country's scientific community, this fact should not come as a surprise. From a dynamic viewpoint, the rate of increase has been higher in the US and Japan than in European countries, but this is due to the fact that the US has lowered the growth of national scientific articles (see NSF 2002: Table 5.41). These data clearly show that the academic community in Europe is a valuable asset for the acquisition of knowledge and expertise beyond the borders of their countries.

Does the academic community also share the same preference of European firms for American rather than for European partners? Table 5.12 reports the distribution of internationally co-authored collaborations in the triad: Europe is by far the greatest collaborator for the American aca-

Table 5.11 Percentage of internationally coauthored scientific papers in selected countries in all scientific papers, 1986 and 1999

	Percentage internationally coauthored in 1999	*Percentage internationally coauthored in 1986*	*Annual growth rate from 1986 to 1999 (%)*
The USA	21.6	9.2	6.8
Japan	17.6	7.5	6.7
Austria	47.6	25.2	5.0
Belgium	52.5	29.9	4.4
Denmark	48.5	24.4	5.4
Finland	42.0	18.7	6.4
France	39.6	21.0	5.0
Germany	38.4	20.1	5.1
Greece	42.1	26.6	3.6
Ireland	44.7	26.7	4.0
Italy	39.4	22.9	4.3
The Netherlands	41.2	19.8	5.8
Portugal	52.8	34.8	3.3
Spain	36.2	17.0	6.0
Sweden	44.1	22.2	5.4
The UK	34.1	15.7	6.1
Canada	35.4	18.9	5.0
Norway	44.9	21.9	5.7
Switzerland	52.4	32.2	3.8

Source: Authors' elaboration from NSF (2002), data from Institute for Scientific Information.

Notes
National rates are based on total counts: each collaborating country is assigned one paper (a paper with three international coauthors may contribute to the international coauthorship of three countries).
We could not calculate the EU total, as it would contain multiple counting.

Table 5.12 Distribution of internationally coauthored papers across collaborating countries, 1986–1988 and 1995–1997

Country	1995–1997			1986–1988		
	USA	Japan	EU	USA	Japan	EU
USA	–	9.6	60.3	–	8.2	54.9
Japan	45.6	–	39.4	54.0	–	33.3
EU	29.0	4.5	69.4	31.9	3.1	56.6

Sources: Our elaboration from NSF (2000), data from Institute for Scientific Information.

Notes
Row percentages may add to more than 100 because articles are counted in each contributing country and some may have authors in 3 or more countries. With regard to European Union, internationally coauthored articles also include those among members countries.
Rows report the percentage of the total number of international coauthorships of the country. Columns indicate the relative prominence of a country in the portfolio of internationally coauthored articles of every country.

demic community. From 1995 to 1997 as much as 60.3 percent of internationally co-authored papers in the US involved a partner in the EU. Additionally, Europeans have a strong propensity to collaborate among each other. This fact could be misleading if we think that a paper co-authored by a Dutch and a Belgian scientist is classified as "international," while a paper co-authored by a Californian and a New Yorker is classified as national. Still, the US remains the single most important nation for Europeans to collaborate with.

But the data's significance lies in the time evolution (and this is not affected by the different size of the countries): by comparing the first period (1986–1988) to the last one (1995–1997), it becomes evident that intra-EU collaborations are increasing (from 56.6 to 69.4 percent of all internationally co-authored papers), while EU–US collaborations are decreasing for the EU as a whole (from 31.9 to 29.0 percent) as well as for each EU member country. Looking at the data from an American perspective, the above tendency is enhanced: the share of intra-US articles in all US co-authored articles declines from 78 to 68 percent, while the co-authorship with authors based in the EU grows from 11 to 19 percent (NSF 2000: Table 6.51).

We therefore note an inverse tendency: the European business community has an increasing propensity for technological alliances with US firms, while the European academic community has an increasing propensity for intra-European partnership. One of the main policies used by the European Commission in the last decade has been to promote collaborations among European institutions and firms through the instrument of the Framework Programs. The data reported suggest that these policies have been much more successful in academia than in business. It seems as if the limited resources the European Commission disposes (about 4,000 million euro a year in the last approved Sixth Framework Program) have not been enough to face the needs of European industry, while they have revealed to be more effective in the training and mobility of researchers.

A single Europe for science and technology?

The evidence provided confirms that in some vital areas of knowledge and competence building Europe is lagging behind. Contrary to what happened for many periods after the end of the Second World War, the gap between Europe and the US has increased in the 1990s. It is therefore understandable that a major policy concern in Europe is to identify strategies that would allow for the catching up and upgrading of its scientific and technological competence.

Europe is dominated by vast regional disparities and they are much wider in terms of scientific and technological competencies than in income, production or consumption. Germany, which for long has been the technological engine of Europe, has to face a major regional problem: the integration of the former German Democratic Republic. The UK, soul of many centers of scientific excellence, has under-funded its universities for more than twenty years. The EU's enlargement to 15 countries has integrated some small and highly dynamic countries such as Sweden and Finland, but future enlargements will not bring nations with this kind of sophisticated dowry of scientific and technological infrastructures. The candidates to join the EU are nations in which the scientific community suffered hardship for many years while the business world is still far from the competitive proficiency of the EU's more advanced countries. Future enlargements will lead to a EU with a larger population and an expanded market, but with a somewhat reduced intensity of scientific and technological capabilities.

At the Council Summit held in Lisbon in March 2000, European governments set themselves a very ambitious goal: to make Europe the most competitive and dynamic knowledge-based economy in the world. As it often happens with political statements, there is a certain divergence between the target announced and the instruments made available. Too little commitment has been expressed to reach this target. More recently, at the summit of March 2002 held in Barcelona, the EU has set the more ambitious target to raise R&D expenditure to 3 percent of the GDP by 2010. Further, it has set itself the goal to increase the presence of the business sector, which, by 2010, should finance two-thirds of total R&D expenditure. As we know, R&D intensity has a positive relation with economic growth, but such an objective appears very difficult to reach if we simply consider its evolution in the last decade (Schibany and Streicher 2003). One of the results is that it would imply a strongly needed, but hard to realize, increase in research personnel of about 100,000 units per year.

An ambitious goal like this requires serious policy measures: an important one is the direct financing by governments. This is limited by the Maastricht criteria on public balance on the one hand and, on the other, by the aim to increase the private presence at the expense of the public. Indirect measures include tax incentives for the industry, but there are doubts about the leverage effects they will display. Surely a greater effort by the private sector is necessary, as it is also testified by the low level of venture capital financing in Europe with respect to US and Japan (EC 2002). This form of financing is particularly significant for the promotion of innovative activities by small firms (the so-called *start-ups*).

Thus, what are the possible actions to pursue in order to increase Europe's level of innovation? It is difficult to give a unique answer: we can take for granted the fact that institutions play a fundamental role in fostering and creating the premise for technical change. Recently, the concept of Innovation Systems (IS) is being replaced by the more complex one of Social System of Innovation and Production (SSIP). This means that not only direct scientific institutions must be considered for the technological upgrading of an area, but rather the economic system as a whole, including the relations in the markets of production factors (such as labor market connections), the educational and the financial institutions which are all linked by mechanisms of reciprocal complementarities (Amable and Petit 2001). A second consideration to keep in mind is that ICT must be considered as a strategic sector of long-term growth.

As a result, the initiatives of the EU, expressed in the various Framework Programs, are indeed welcomed and well-posed, but they are certainly not sufficient to achieve the targets set by the European Council. This frequently-cited instrument is promoted every four years and allows the European Commission to progressively revise and enlarge the areas of intervention. In this, it follows the leading principle to enhance intra-European co-operation in the so-called pre-competitive research fields. In the last approved Sixth Framework Program, the greatest bulk of resources has been dedicated to Informative Society Technology and Nano-technologies (4,925 million euro over the next four years). Thus, the strategic importance of this sector has indeed been recognized, not only for the new jobs and business that the 3G wireless communication systems, the software architectures and the opto-electronics networks can create, but also because it perfectly meets the request of "ambient intelligence," that is the target to link economic growth with welfare purposes. The other research areas are devoted to the same aim: biotechnology, environment and energy.

However, if these are the actions that the EC wants to engage in, its budget is too limited. The ambitious targets will require a much larger commitment of national resources in terms of funding of the existing centers of excellence (especially when they have been kept under severe financial restriction), to generate the human resources needed for both the public and the business institutions and to start up new problem-oriented institutions. In addition to the (limited) financial instruments, regulations, standards, procurement, competition, real services and large-scale co-operative civilian projects are essential instruments to create a European Research Area (Lundvall 2002).

Parallel to the European commitment, each country makes its own attempts to upgrade its scientific and technological potential. A small country such as Ireland, for example, has managed to improve its technological potential by making the country attractive for multinational corporations. This is not the first time that European governments have preferred to follow an autonomous route. But in an era increasingly dominated by social and economic globalization, the linkages between European nations are so strong that many science and technology policies must be bound to a common European faith. The Commission's schemes have the advantage to reward excellence and to foster the crucial fields where Europe is lagging behind and to involve Europe's least developed regions. The difficulty to implement these policies in an EU of 15 – soon to be 27 – member countries, will continuously increase.

The enormous differences between European member countries show that in order to fully exploit the advantages of knowledge, it is crucial to develop strategies for the transmission and diffusion of competencies across areas. Only by reducing regional disparities it will be possible to obtain a European scientific and technological competence comparable to that of the US and Japan. In this regard, the only risk of ICT development is that it could enlarge the already existing gap between northern and southern European countries. A stronger integration between the academic and the business community is needed, which in turn requires major changes in the institutional setting and in the incentives of the existing publicly funded research centers.

The evidence reported in this chapter has clearly indicated that a small club of European countries has a scientific and technological intensity on par with, and often superior to, the US. The Scandinavian countries have followed a distinctive approach to competence building based on a highly competent and qualified labor force, generated through massive investments in education and training. This model should serve as the model for European policy-making rather than the American model based on firms competing for market shares and R&D public investment concentrated in national priorities such as defense and space. In this regard, the last Framework Program embarked on the right path.

It is evident that successful management of the learning economy will require a much higher political commitment, which should be comparable to the efforts European governments have devoted to creating a single currency. Lundvall (2002) has suggested the creation of a European High Level Council on Innovation and Competence Building chaired by the president of the EU. Its political weight should not be less than that of the European Central Bank. This would be a clear sign that there is a European political commitment to become "the most competitive and dynamic knowledge-based economy in the world" within the next decade. But words without actions will only allow us to observe that at the end of the decade the aim to increase R&D to 3 percent of the GDP has not been achieved and the European technology gap has further widened.

Notes

1 Amable and Petit (2001), Maurseth and Verspagen (1999), Garcia-Fontes and Geuna (1999) and, more broadly, the chapters collected in Archibugi and Lundvall (2001) present some evidence and considerations relating to the lack of a proper European Innovation System.
2 For an assessment of these targets, see Soete 2002; Schibany and Streicher 2003.

Bibliography

Amable, B. and Petit, P. (2001) *The Diversity of Social Systems of Innovation and Production During the 1990s*, Paris: La Defense.

Archibugi, D. (1992) *The Technological Specialisation of Advanced Countries: A Report to the EEC on International Science and Technology Activities*, Boston: Kluwer.

Archibugi, D. and Lundvall, B.-Å. (eds) (2001) *The Globalising Learning Economy*, Oxford: Oxford University Press.

Archibugi, D. and Pianta, M. (1992) *The Technological Specialisation of Advanced Countries: A Report to the EEC on International Science and Technology Activities*, Boston: Kluwer.

Archibugi, D., Howells, J. and Michie, J. (eds) (1999) *Innovation Systems in the Global Economy*, Cambridge: Cambridge University Press.

Bank, W. (2001) *World Development Indicators 2001*, Washington, DC: World Bank.

Cantwell, J.A. and Iammarino, S. (2001) *Multinational Enterprises and Regional Systems of Innovation in Europe*, London: Routledge.

Chesnais, F., Ietto-Gillies, G. and Simonetti, R. (eds) (2000) *European Integration and Global Corporate Strategies*, London: Routledge.

Community Research and Development Information Service (CORDIS) (2002) *Sixth Framework Program*, Luxembourg: CORDIS.

Daveri, F. (2002) *The New Economy in Europe (1992–2001)*, Milan: IGIER.

David, P. and Foray, D. (1995) "Accessing and Expanding the Science and Technology Knowledge-Base," *Science, Technology Industry Review* 16: 13–68.

European Commission (2002) *Key Figures: Towards a European Research Area*, Luxembourg: European Commission.

European Informative Telecommunications Observatory (EITO) (2001) *Yearbook 2001*, Frankfurt a.M.: EITO.

European Patent Office (EPO) (1995–2001) *Annual Report*, Munich: EPO.

Fagerberg, J., Guerrieri, P. and Verspagen, B. (eds) (1999) *The Economic Challenge for Europe: Adapting to Innovation-Based Growth*, Aldershot: Edward Elgar.

Freeman, C. (1987a) *Technology Policy and Economic Performance: Lessons from Japan*, London: Pinter.

—— (ed.) (1987b) *Output Measurement in Science and Technology*, Amsterdam: North Holland.

Gambardella, A. and Malerba, F. (eds) (1999) *The Organization of Economic Innovation in Europe*, Cambridge: Cambridge University Press.

Garcia-Fontes, W. and Geuna, A. (1999) "The Dynamics of Research Networks in Europe," in Gambardella, A. and Malerba, F. (eds) *The Organization of Economic Innovation in Europe*, Cambridge: Cambridge University Press.

Hagedoorn, J. (1996) "Trends and Patterns in Strategic Technology Partnering since the Early Seventies," *Review of Industrial Organization* 11(5): 601–616.

Held, D., McGrew, A., Goldblatt, D. and Perraton, J. (1999) *Global Transformations: Politics, Economics and Culture*, Cambridge: Polity Press.

Kennedy, P. (1987) *The Rise and Fall of the Great Powers*, New York: Random House.

Lundvall, B.-Å. (2002) "Innovation Policy in the Globalising Learning Economy," in Archibugi, D. and Lundvall, B.-Å. (eds) *The Globalising Learning Economy*, Oxford: Oxford University Press.

Lundvall, B.-Å. and Borrás, S. (1998) *The Globalising Learning Economy: Implications for Innovation Policy*, Brussels: European Commission, D.G. XII.

Mathews, J. (2000) *Tiger Technology: The Creation of a Semiconductor Industry in East Asia*, Cambridge: Cambridge University Press.

Maurseth, P.B. and Verspagen, B. (1999) "Europe: One or Several Systems of Innovation? An Analysis Based on Patent Citations," in Fagerberg, J., Guerrieri, P. and Verspagen, B. (eds) *The Economic Challenge to Europe. Adapting to Innovation-Based Growth*, Aldershot: Edward Elgar Publishing.

Molero, J. (ed.) (1995) *Technological Innovation, Multinational Corporations and the New International Competitiveness*, Reading: Hardwood Academic Publishers.

Mytelka, L.K. (1991) *Strategic Partnership. States, Firms and International Competition*, London: Pinter Publishers.

—— (2001) "Mergers, Acquisitions, and Inter-Firm Technology Agreements in the Global Learning Economy," in Archibugi, D. and Lundvall, B.-Å. (eds) *The Globalizing Learning Economy*, Oxford: Oxford University Press.

National Science Foundation (NSF) (2000) *Science and Engineering Indicators 2000*, Washington, DC: US Government Printing Office.

—— (2002) *Science and Engineering Indicators 2002*, Washington, DC: U.S. Government Printing Office.

Nelson, R. (1990) "Technological Leadership. Where Did It Come From and Where Did It Go?," *Research Policy* 19(2): 117–132.

Niosi, J. (1999) "The Internationalization of Industrial R&D," *Research Policy* Special Issue, Guest Editor J. Niosi, 28(2–3): 107–336.

OECD (2001) *Main Science and Technology Indicators 2001–2002*, Paris: OECD.

Patel, P. and Pavitt, K. (1987) "Is Western Europe Losing the Technological Race," in Freeman, C. (ed.) *Output Measurement in Science and Technology: Essays in Honor of Yvan Fabian*, Amsterdam: North Holland.

Pianta, M. (1988) *New Technologies Across the Atlantic: U.S. Leadership or European Autonomy?*, Hemel Hempstead, Hertfordshire: Harvester-Wheatsheaf.

Schibany, A. and Streicher, G. (2003) *Aiming High: An Assessment of the Barcelona Targets*, Vienna: Institute of Technology and Regional Policy, Working Paper no. 06.

Servan-Schreiber, J.-J. (1968) *The American Challenge*, New York: Atheneum.

Sharp, M. (2001) "The Need for New Perspectives in European Commission Innovation Policy," in Archibugi, D. and Lundvall, B.-Å. (eds) *The Globalizing Learning Economy*, Oxford: Oxford University Press.

Soete, L. (2001) "The New Economy: A European Perspective," in Archibugi, D. and Lundvall, B.-Å. (eds) *The Globalizing Learning Economy*, Oxford: Oxford University Press.

—— (2002) *The European Research Area: Perspectives and Opportunities*, paper presented at the International Workshop on Research Policy: Incentives and Institutions, Rome, November 28.

Stubbs, P. (1997) "Science and Technology Policy," in Artis, M. and Lee, N. (eds) *The Economics of the European Union*, Oxford: Oxford University Press.

United Nations Development Program (UNDP) (2001) *Human Development Report*, New York: United Nations.

US Patent and Trademark Office (USPTO) (2001) *Patent Database*, Washington, DC: USPTO.

Vivarelli, M. and Pianta, M. (eds) (2000) *The Employment Impact of Innovation*, London: Routledge.

Worldbank (2000) *Worldbank Development Indicators 2000*, Worldbank. Available online at http://www.worldbank.org/data/wdi2000/index.htm (September 27, 2004).

6 Innovation and social security

An international comparison*

Martin Heidenreich

Introduction

> There is no more of paradox in this [in intellectual property protection] than there is in saying that motorcars are traveling faster than they otherwise would *because* they are provided with brakes.
>
> (Josef A. Schumpeter 1976: 88)

A central characteristic of modern society is the crucial importance of innovations. In the current knowledge society, welfare and economic prosperity are based to a lesser extent on *territorial* barriers erected along national borders for the free trafficking of people, goods, capital and services and to a larger extent on *temporary* advantages gained through innovation. This poses the question if current forms of welfare – which are closely connected to national governance structures – can be maintained.[1] On the one hand, this could be expected if social expenditures were to slow down a country's innovation dynamics. On the other hand, if social security facilitates the acceptance of innovations, then even increasing social expenditures should be expected since the uncertainties associated with innovations would thus be compensated.

The relationship between innovations and social security is crucial especially for Europe, as most European countries are characterized by high social expenditures.[2] If social security systems should prove to be an impediment to innovation, this, in the long term, could lead to an erosion of the European social model. Otherwise, the European welfare states could even envisage competitive and innovative advantages due to their specific production and innovation capabilities (see Heidenreich 1999; Hall and Soskice 2001). Thus, this chapter examines the relationship between innovations and social security on the basis of internationally comparable data.

In its first section, this chapter will develop two opposed hypotheses capturing the relationship between innovation and social security. Following the introduction of these hypotheses, the research design used to test these hypotheses is presented. The third section analyzes the relationship between public spending on social security and education and three different groups of innovation indicators (research, development and education expenditure, international patents, relative weight of knowledge-based industries and services). The last section provides a short summary of the results.

Social security: a prerequisite or a barrier to innovation?

For market economies, social security is in no way an external factor imposed from the outside. Since the end of the nineteenth century, market economies have learned to counterbalance the destructive potential of a disembedded industrial society whose traditional ties have been eroded by new forms of social security "beyond the family and village" (Schmidt 1988).

The current welfare state was not the only possible answer to the demands for new forms of social security. Europe had favored collective work relationships and the welfare state since the 1880s in order to cushion the social effects of a long period of fundamental industrialization (Therborn 1995). The USA, however, at a very early stage, had already decided upon the expansion of the educational sector as a means of raising individual employability. Furthermore, private and voluntary forms of social security and protectionist trading policies can also be interpreted as an answer to the demand for new forms of social security (Rieger and Leibfried 2003). In Japan, the demand for new forms of social security was covered above all by corporate welfare, by a system of life-long employment guarantees for the employees of bigger firms. Employees and citizens were therefore protected from the uncertainties of the market economy by entrepreneurial, educational, commercial and welfare state correction of market results. Social security, therefore, is an integral part of the public, family, economic and labor market structures of developed countries.

There is one common factor linking the different forms of social security: education, laws against unfair dismissal, or social security payments can be interpreted as forms of insurance against risks to employment and income (Sinn 1995). However, this insurance is provided in very different ways (cf. Table 6.1). On the one hand, it can be provided on the basis of individual rights, on the other hand, it can be provided to collectivities without individual rights. In this dimension, individually assessed income compensation payments (social assistance, unemployment and sick pay, pensions) but also education can be distinguished from innovations and laws against collective dismissals. Laws against collective dismissals reduce the risk of loss of employment in selected companies. Through innovations, the competitiveness and capability of businesses, industries, regions and countries is enhanced; thereby the risks of loss of employment and income to the corresponding groups of employees are reduced.

Furthermore, one can distinguish between ex ante and ex post types of social security.[3] On the one hand, the citizens of a country can be protected from the vagaries of the market ex post by the correction of market results. The social effects of a modern economy seen as problematic will be compensated for by supplementary welfare state income payments and benefits. The ex post correction of market incomes is in general seen as a central task of the welfare state. On the other hand, the provision of the conditions for a successful participation in working life, for instance through education and innovations, can also be considered as part of public security. In this sense, already during the 1950s Thomas H. Marshall emphasized that social rights can be guaranteed not only through social security systems, but also through the education system:

> Education is a necessary prerequisite of civil freedom (...) It was increasingly recognized, as the nineteenth century wore on, that political democracy needed and educated electorate, and that scientific manufacture needed educated workers and technicians. The duty to improve and civilize oneself is therefore a social duty, and not merely a personal one.
>
> (Marshall 1977: 90)

Marshall already refers to the fact that the principal goal of welfare state arrangements is not primarily to guarantee a fair distribution of income – a hopeless task in view of conflicting standards of justice – but the inclusion of the population in the different, functionally-differentiated subsystems of a modern society (Kaufmann 1999: 806): inclusion instead of justice. Taking the example of entrepreneurial human resource policies, Kanter describes this as a shift from employment guarantees to an employability-centred strategy:

> If security no longer comes from being employed, it must come from being employable. Large organizations can no longer guarantee long-term employment (...) But employability security – the knowledge that today's work will enhance the person's value in terms of future opportunities – is a promise that can be made and kept. Employability security comes from the chance to accumulate human capital – skills and reputation – that can be invested in new opportunities as they arise.
>
> (Kanter 1995: 157)

Employment chances no longer depend on the inclusion in a specific organization but on the inclusion in the labor market as a whole. This can be generalized: in a knowledge society, social security does not depend only on the ex post protection against income and employment risks, but also on the individual employability of the labor force and on the innovativeness of nations. Innovations can be considered also as a collective protection against income and employment risks. While education can be interpreted as a means of reducing the employment and income risks of individuals, the competitiveness and innovativeness of businesses can be interpreted as a collective provision against employment and income risks (cf. Table 6.1).

Social security cannot therefore be equated with the welfare state's organized redistribution of resources (Esping-Andersen 1994: 726). The inclusion into the labor market by enhancing the employability of individuals and the competitiveness of firms can also be considered as functionally equivalent solutions to the demand for social security. This raises the question of the relationship of these different forms of social security.

This question will be discussed in the following taking the example of the relationship between social security expenditures and innovation expenditures. Concerning the relationship of these two types of expenditures, two different theses can be formulated, which will be reconstructed in the following as *efficiency and compensation hypotheses* (Schwarze and Härpfer 2003). On the one hand, on the basis of neoclassical assumption (cf. for example Siebert 1997) it can be predicted that a higher level of social security has a negative impact on the innovation dynamics of a country, since the incentives for potential innovators will be reduced. Potential "innovation losers" are offered "side payments" and institutional guarantees (for example protection from dismissal and co-determination possibilities) in order to avoid possible resistance to innovations. Such guarantees act much like a tax on innovations. Hereby, the advantages of innovations decrease. If the anticipated benefits of innovations are less than the anticipated costs of innovations, then potential innovators will stop their activities. Therefore, from a neoclassical perspective, a trade-off between innovations and social security is expected (cf. in a somewhat similar vein the relationship of efficiency and social security, Esping-Andersen 1994).

This efficiency hypothesis can also be formulated from a different, more sociological perspective. Innovations are processes of creative destruction;

Table 6.1 Different forms of social security

	Individual security	*Collective security*
Parity of results	Income replacement schemes (sickness and unemployment benefits etc.)	Collective protection against dismissals, family ties
Equal opportunity, employability and competitiveness	Educational facilities	Research and development facilities and innovations

therefore, they endanger previous securities. "The transformation of an idea into a marketable product or service, a new or improved manufacturing or distribution process, or a new method of social service"[4] threatens previous investments, competences and sources of influence: "Capitalist innovation means creation of new combinations of methods and machines and at the same time radical devaluation of all produced values, including well-functioning machines, effective production methods, and highly qualified workforce." (Rammert 2000: 3). This process of creative destruction could be made more difficult by social protection rights for less efficient employees and businesses.

On the other hand, a complementary or even a reciprocal reinforcement of innovations and social security can be assumed. This hypothesis can be developed on the basis of the works of Schumpeter (1976).[5] The underlying argument is known as compensation hypothesis; is has been developed taking the example of the relationship between globalization and social security. Sinn (1995), Rodrik (2000) and Rieger and Leibfried (2003), for example, analyze social security as a counterpart to economic globalization and liberalization processes:

> there is a striking correlation between an economy's exposure to foreign trade and the size of its welfare state [...] This is not to say that the government is the sole, or the best, provider of social insurance. The extended family, religious groups, and local communities often play similar roles. My point is that it is a hallmark of the postwar period that governments in the advanced countries have been expected to provide such insurance.
>
> (Rodrik 2000: 324–325)

The welfare state was the prerequisite which has allowed governments to lower import barriers, to moderate them or lift them completely (Rieger and Leibfried 2003: 75). Sinn (1995: 524) analyzes the welfare state "as a device for stimulating risk taking, thereby liberating productive forces and increasing aggregate income."

These considerations can be applied to the relationship between innovations and social security: it could be expected that innovations can be pushed through more easily, the more potential innovation losers are protected from the negative consequences of innovations. This supposition is supported by the positive correlation between the capability of national innovation regimes in Europe and an egalitarian distribution of income. The European commission therefore surmises: "the outstanding innovation performances of the small welfare economies in Europe could partly be due to giving their citizens more economic security. A more conservative interpretation would be that policies preventing social exclusion need not interfere with innovation." (European Commission 2001: 18). An appropriate social safeguarding could therefore be a central prerequisite for the innovation ability of a country. Conversely, a distinctive technical, scientific and economic capability is a necessary (even if not adequate) condition for a developed social state.

Therefore, the relationship between innovations and social security can be predicted in two completely different ways: the efficiency hypothesis and its sociological counterpart point to a conflict between innovations and security and therefore expect a trade-off between social security and innovations. Meanwhile on the basis of the compensation hypothesis a reciprocal increase in the relationship between welfare state social security payments and public innovation expenditure can be expected.

For each of these two hypotheses, empirical evidence can be found: while the USA and Japan are characterized by a high share of research and development (R&D) expenditures and a low level of social security expenditures, some Scandinavian countries – especially Finland and Sweden – combine high research and development expenditures and a high proportion of research-intensive industries with high social expenditures. The controversy outlined above, therefore, cannot be decided on the basis of single case studies. It is necessary to include a larger group of countries.

The method and the data

The connection between innovations and social security provisions will be analyzed on the basis of internationally comparative data. On the basis of the data[6] collected by the Organization for Economic Co-operation and Development (OECD), this task could simply be solved by bivariate analyses – for example by a regression or a scatter diagram (cf. Figure 6.1). It turns out that the relationship between social security and research and development expenditure exhibits a very strong correlation coefficient of $r^2 = 0.22$. This can be understood as a confirmation of the compensation hypothesis. However, such an interpretation would not take into account that the strong correlation is perhaps only the result of a third variable not being taken into account – for example the result of the economic prosperity or the integration into the world markets: richer countries, who are more integrated in the world market invest more in research and social security. Due to the small number of developed countries, the control of such intervening variables is normally not possible, because the number of advanced industrial countries is too low: the required data will hardly be available for all 30 OECD countries.

Nevertheless, multivariate analyses can be carried out if the necessary data are available for several years. If, for example, data for 20 countries are available for 20 years (in our case: for two decades, the 1980s and 1990s[7]), then the number of observations can be increased to a maximum of 400. Classic linear regressions could be carried out through this "pooling" of data, if the observations for one variable for one country at

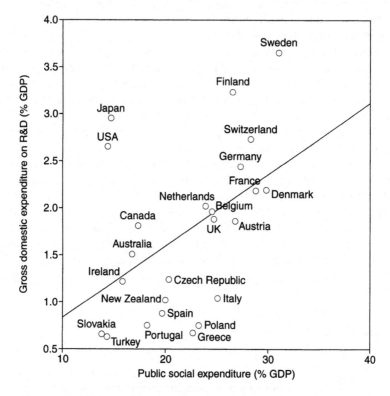

Figure 6.1 Public social expenditure and gross domestic expenditure for research and development (in percentage of gross domestic product, 24 OECD countries, 1999) (sources: OECD Statistical Compendium own calculations).

different times were independent from each other. However, this assumption (technically speaking: the assumption of no unobserved heterogeneity) is extremely implausible; it implies, for example, that there is no connection between the income inequalities in a country in the years 1980 and 1981. This assumption can be checked with the Breusch–Pagan Test (Schwarze and Härpfer 2003; Breusch and Pagan 1980). Normally, this assumption will be rejected. It is not only implausible, but also statistically refutable. In this case, different panel regressions can be used – above all models of fixed or random effects.

Models of fixed and random effects differ regarding the assumptions concerning the error terms: models with fixed effects assume country-specific constant error terms over a period of time; in models with random effects, the country-specific effects are considered as random variables. Whether one or the other assumption applies can be checked with the Hausman Test. The zero hypothesis of the Hausman Test is: the country-specific errors and the explanatory variables are not correlated. If this hypothesis cannot be rejected, because the differences between estimated coefficients of the random-effects model and the fixed-effects model are not systematically different from zero, a model with fixed effects as well as a model with random effects can be used. If the zero hypothesis is rejected, then a model with fixed effects is preferred (Greene 2000: chapter 14; Baltagi 2001). An advantage of using exclusively the model with fixed effects is that the estimations are unbiased even if the fixed effects and the explanatory variables are correlated; a disadvantage is that influences of time-constant variables (for example the culture of a specific country) cannot be identified, because it cannot be distinguished from the fixed error terms.

After the Breusch–Pagan Test and the Hausman Test, a third test must be carried out to determine whether the error parameters of the variables are time-dependent. A conventional procedure for this is the application of a modified Durbin–Watson Test (cf. Baltagi 2001: 95). If the corresponding value clearly deviates from 2, this can be interpreted as a correlation of the residuals over time. The rho value also shown in the following tables indicates the strength of these auto correlations (zero: no auto correlation). The squared correlation coefficient (r^2) indicates the amount of variance explained by the entire model (including the 19 dummy variables for the years not listed in Tables 6.3–6.5). With regard to these tests, Tables 6.3–6.5 use fixed-effects models with first-order autoregressive disturbance terms (AR1). The estimates of these models are carried out using the procedure *xtregar* of the program STATA 8. The median values of the variables used in the following tables are portrayed in Table 6.2.

Innovations and social security: the empirical results

In order to analyze the relationship between social security and innovations, two groups of dependent variables have to be distinguished. On the one hand, there are the indicators measuring the input of innovation processes, for example the expenditures for research, development and education. On the other hand there are the output indicators, for example the number of patents or the share of advanced technologies. In this chapter, the connection between social security systems and innovations is discussed on the basis of three different groups of dependent variables. First, the relationship between social security and innovation expenditure, then the connection between social security and patents and finally the connection between public social security expenditure and the relative weight of knowledge-based industries and services.

Table 6.2 Innovations and social security: mean values and standard deviations (20 OECD countries; 1980–1999)

	Australia	Austria	Belgium	Canada	Denmark	Finland	France
Gross domestic product per head, at the price levels and PPPs of 1995	19.595	19.546	19.955	21.814	21.163	18.424	18.793
Total trade (exports and imports/GDP)	35.8	76.6	135	60.0	67.6	58.7	44.2
Public social expenditure (% GDP)	14.7	25.5	25.6	17.6	29.9	25.8	26.4
Social security transfers (% GDP)	7.8	18.4	17.2	11.7	17.8	16.7	17.6
Expenditure for public services (% GDP)	6.9	7.1	8.4	6.0	12.1	9.1	8.8
Family cash benefits (% GDP)	1.5	2.3	2.4	0.7	1.3	1.8	2.1
Family services (% GDP)	0.2	0.8	0.1	0.1	1.9	1.3	0.6
Active labor market programs (% GDP)	0.5	0.4	1.3	0.5	1.3	1.2	0.9
Health (% GDP)	5.2	5.4	6.3	6.4	7.3	5.8	6.7
Expenditure from public and private sources for education (% GDP)	5.1	5.8	5.3	6.4	6.7	5.7	5.7
Gross domestic expenditure on R&D (% GDP) (GERD)6	1.3	1.4	1.7	1.5	1.5	2.0	2.2
Expenditure on R&D in the higher education sector (% GDP)	0.3	0.4	0.4	0.4	0.4	0.4	0.4
Industry-financed GERD (% GDP)	0.5	0.7	1.1	0.6	0.8	1.1	1.0
Government-financed GERD (% GDP)	0.7	0.6	0.5	0.7	0.6	0.7	1.0
Number of patent applications to the EPO (per million inhabitants)	25.1	80.2	62.6	22.9	71.3	95.2	78.4
Number of patents granted by the USPTO (per million inhabitants)	31.9	50.4	44.5	77.1	55.5	86.7	54.1
Number of "triadic" patent families (per million inhabitants)	10.7	24.2	25.3	10.8	25.8	36.5	30.4
High technology industries[a]	0.0	2.0	1.9	1.6	1.7	2.1	2.5
Medium high technology industries[a]	3.7	6.2	7.7	5.6	5.1	6.6	7.5
Knowledge-based services[a]	13.6	13.7	6.3	14.1	12.9	10.3	18.0

Note

a The proportion of real net output of high-technology industries (aircraft and spacecraft, pharmaceuticals, office, accounting and computing machinery, radio, television and communications equipment, medical, precision and optical instruments), of medium-high-technology industries (electrical machinery and apparatus, motor vehicles, trailers and semi-trailers, chemicals excluding pharmaceuticals, railroad equipment and transport equipment, machinery and equipment) and from market-related knowledge-based services (post and telecommunications, finance and insurance, business services) can be calculated on the basis of the OECD STAN database (cf. also OECD 2003).

Germany	*Greece*	*Ireland*	*Italy*	*Netherlands*	*New Zealand*	*Norway*	*Portugal*	*Spain*	*Sweden*	*Switzerland*	*United Kingdom*	*USA*
9.204	12.491	15.082	18.317	19.393	16.274	20.776	11.977	13.626	19.663	25.132	17.024	25.502
3.3	46.6	121	43.6	108	58.1	73.6	66.3	40.7	66.3	68.6	52.9	20.6
3.4	19.0	18.8	22.8	27.2	20.2	23.7	14.7	18.9	31.7	20.8	22.6	14.0
7.1	14.3	13.5	15.7	23.3	0.0	14.3	11.5	15.4	19.6	12.2	13.9	11.8
6.3	4.7	5.3	7.1	3.9	20.2	9.4	3.2	3.6	12.0	8.6	8.7	2.3
1.4	0.7	1.5	0.7	1.3	2.3	1.8	0.7	0.3	1.9	1.1	1.8	0.3
0.6	0.4	0.1	0.2	0.4	0.1	0.9	0.2	0.1	2.2	0.1	0.5	0.3
1.0	0.3	1.4	0.7	1.0	0.8	0.8	0.6	0.6	2.0	0.3	0.6	0.2
5.8	4.8	5.4	5.7	5.9	6.0	6.4	4.1	5.0	7.6	6.0	5.3	4.9
4.7	2.9	5.6	5.0	5.9	5.3	6.6	4.5	5.0	7.0	5.2	4.9	5.2
2.5	0.4	1.0	1.1	2.0	0.9	1.5	0.7	0.7	2.9	2.6	2.1	2.6
.4	0.1	0.2	0.2	0.5	0.2	0.4	0.2	0.2	0.8	0.5	0.3	0.4
.5	0.1	0.5	0.5	1.0	0.3	0.7	0.3	0.3	1.8	1.9	1.0	1.4
.9	0.2	0.3	0.5	0.9	0.6	0.7	0.4	0.3	1.0	0.6	0.8	1.1
	2.3	20.3	35.8	102	15.6	40.0	1.2	7.2	136	246	62.8	63.9
	1.3	19.5	22.7	66.1	21.5	36.8	0.6	4.4	120	187	51.9	225
.4	0.4	6.8	10.6	43.5	5.4	13.9	0.3	1.6	62.2	113	24.9	40.6
.7	0.6	–	2.1	1.3	–	0.9	1.0	1.2	2.8	–	3.1	3.7
.9	2.3	–	7.6	5.1	–	3.3	4.3	6.3	7.4	–	7.5	5.9
.6	10.4	–	10.8	13.2	12.2	11.8	7.9	12.0	12.6	–	12.5	16.6

Social security an innovation expenditure

Research and development expenditure in percentage of the gross domestic product is a central indicator for the input to innovation processes. However, a weakness of this indicator is that it focuses only on systematic innovation activities especially in larger businesses. Therefore, the inclusion of additional indicators, which measure the role of technical knowledge based on investments in machinery and equipment, software or higher education would be highly desirable. In a recent study, the OECD (2003) proposed a more comprehensive concept of innovation expenditure taking into account all these expenditures. It has been estimated that in the year 2000 in the 30 OECD countries, 2.3 percent of the gross domestic product (2000) was spent on research and development, 1.3 percent on software, 1.3 percent on higher education and 8.4 percent on machinery and equipment. However, the last three types of expenditure can only be estimated for some recent years.

Therefore, it is necessary to use other input indicators: the indicator "knowledge investments" will be made up of the expenditure for research and development and for education (subtracting the share of research and development expenditure in higher education, since this expenditure is included in both positions). On the one hand, these two indicators overestimate the investment in knowledge, since the expenditure for primary school education can hardly be counted as innovation expenditure. However, since the educational expenditure and the expenditure for higher education in the second half of the 1990s are closely correlated ($r = 0.63$), the changes in educational expenditure can be taken as indicators for the size of innovation-relevant investments in human capital. On the other hand, the innovation expenditure is underestimated since the investments in software and into new machinery and equipment are blanked out. The OECD (2003: 74) submitted estimations of the investment in software for the last years. However, these data are not available for all the eighties and nineties. In the following, we will therefore take the educational and research expenditure as input indicators.

In Table 6.3, different models are reported, in which the connection between innovation expenditure and public social security expenditure is captured in different ways. In each case, the purchasing-power-adjusted gross domestic product (GDP), the integration into the world market (the sum of the import and export quotas), and the dummy variables for the different years (with the exception of the reference year 1980) are included as control variables. The coefficients of the constant and these dummy variables are not reported in the following tables.

In the first column of Table 6.3, a model is introduced, which – with the exception of the additional control variables – essentially corresponds to the model portrayed in Figure 6.1. The results are surprising: in contrast to Figure 6.1, there is no significant correlation between research expenditure and social security expenditure. When the economic performance and the integration into the world market are taken into consideration, there is no connection between the two variables. This points to the previously indicated limitations of bivariate analyses. In international comparisons, bivariate analyses can be used only with the utmost caution.

However, only 29 percent of the research and development expenditure in OECD countries is financed by governments (OECD 2003: 21). 64 percent (2000) of R&D expenditure is carried by the private economy. If only the government-financed R&D expenditure (column 2) are included, a significant connection emerges between R&D and social security expenditure. The connection between public social security expenditure and public and private educational expenditure is also significant (column 2):

Table 6.3 The relationship between educational and research expenditure and social expenditure (20 OECD countries, 1980–1999)

	R&D expenditures	Government-financed R&D expenditures	Public and private expenditures for education	Public and private expenditures for education and R&D	Public financed education and R&D expenditures	Public expenditures for education and R&D	Public expenditures for education and R&D	Public expenditures for education and R&D
	(1)	(2)	(3)	(4)	(5)	(6)	(7)	(8)
GDP (per head, PPP, 1995)	−0.01 (0.67)	−0.00 (0.09)	−0.06 (1.14)	−0.07 (1.26)	−0.19 (3.31)‡	−0.18 (3.08)‡	−0.24 (4.55)‡	−0.25 (4.51)‡
Total trade	0.00 (0.69)	0.00 (0.64)	0.00 (0.50)	0.00 (0.73)	0.00 (0.43)	0.00 (0.42)	0.00 (0.52)	0.00 (0.13)
Public social expenditures	0.00 (0.49)	0.01 (3.11)‡	0.04 (2.00)†	0.03 (1.48)	0.08 (3.15)‡	—	—	—
Social security transfers	—	—	—	—	—	0.10 (3.19)‡	—	—
Public social services	—	—	—	—	—	0.07 (2.58)†	—	—
Family services and cash benefits	—	—	—	—	—	—	0.07 (0.50)	—
Active labor market programs	—	—	—	—	—	—	0.22 (1.17)	—
Health expenditures	—	—	—	—	—	—	0.18 (2.00)†	—
Taxes on income, profits and capital gains	—	—	—	—	—	—	—	−0.01 (0.21)
Social security contributions	—	—	—	—	—	—	—	0.03 (0.71)
Taxes on goods and services	—	—	—	—	—	—	—	−0.01 (0.22)
Breusch–Pagan Test	1,940‡	1,743‡	1,255‡	1,218‡	1,533‡	1,245‡	949‡	1,221‡
Hausman Test	44.34	29.79	6.22	13.44	36.90	92.59	69.34	67.07
DF	22‡	22	22	22	22*	23‡	24‡	24‡
Modified Durbin–Watson Test	0.21	0.22	0.38	0.38	0.57	0.57	0.58	0.48
Rho_ar	0.91	0.89	0.84	0.83	0.73	0.73	0.74	0.77
R²	0.09	0.10	0.24	0.23	0.24	0.24	0.23	0.22

Sources: OECD: Statistical Compendium and own calculations.

Notes

Absolute value of t statistics in parentheses; balanced fixed-effects model when the disturbance term is first-order autoregressive; data for 20 OECD countries from 1980–1999. Time dummies and constants included but not portrayed in the table. * significant at 10%; † significant at 5%; ‡ significant at 1%. Breusch–Pagan Test on the existence of country-specific effects (chi-square distributed with a degree of freedom). Hausman Test on failure specifications using a model with random effects (chi-square distributed; number of degrees of freedom shown in the table).

an active state invests in education as well as in research and in the social security of its citizens.

If the public and private educational and research expenditure is added and the overlapping expenditure for research in higher education is deducted (column 4), the correlation between knowledge investments and social security expenditure is no longer significant. If the public and the private research and educational expenditure is taken as an indicator for the input of innovation processes, neither the efficiency nor the compensation hypothesis can be confirmed.

However, this is not valid if only public educational and research expenditure (column 5) is included: the correlation between public social security and educational and research expenditure is highly significant. The compensation hypothesis therefore applies if it is understood as a statement about political actors: states that invest a great deal in social security also invest a great deal in education and research. However, a general correlation between innovation expenditure and social security expenditure – as predicted by the compensation hypothesis – cannot be proved.[8]

In the last three columns of Table 6.3, the connection between social security expenditure and public educational and research expenditure is examined more closely. At first, the public social security expenditure is divided into transfer payments and into expenditure for the public provision of services (column 6). Both indicators are significantly correlated with research and educational expenditure. A state which invests in research and education does not have any preference for transfer payments or for a developed public service.

In the seventh column, the hypothesis is tested that "future-oriented" social expenditure (expenditure for families, for active labor market policies and for health services) in comparison to ex post measures (unemployment benefit, pensions, etc.) are more closely associated with research and educational expenditure. After the inclusion of three different "ex ante" types of social expenditure it can be seen that only the expenditure of publicly-financed health services is correlated significantly with the amount of the research and educational expenditure. This indicates the importance of "life sciences," which will be one of the future growth markets in view of the older population of most OECD-countries.

In the last column, the hypothesis is examined that the relative weight of social security contributions and of taxes on income and goods and services influences the state commitment to education and research. It could be supposed that a high share of social security contributions limits the possibilities of the state to finance research and education investments. This hypothesis cannot be confirmed.

In conclusion: neither the negative correlation between social security and innovation expenditure predicted by the efficiency thesis nor the positive correlation predicted by the compensation thesis can be adequately proven. However, a positive correlation between public social security and educational and research expenditure can be proved. This connection cannot be interpreted – in the sense of the compensation hypothesis – as expression of functional requirements, but it reflects the fact that welfare states are engaged in education and research as well.

Social security and international patents

In the next stage, the relationship between social security expenditure and the results of innovation processes will be analyzed, considering the patent activities of the respective national economies. These patent activities can be detected by using three different patent categories: firstly, by the number of applications for patents (per million residents) to the European Patent Office (EPO); secondly, by the number of the patents approved by the United States Patent and Trademark Office (USPTO); and finally through the number of the patents approved in Japan, the European Union and the USA ("triadic patents").

The number of the European patents is negatively correlated with the proportion of public social security expenditure (Table 6.4, column 3). However, this is not true for triadic and US patents (columns 1 and 2). Contrary to the European experience, in the USA and the American-European-Japanese triad, high social security expenditure does not have any negative effects on the patent applications. Even if, additionally, the amount of the educational and research investments is included, the correlation between social security expenditure and European patent activities remains significant (column 6). Such a relationship cannot be proved with the triad and US patents (columns 4 and 5). This points to a European particularity – a negative impact of welfare state activities on patent activities.

In the next stage, the educational and research expenditure is divided into three components (columns 7–9): public and private educational expenditure; industry-financed R&D expenditure; and government-financed R&D expenditure. In all cases, the R&D expenditure of businesses has a clear positive influence on the patent intensity in the triad, in the USA and in Europe. Public research, however, is negatively correlated with patent intensity. In the USA, the corresponding coefficient is even significant at the 5 percent level (column 8). The influence of social security expenditure on the patent level is no more significant.

At first sight these results are calming: on the basis of a central output indicator, the patent applications, the expected negative effects of the efficiency hypothesis on the innovativeness of the respective national economies could not be confirmed. However, this is not applicable to the patent registrations with the EPO. If it is assumed that there is a "home bias," and therefore a propensity to apply for patents in one's own economic area, then this can be interpreted as a minor innovativeness of the relatively strongly developed European welfare states.

Table 6.4 The relationship between patent applications and social security expenditure (20 OECD countries, 1980–1999)

	Triadic patents	US patents	EPO patents	Triadic patent families	US patents	EPO patents	Triadic patents families	US patents	EPO patents
	(1)	(2)	(3)	(4)	(5)	(6)	(7)	(8)	(9)
GDP (per head, PPP, 1995)	−1.60 (3.2)‡	−2.11 (2.19)†	−3.09 (2.47)†	−1.55 (3.1)‡	−2.04 (2.11)†	−2.93 (2.35)†	−1.50 (3.1)‡	−1.92 (2.00)†	−2.84 (2.30)†
Total trade	0.03 (0.60)	0.01 (0.07)	−0.02 (0.21)	0.02 (0.54)	0.00 (0.03)	−0.03 (0.31)	0.03 (0.60)	0.01 (0.11)	−0.02 (0.21)
Public social expenditures	−0.28 (1.42)	−0.34 (0.90)	−1.12 (2.26)†	−0.30 (1.53)	−0.37 (0.97)	−1.18 (2.40)†	−0.24 (1.17)	−0.15 (0.38)	−0.82 (1.60)
Expenditures for education and R&D	–	–	–	0.81 (1.78)*	1.09 (1.26)	2.59 (2.27)†	–	–	–
Industry-financed R&D (GERD)	–	–	–	–	–	–	4.08 (1.82)*	7.22 (1.67)*	19.51 (3.48)‡
Government-financed R&D	–	–	–	–	–	–	−2.64 (0.72)	−14.38 (2.06)†	−12.54 (1.38)
Expenditure for education (public/private)	–	–	–	–	–	–	0.68 (1.38)	0.84 (0.90)	1.71 (1.40)
Observations	380	380	380	380	380	380	380	380	380
Breusch–Pagan Test	2,704‡	2,073‡	2,439‡	2,723‡	2,208‡	2,412‡	1,635‡	1,127‡	1,548‡
Hausman Test	29.28	24.85	18.39	19.83	24.59	16.91	33.38	34.06	19.70
DF	22	22	22	23	23	23	25	25	25
Modified Durbin–Watson Test	0.16	0.11	0.14	0.18	0.15	0.14	0.37	0.29	0.26
Rho_ar	0.92	0.95	0.93	0.92	0.95	0.93	0.90	0.94	0.92
R^2	0.25	0.29	0.37	0.26	0.29	0.38	0.27	0.31	0.41

Sources: OECD: Statistical Compendium and own calculations.

Notes
See Table 6.3.

Furthermore, if the fact, that public research and educational investments do not have any positive effect on the patent intensity of a country is taken into consideration, then the positive correlation between social security and educational and research expenditure described in the previous section can no longer be evaluated as positive evidence. Only industrial research and development expenditure seems to have an immediate and positive influence on the patent activities of a country. Altogether, at least for Europe this evidence seems to confirm the negative relationship between social security and innovations postulated by the efficiency hypothesis.

Social security and the share of knowledge-based industries and services

A further indicator of the innovativeness of a national economy is the relative share of knowledge-based industries and service industries as a percentage of the respective national GDP. Industries characterized by particularly high expenditure for research and development are regarded as knowledge based (see footnote to Table 6.2). The relative weight of high-technology- and medium-high-technology industries and knowledge-based services can be calculated on the basis of the OECD STAN database.

The connection between social, educational and research expenditure and the branch structure of the respective countries is examined in Table 6.5. The first column shows, that industry-financed research and development activities are positively correlated with the relative weight of leading-edge technology industries (column 1). This is not surprising, since these industries invest at least 18 percent of their value added in research and development (OECD 2003: 156). Public research and educational expenditure, however, does not have any recognizable effect on the share of the value-added of knowledge-based industries.

Social security expenditure is also not significantly correlated with the share of high-technology industries. This is a surprising result, since other studies describe a lower degree of economic coordination and social embedding, for example in the USA, as a prerequisite for the strong position of the American high-technology industries (Hall and Soskice 2001). The panel regression introduced in this chapter cannot confirm this supposition: countries with a developed system of social security (for example, Germany, Sweden, Finland) are also characterized by a considerable share of leading-edge technologies. The efficiency hypothesis – just as the compensation hypothesis – cannot be confirmed for this group of output indicators.

However, social security expenditure and the relative share of medium-high-technology industries (for example, vehicle and mechanical engineering), are negatively correlated (column 2). This could be assessed as confirmation of the efficiency hypothesis. The positive correlation with the relative openness of the countries suggests another interpretation: the

Table 6.5 The relationship between knowledge-based industries and social security expenditure (20 OECD countries, 1980–1999)

	High-technology industries (VA) (1)	Medium-high-technology industries (2)	Knowledge-based industries (VA) (3)	Knowledge-based services (VA) (4)
GDP (per head, PPP, 1995)	−0.02 (0.52)	0.08 (1.44)	0.07 (o,94)	−0.14 (0.60)
Total trade	0.00 (0.06)	0.02 (4.46)‡	0.02 (3.33)‡	−0.02 (0.67)
Public social expenditures	−0.02v	−0.06 (2.73)‡	−0.07 (2.54)†	0.09 (0.93)
Industry-financed R&D (GERD)	0.80 (4.49)‡	−0.10 (0.43)	0.56 (1.82)*	0.93 (0.86)
Government-financed R&D	−0.11 (0.42)	0.00 (0.00)	−0.24 (0.52)	−1.56 (0.98)
Expenditure for education (public/private)	−0.00 (0.10)	−0.06 (0.13)	−0.06 (0.92)	0.15 (0.72)
Observations	323	323	323	342
Breusch–Pagan Test	1,723‡	2,196‡	2,065‡	196‡
Hausman Test	4.92	112†	57†	56‡
DF	25	25	25	25
Modified Durbin–Watson Test	0.43	0.33	0.33	0.27
Rho_ar	0.83	0.87	0.89	0.88
R^2	0.15	0.34	0.29	0.12

Sources: OECD: Statistical Compendium and own calculations.

Notes
See Table 6.3.

international competition, especially in industries with higher-quality technologies, is particularly intensive. The lower share of social security expenditure, particularly in those countries that specialize in medium-high technologies, could also be explained by the fact that the intensive international competition, especially in higher-quality technologies, restricts the scope of welfare state activities (cf. Alber and Standing 2000). This effect cannot be observed, however, in high-technology industries (column 1), since there is less pressure of competition in these industries.

There is no significant relationship between the share of knowledge-based services and the amount of expenditure on social security, research and education (column 4).

In conclusion, that higher social security expenditure goes hand in hand with a lower share of medium-high-technology industries. Since this effect cannot be observed in the case of high technologies, this result cannot be considered as a confirmation of the efficiency hypothesis. More likely, this result can be explained by the stronger competition in the field of medium-high technologies: nations with a higher share of advanced technologies are confronted with the limits of growth of welfare state expenditures in an increasingly globalized economy.

Summary

In this chapter, the relationship, already put forward by Schumpeter, between social security and innovations was pursued on the basis of internationally comparative data for 20 developed industrial countries. At first, two different hypotheses were introduced: the efficiency hypothesis emphasizes that the inclination to take economic risks is hampered by higher standards of social security; there are less incentives for innovation. The compensation hypothesis however, presumes that higher risks conditional to innovation require higher standards of social security. Without a political compensation for innovation losers, the resistance to innovations could become so great that they would no longer be implemented in developed democratic societies.

These two hypotheses were checked on the basis of three different innovation indicators with the assistance of panel data for 20 countries over two decades. First, the amount of research and development expenditure and the amount of the educational expenditure were included as indicators of the input of innovation processes, then the patent quotas in Europe, in the USA and in the triad added and finally the share of value added in knowledge-intensive industries and service sectors. Here too, as with every empirical analysis, the limitations of the data used must also be emphasized. The input for innovations is only partially taken into account since, among others, the investments in software, in new machinery and in highly-qualified employees are not available for the 1980s and 1990s. With social security expenditure, only public expenditure was taken into account and not private, family or entrepreneurial expenditure. Also, no non-linear connections between the variables were modeled.

This chapter demonstrated that the compensation hypothesis predicts correctly the connection between public social security and research expenditure. States that invest in research and development, also invest strongly in social security. However, in both groups of output indicators used, the compensation hypothesis could not be confirmed. A higher share of patents and knowledge-intensive industries is not positively correlated with higher social security expenditure. Given the positive correlations between social security, educational and research expenditure, this result comes as a surprise. This surprising result can be explained by the fact that higher governmental research and development expenditure does not lead to significantly higher patent successes or to a significantly higher value added of knowledge-intensive industries. Only business expenditure on research and development has a positive impact on the patent activities of a country and the share of knowledge-intensive industries. In addition, an active state cannot contribute directly to innovations through the support of research and education.

The negative relationship between social security expenditure and the applications to the European patent office can be considered as a partial confirmation of the efficiency hypothesis. This relationship was interpreted as an indication of a lesser propensity for innovation in the relatively strongly-developed European welfare states. However, the negative correlation between social security expenditure and the share of medium-high technology industries rather refers to the higher competition in the international markets for these technologies.

In conclusion: neither the negative relationship predicted by the efficiency hypothesis nor the positive one by the compensation hypothesis between social security and innovations can be confirmed in all circumstances. Neither can a conclusion be drawn (as a consequence of the efficiency hypothesis) that the welfare state, which is the result of over 100 years of conflicts, negotiations, compromises and reforms, has become functionless in a globalized knowledge society and will gradually vanish due to international competition. However, there is also little in support of the conclusion (which would be the implication of the compensation hypothesis) that the shift from territorially-based strategies of social closure to innovation-based, temporary competitive advantages in innovations will be possible without a fundamental redesign of the current, national systems of social security. The importance of qualification and innovation-centered state policies will increase but the state cannot hope to directly increase the innovativeness of the national economy. There is therefore no reason for political fatalism; social state security in a global knowledge economy is not a locational disadvantage per se, nor is it an advantage. The fate of social security probably depends on how successfully the different countries manage to walk the tightrope between lower innovation incentives and the higher preparedness to take risks.

Notes

* I am grateful to Johannes Schwartze for his methodical support and to Marc Rohr for the translation of this chapter.

1 A central result of the debate regarding the relationship between globalization and social security is that neither a race to the bottom nor a further extension of the welfare state as a compensation for losses due to globalization can be observed (cf. Kittel and Obinger 2003; Alber and Standing 2000; Genschel 2003). Garrett and Mitchell (2001: 176) summarize their empirical analyses as follows: "Globalization has not induced a pervasive race to the bottom in welfare state regimes. Nor have governments responded to market integration by increasing their welfare state effort across the board. The reality surely lies somewhere between these two extremes."

2 The public social spending in the EU countries amount to 24.2 percent of the gross domestic product (GDP) in 1998 in comparison with 20.8 percent in all the OECD countries.

3 The distinction between two concepts of fairness, or solidarity, characterized as result-equity and opportunity-equity by Münch (2001) focuses on the same issue. *Result-equity* is intended to equalize, to some degree, the market compensation, between people who have achieved different results on the basis of unequal performance – for example, the redistribution of wealth in a family, or a welfare state. Such redistributions require a feeling of unity, or "mechanical solidarity." The stronger members of a society must be prepared to share, while the weaker members may not take advantage of the situation. A shared understanding of members' rights and privileges must effectively counter free-riders. In *opportunity-equity* societies the emphasis is on the definition of procedures and the creation of prerequisites, which ensure that everyone has the same opportunity to achieve his or her goals through individual performance – without hindering others. In the first instance inequality is addressed ex post, while in the second, an attempt is made to correct inequality ex ante.

4 This is the definition of the term "innovation" which can be found in the green paper on innovation published by the European Commission (OECD 1995: 4). This definition is based on the OECD's Frascati Handbook. The subsequently developed *Oslo Handbook* (1997), also published by OECD, limits the concept of innovation to technical innovations.

5 Innovations undermine not only the basis of existing technologies and businesses, but they also threaten the customs, qualifications, the social status and the sources of influence of employees and professional associations. Schumpeter has already stated that those affected by innovations offer resistance to them; "it was [...] in general not the postmasters, who founded the railways." (Schumpeter 1935: 101) Schumpeter therefore defines innovations as the pushing through of new combinations *against resistances* (Schumpeter 1935: 124–126).

6 This data can be downloaded from the various databases of the OECD available on the Internet (http://195.145.59.167) if the corresponding access authorization is available. This chapter employs the databases "National Accounts and Historical Statistics" and "Labor Market and Social Issues").

7 In this chapter, data for the following 20 countries are used for the 1980s and 1990s: Australia, Austria, Belgium, Canada, Denmark, Finland, France, Germany, Greece, Ireland, Italy, the Netherlands, New Zealand, Norway, Portugal, Spain, Sweden, Switzerland, United Kingdom and the United States. The 1980s and 1990s were chosen because the years 1979/1980 were a particular turning point in most industrial countries: the extraordinary phase of prosperity of the post-war period had definitely come to an end. Since then the number of unemployed has risen continuously to levels previously unknown. The second

major rise in the price of oil signalled the end of the previous period of cheap fuel and with the necessity to recycle petrodollars, created the conditions for the liberalization of the financial markets (Eurodollar markets). Since the beginning of the Reagan and Thatcher eras the national collective bargaining systems had come under considerable pressure to change. The global networking of the economy permanently exceeded levels achieved prior to the First World War (Hirst and Thompson 1996) and the Taylorist, bureaucratically-organized mass production of the post-war period was threatened increasingly by new flexible forms of production and organization.

8 This diagnosis, however, may also be a consequence of insufficient data. While the compensation hypothesis applies to all social security expenditure, only the public spending on social security was included in the analysis, as private social security expenditure is only available for a few OECD countries over the period of a few years (Adema 1999).

Bibliography

Adema, W. (1999) *Net Social Expenditure*, Paris: OECD.

Alber, J. and Standing, G. (2000) "Social Dumping, Catch-up or Convergence? Europe in a Comparative Global Context," *European Journal of Social Policy* 10(2): 99–119.

Baltagi, B.H. (2001) *Econometric Analysis of Panel Data*, 2nd edn, New York: John Wiley and Sons.

Breusch, T.S. and Pagan, A.R. (1980) "The Lagrange Multiplier Test and Its Applications to Model Specification in Econometrics," *Review of Economic Studies* 47(1): 239–253.

Esping-Andersen, G. (1994) "Welfare States and the Economy," in Smelser, N. and Swedberg, R. (eds) *Handbook of Economic Sociology*, Princeton: Princeton University Press.

European Commission (1995) *Green Paper on Innovation*, Brussels: European Commission.

—— (2001) *2001 Innovation Scoreboard*, Brussels: European Commission.

Garrett, G. and Mitchell, D. (2001) "Globalization, Government Spending and Taxation in the OECD," *European Journal of Political Research* 39(2): 145–177.

Genschel, P. (2003) "Globalisierung als Problem, als Lösung und als Staffage," in Hellmann, G., Wolf, K.D. and Zürn, M. (eds) *Die Neuen Internationalen Beziehungen – Forschungsstand und Perspektiven in Deutschland*, Baden-Baden: Nomos.

Greene, W.H. (2000) *Econometric Analysis*, 4th edn, London: Prentice Hall International.

Hall, P.A. and Soskice, D.W. (2001) "An Introduction to Varieties of Capitalism," in Hall, P.A. and Soskice, D.W. (eds) *Varieties of Capitalism: The Institutional Foundations of Comparative Advantage*, Oxford: Oxford University Press.

Heidenreich, M. (1999) "Gibt es einen europäischen Weg in die Wissensgesellschaft?," in Schmidt, G. and Trinczek, R. (eds) *Globalisierung: Ökonomische und soziale Herausforderungen am Ende des Zwanzigsten Jahrhunderts*, Sonderband 13 der 'Sozialen Welt,' Baden-Baden: Nomos.

Hirst, P. and Thompson, G. (1996) *Globalization in Question: The International Economy and the Possibility of Governance*, Cambridge: Polity Press.

Kanter, R.M. (1995) *World Class: Thriving Locally in the Global Economy*, New York: Simon & Schuster.

Kaufmann, F.-X. (1999) "Sozialstaatlichkeit unter den Bedingungen moderner Wirtschaft," in Korff, W. (ed.) *Handbuch der Wirtschaftsethik*, Gütersloh: Gütersloher Verlagshaus.

Kittel, B. and Obinger, H. (2003) "Political Parties, Institutions, and the Dynamics of Social Expenditure in Times of Austerity," *Journal of European Public Policy* 10(1): 20–45.

Marshall, T.H. (1977) "Citizenship and Social Class," in Marshall, T.H. (ed.) *Class, Citizenship, and Social Development (with an Introduction by Seymour Martin Lipset)*, Chicago: University of Chicago Press.

Münch, R. (2001) *Offene Räume. Soziale Integration diesseits und jenseits des Nationalstaats*, Frankfurt a.M.: Suhrkamp.

OECD (1997) *The Measurement of Scientific and Technical Activities: Proposed Guidelines for Collecting and Interpreting Technological Innovation Data (Oslo Manual)*, Paris: DSTI, OECD.

—— (2003) *OECD Science, Technology and Industry Scoreboard*, Paris: OECD.

Rammert, W. (1997) "Innovation im Netz: Neue Zeiten für technische Innovationen: Heterogen verteilt und interaktiv vernetzt," *Soziale Welt* 48(4): 397–416.

—— (2000) "Ritardando and Accelerando in Reflexive Innovation, or How Networks Synchronise the Tempi of Technological Innovation," Technical University Technology Studies Working Papers No. WP-7-2000.

Rieger, E. and Leibfried, St. (2003) *Limits to Globalization*, Cambridge: Polity.

Rodrik, D. (2000) "Has Globalization Gone Too Far?" in Held, D. and McGrew, A. (eds) *The Global Transformations Reader: An Introduction to the Globalization Debate*, Cambridge: Polity Press.

Schmidt, M.G. (1988) *Sozialpolitik: Historische Entwicklung und internationaler Vergleich*, Opladen: Leske und Budrich.

Schumpeter, J. (1935) *Theorie der Wirtschaftlichen Entwicklung*, 4th edn, Leipzig: Duncker and Humblot.

—— (1976) *Capitalism, Socialism and Democracy*, 5th edn, London: Allen & Unwin.

Schwarze, J. and Härpfer, M. (2003) *Are People Inequality Averse, and Do They Prefer Redistribution by the State? Evidence from German Longitudinal Data on Life Satisfaction*, Bamberg: University of Bamberg.

Siebert, H. (1997) "Labor Market Rigidities: At the Root of Unemployment in Europe," *Journal of Economic Perspectives* 11(3): 37–54.

Sinn, H.-W. (1995) "A Theory of the Welfare State," *Scandinavian Journal of Economics* 97(4): 495–526.

Soskice, D. (1999) "Divergent Production Regimes: Coordinated and Uncoordinated Market Economies in the 1980s and 1990s," in Kitschelt, H., Lange, P., Marks, G. and Stephens, J.D. (eds) *Continuity and Change in Contemporary Capitalism*, Cambridge: Cambridge University Press.

Therborn, G. (1995) *European Modernity and Beyond: The Trajectory of European Societies 1945–2000*, London: Sage.

7 Transnationalization of European governance in the information age

The role of *policy networks*

David Gibbs

Introduction

This chapter is concerned with the role of policy networks in shifting power relationships in local, regional, national and supra-national governance, together with the impact of such networks upon the promotion of innovative policies on information and communication technologies (ICTs). At the policy-making level, the perceived importance of ICTs to the future development of localities has engendered a range of responses to try and harness the new economy for the benefit of local populations and the local economy. Thus several cities, towns and regions have developed their own policies on ICT to try and foster the development of new sectors and the take-up of ICTs by existing sectors. One response has been to encourage the development of institutional capacity within areas to develop ICT initiatives, as part of broader arguments about the potential of "associationist" development and "learning regions" (Amin and Thrift 1995; OECD 2001).

It has been argued that ICTs as a technology have the power to coalesce groups, in this case as groups of actors seeking to shape the "space of flows" (Castells 1989). Increasingly urban and regional partnerships that synthesize ICTs and governance have emerged. These partnerships are attempting to shape the "space of flows" through trying to exert some form of control over exogenous and endogenous features of the informational age (Southern 2000). While much of this falls outside local control, for example in the construction of infrastructure, there are still attempts to enforce territorial control over the process (see Gillespie *et al.* 2001). How such control is exerted and the success or otherwise in doing so, may vary substantially from place to place. In the European Union, such developments have been encouraged and assisted by EU policy makers in their attempts to promote an EU "Information Society" (Gibbs 2001). These developments can be seen in the context of broader debates about changing governance structures. These include shifts from government to governance, the "hollowing out" of the nation state and the rise of multi-level governance. The structure of the chapter is as follows. The next section provides an overview of the development of ICT policies within the European Union and outlines the specific measures taken to try and encourage the development of a European Information Society. Following these sections, the focus shifts to an examination of debates on changing governance structures in an effort to contextualize EU policies within such debates. Evidence from the two main EU Information Society policy networks is then presented and a final section provides some conclusions from the analysis.

European Union policies on ICTs: developing the information society

From the 1990s onwards, the European Commission (EC) has developed a range of policies and initiatives which form a strong political drive or "policy push" to develop a European Information Society (Dai 2000a). These are embodied in a series of reports and white papers, including the Delors' White Paper *Growth, Competitiveness and Employment* (CEC 1993), the Bangemann Report *Europe and the Global Information Society* (CEC 1994) and *First Reflections of the High Level Group of Experts* (CEC 1996d). They deal with the social and societal aspects of the information society and propose a range of regulatory, technological and structural initiatives to stimulate its development. Such initiatives have encouraged experimentation with ICT uptake and have focused on such developments as providing infrastructure for peripheral areas, enabling them to be more pro-active in working with core areas, as well as regional initiatives aimed at promoting an integrated approach to policies for an Information Society. The European Commission argues that new jobs and more efficient services will arise from the plethora of new technologies now coming to maturity. A European strategy on the Information Society is essential, it is argued, given estimates that half of all jobs will be in industries that are either major producers or intensive users of information technology products and services (McQuaid 2002). The European Union's approach to the Information Society is illustrated in the following quotation:

> The information society is on its way. A "digital revolution" is triggering structural changes comparable to last century's industrial revolution with the corresponding high economic stakes. The process cannot be stopped and will lead eventually to a knowledge-based economy.
>
> (CEC 1994)

In consequence, the EU proposes that a crucial policy goal is to transform Europe into an Information Society. The importance attached to this is also associated with its perceived relevance in achieving other EU objectives, notably greater integration and cohesion, as well as being related to the demands of economic competitiveness – especially vis-à-vis the USA (Dai 2000b). Official EU literature leaves one in little doubt as to the inevitability of such a process: "the challenge is to manage the transition to the information society in order to optimize the number of jobs retained and created. It is not a question of *whether* the information society is achieved, but *how, when and where* it is achieved" (CEC 1995a, emphasis added). This goal and the implications for local and regional development are outlined in a number of policy documents. The Delors' White Paper viewed the information society as a powerful engine for employment growth that would bring benefits to all regions and all parts of society. The highly influential Bangemann Report similarly viewed the development of an information society as a positive development for regions, particularly peripheral regions. Exactly how these benefits were to be achieved is not evident in the report, although considerable stress is placed upon the capacity of the free market and liberalization to deliver economic growth. The report was presented to a European Council meeting in Corfu (1994) which recommended that Bangemann's proposals should be taken forward through designating a responsible ministerial level appointment in each member state, thus creating a Council of Ministers to direct the information society proposals.[1] The next step was the publication of the EC's action plan (1994) entitled *Europe's Way to the Information Society*, which summarized information society initiatives already under way, or planned, by the Commission. In this action plan the major emphasis was placed upon developing a new EU-wide regulatory framework, with limited mention of regional imbalances. The regional consequences of the information society were largely left to the operation of the EU's regional development funds, with a greater emphasis upon the information society in the Community Support Frameworks and in the Single Programming Documents agreed for Objective 1 regions for 1994–1999.[2] The Commission launched a study of the impacts and benefits of the information society for regional, economic and social cohesion. At this stage, only pilot projects and specific networks were envisaged in co-operation with cities and regions.

In 1994, EU policy was further developed at a European Council meeting in Essen where it was proposed that the information society would bring new jobs, stronger regional cohesion and facilitate greater solidarity between rich and poor regions. One concrete development from the meeting was the inauguration of a Forum on the Information Society and the installation of a group of High Level Experts to deal with social and societal issues. This latter group produced the *Working Document on the Social and Societal Aspects of the Information Society* in 1995. Six key themes were identified as the major agenda items for the Commission in the short to medium term: the quantity and quality of work; the way work is organized; the efficiency of the labor market; education and training; upgrading systems of healthcare; and improving regional and urban cohesion. The document stated that economic cohesion could be enhanced through the use of electronic networks by:

- Improving access to markets and sources of information;
- Bringing work to areas of high unemployment;
- Increasing the competitiveness of businesses at a regional level;
- Reinforcing positive externalities through shared infrastructures;
- Enhancing social cohesion through ICT usage;
- Reducing exclusion by making health, education, the arts and cultural services more accessible;
- Using the power of ICTs to provide on-line forms of these services to all groups in society.

This group pointed out that ICT usage may not automatically lead to enhanced cohesion and that they could lead to greater centralization of jobs and services and to a "fast" and "slow track" information society. The questions asked by the group in relation to spatial development were:

- What are the regional and urban development consequences of disparities in infrastructure provision and service levels? What can be done to assist less well-equipped regions and areas?
- How do different levels of provision affect social cohesion at both regional and urban levels? What can be done to increase the accessibility of these new essential services?
- How can regions and towns be helped to optimize their use of the new possibilities of ICT services?
- How can ICTs be used to improve the quality of life in the towns and regions of Europe, by allowing innovation in urban government and greater accessibility of services?

Preliminary answers to these questions were given in the Interim Report of the High Level Group of Experts *Building the European Information Society for Us All: First Reflections of the High Level Group of Experts* (CEC 1996d). This outlined both the threats and opportunities that ICTs present for peripheral regions and suggested a number of policy measures. They stressed the need for an integrated EU approach to the information society in order to increase social cohesion, as well as the need for a more focused approach to infrastructural support and to secure access to a reasonable service level at a reasonable price for different social groups. The group proposed that social policy merited at least equal consideration with economic policy in formulating a European approach to the information society.

A subsequent development was the establishment of the Information Society Forum by the EU which produced its first report in 1996 which encouraged the Commission to launch EU-wide awareness raising initiatives, promote ICT usage and access and explore the social and economic implications of the Information Society (CEC 1996c). In relation to the latter point, in 1996 the Commission adopted a green paper on *Living and Working in the Information Society: People First.* The paper's purpose was to deepen the dialogue on such social and societal aspects, with an aim to implementing specific proposals in 1997.

Further measures "to place Europe at the forefront of the Information Society" are outlined in CEC (1996b):

- Liberalization of Europe's telecommunications market, which was intended to lead to the development of new services and promote the uptake of ICTs;
- Supporting regional Information Society initiatives to enhance cohesion and to take social and societal aspects of the Information Society into account;
- Recognition of the role of education and training through the development of a Europe-wide learning action plan (CEC 1996e);
- Supporting the development of a strong EU multimedia content industry, which was expected to create 1 million new jobs in the next 10 years[3];
- Incorporating a specific ICT element into the EU's Fourth Framework Program for Research and Technological Development, which has been continued within the Fifth and the new Sixth Framework Program;
- Playing a role in developing and shaping the international context of the information society.

Finally, the European Commission launched an *e*Europe initiative intended to ensure that European economies exploit the opportunities offered by new technologies and do not lose out to competition, particularly from the USA (CEC 2000). This has three main objectives, with a number of sub-measures within each (see Table 7.1).

EU policy initiatives have begun to directly emphasize the *spatial* consequences of the Information Society program. As the CEC (1996a: 8) states: "the relevant disadvantage of peripheral regions [...] can be reduced through direct connection [...] However, the participation in the information society of *all* European regions will not happen automatically, but requires active policy measures" (emphasis in the original). These policy measures are envisaged as involving local, regional and national initiatives, not only to attract infrastructure investments but also to stimulate the demand for new information services. Emphasis is placed on the transfer of experiences and best practice already developed by advanced regions (e.g. in strategy development, in the use of "telecottages" and in teleworking). Meanwhile, rural areas and less-favored regions are encouraged to facilitate private–public or cross-regional partnerships, elaborate

Table 7.1 Objectives of the *e*Europe Initiative Action Plan

A cheaper, faster, secure Internet
- Cheaper and faster Internet access
- Faster Internet for researchers and students
- Secure networks and smart cards

Investing in people and skills
- European youth into the digital age
- Working in the knowledge-based economy
- Participation for all in the knowledge-based economy

Stimulate the use of the Internet
- Accelerating e-commerce
- Government online: electronic access to public services
- Health online
- European digital content for global networks
- Intelligent transport systems

Source: CEC 2000.

regional strategies and launch pilot applications (CEC 1996a). The document proposes that future policies will build on those local initiatives that have already been supported and to integrate policy initiatives on the Information Society with Structural Funds policies. The more recent *e*Europe Action Plan, *An Information Society for All*, similarly stresses the Structural Funds' role in improving ICT infrastructure (CEC 2000).

Governance, policy networks and EU policy

A particular feature of the EU's Information Society policy has been the emergence of networks of cities and regions to link together locally based partnerships. Such policy networks have become an increasingly important approach to the development of EU policy (Bennington and Harvey 1998). These policy networks can be defined as "a (more or less) structured cluster of public and private actors who are stakeholders in a specific sector of policy and possess resources which allow them to affect policy outcomes" (Peterson 1997: 7). The growth of policy networks is part of a broader shift from govern*ment* to govern*ance* or from a more linear, state-dominated political system to one which involves non-hierarchical, multi-level governance by a mix of public and private actors (Jordan 2001). Thus, "political power and institutional capability is less and less derived from formal constitutional powers accorded the state but more from a capacity to wield and co-ordinate resources from public and private actors and interests" (Peters and Pierre 2001: 131). This shift has led to a much greater recognition of the roles played by supra-national and sub-national state and non-state actors and the complex interactions between them. Institutional relationships need not be vertical and "do not have to operate through intermediary levels but can take place between, say, transnational and regional levels, thus bypassing the state level" (Peters and Pierre 2001: 132).

These changes have been recognized as reflecting new "geographies of governance" as state functions are redistributed vertically, both upwards to supranational organizations and downwards to cities and regions, as well as horizontally to non-state actors (MacLeod and Goodwin 1999). This does not, however, necessarily reflect the decline of the nation state, rather that "the continuous reshuffling and reorganizations of spatial scales are an integral part of social strategies and struggles for control and empowerment" (Swyngedouw 2000: 70), where the nation state continues to play a key role. However, the tendency for national governments to become less interventionist in some spheres has encouraged sub-national authorities to develop their own strategies to deal with adjustment problems consequent upon new economic circumstances (OECD 2001). There is thus a complex interrelationship between changing governance structures and the development of new economic forms based upon new technological developments.

Theoretically, "the workings of policy networks are critical for promoting the diffusion of policy innovations" (Mintrom and Vergari 1998: 128). Such networks may act to promote policy learning in the regions, though this depends on the structure of the network and the patterns of interaction (Benz and Fürst 2002). Such networks are a key means of exercising power by the EU (through the European Commission), but where policy making is achieved through sharing power with a range of actors from European, national and local levels. As the recent EU White Paper on governance states "the Union cannot develop and deliver policy in the same way as a national government; it must build partnerships and rely on a wide variety of actors" (CEC 2001b: 32). Much EU decision making now takes place within policy networks. In describing patterns of multi-level governance in the Europeanization of regional policies, Benz and Eberlein (1999) argue that EU policy making is achieved through power sharing between different levels of government and that policy networks are formed for collaboration based on various combinations of government authorities.

Such relationships are not simply at the level of local-European alliances, signifying the "hollowing out" of the nation state, but rather reflect a shifting mix of national–sub-national alliances, as well as EU–local alliances (Jessop 1994). The EC promotes such networking activity as a means of building coalitions in favor of its own renditions of policy, thus increasing its leverage with the Council of Ministers and the European Parliament (Richardson 1996). The EC has recently argued that networking is also an essential component of legitimating European governance, incorporating local and regional knowledge and conditions and showing "policies in action" (CEC 2001b: 18). The EC expects such policy networks to develop policy proposals and exchange experience, thus mobilizing the regions as potential allies of the Commission in that they seek further funding and/or an extension of European policies (Tömmel 1998). Such developments though are far from a one way process. Regions and urban areas (or at least those fractions that claim to represent or speak for local areas) use such networks as a means of seeking greater autonomy and a voice in EU policy making, sometimes as a means of circumventing nation state control. While Lloyd and Meegan (1996: 78) point out that "the Commission and its advisers are a key source of new scripts about the regional development process – both in the sense of how to and in terms of their views on the most appropriate institutional arrangements," regional authorities are also able to rewrite such scripts for their own purposes. Thus, the rise of multi-level governance may involve the relative empowerment of sub-national actors, providing a means for them to circumvent the formal channels of government (Jordan 2001).

Policy networks and the European information society

The discussion of shifting governance patterns and policy networks is particularly relevant to discussions on European Information Society policy at the local and regional scales, where there has been the initiation of two major policy networks – the Regional Information Society Initiative/eris@ and the TeleCities network. The rationale for developing these was that "European cities and regions needed to access the financial resources available at the European level (handled by the European Commission); they also needed to be better informed of European policy making and learn from the experience of other places in many aspects of local governance in the information age" (Dai 2000a: 70–71). The European Commission also needed these networks, not just to obtain technical information, but also to act as an information network for EU policies (Sidjanski 1997).

The RISI/eris@ network

The EC's initial establishment of the Regional Information Society Initiative (RISI) was a deliberate attempt to shift the basis of policy away from an infrastructural and technological focus toward engaging with the social context of technology and involving a range of social actors. A number of pilot projects were undertaken (through the Inter-Regional Information Society Initiative – IRISI) before the subsequent RISI program involving 22 regions[4] was established. The former was a pilot project co-funded by the former DGs XVI and XIII and involved six regions: North West of England, Nord Pas de Calais, Central Macedonia, Valencia, Saxony and Piemonte. IRISI was supported by the European Commission through a Regional Information Society Unit (RISU) promoting partnership and strategy development at the regional level and a European network stimulating diffusion of experience and facilitating collaboration inter-regionally. IRISI had as its main objective the promotion of universal access to the opportunities and advantages of the Information Society with a view to generating new employment opportunities, improving the quality of life and addressing the challenges of structural adjustment and sustainable development. The priority fields for action were[5]: teleworking, distance learning, university and research center networks, ICT services for small- and medium-sized enterprises, city information highways and healthcare.

Each IRISI region developed a coordinated strategy toward the development of ICT applications and services including: the implementation of advanced applications and services, as opposed to concentrating on research or technology demonstrations; the involvement of potential users of these applications and services in order to base policies around clearly identified user demands; and an attempt to balance economic and social aspects. That is, policy should be aimed not just at improving productivity and performance gains, but should also contribute to creating employment and improving the quality of life (Carter 1996).

> IRISI attempted to demonstrate a methodology based on subsidiarity and a bottom-up approach for creating awareness among the general public and decision-makers. The six participating [regions] had to outline a strategy on the information society by analysing the base-line strategies and assessing the opportunities for building the information society, through a concerted effort bringing together all the relevant regional actors. The innovative nature of the IRISI approach rests on the institutional mechanism by which strategy has been developed i.e. a partnership between all key players in a region. The success of the IRISI initiatives has convinced the Commission to continue in that direction.
>
> (CEC 1996b: 14)

Indeed, the subsequent RISI continued to display a shift in EC policy thinking away from a concern with the narrow technical aspects of the information society toward a viewpoint that it is predominantly about socio-economic processes. This view of the information society conceptualizes it as being as much about learning processes, cultural change, institutional reorganization and developing applications in response to user needs, as it is about technical concerns *per se*. In such a context, the task for regional actors is to avoid engaging with an information society shaped by exogenous forces solely in a reactive manner and to engage with the information society in a proactive fashion. However, it was argued that the "route to the information society" would be different for different regions depending upon pre-existing economic and social circumstances. RISI projects were therefore intended to be part of an active learning strategy to test the best policy options that can subsequently be applied through the Structural Funds. The overall aim was to enable regional partnerships to make better use of existing resources for developing the IS. The objectives were:

- To develop consensus and partnership among key regional actors around a regional information society strategy;
- To outline how regions should respond to the challenges and opportunities offered by the information society;
- To promote commitment and cooperation by regional actors through developing a regional action plan;
- To provide a basis for the better use of existing regional, national and European resources (especially the EU Structural Funds).

The most recent development of the RISI network has been its transformation into eris@, the European Regional Information Society Association, a trans-European network of 34 regions, which incorporates both IRISI and RISI member regions. In addition, eris@ is open to all European regions, including those from central and eastern European countries (Dai 1999). The network involves region-wide partnerships drawn from local business, local government, education and training bodies, trade unions and the voluntary sector. The eris@ network aims to share good practice, information and experience across participant regions with the objective of improving economic and social development by implementing new ICT-based applications and services.[6] The transnational process of policy discussions and learning between member regions are achieved in part by the network's thematic working groups on identified areas including: education and training; rural areas and peripheral areas; tele-medicine and healthcare; small- and medium-sized enterprises and e-commerce; social affairs; public administration and citizens' services; telecommunications policy and infrastructure. There has been substantial inputs made by eris@ into the development of EU policy making, particularly in relation to ensuring that information society issues have a high profile in regional policy funding.

The TeleCities Network

The second major policy networking initiative is the TeleCities Network. This was established in 1993 and formally launched in 1994, with the aim of bringing together towns and cities for the development of ICT applications in an urban context.[7] In organizational terms, TeleCities includes: an elected steering committee; working groups to address major urban issues identified by policy and decision makers; open fora for discussion and information dissemination and pilot projects to promote the exchange of experience and examine the issues related to the development of digital cities. The working groups are intended to collate material and provide examples so as to develop a consensus on "best practice" ICT applications throughout Europe. In 2002 there were five working groups on the following issues: eDemocracy and community building; re-engineering local public administration; eSecurity; e-learning and inclusion; and benchlearning eStrategies in cities (TeleCities 2002a).

In the early stages of development, the aims and objectives of the TeleCities network included using and developing ICT applications and services that supported the regeneration of urban areas. These included: economic development strategies, with a specific focus on tackling unemployment; social and cultural development, aimed at improving the quality of life; and new solutions to fight social exclusion as well as maximizing the resources available to cities to support local demonstration projects (Carter 1996). More recently, TeleCities' key issues are:

- Implementing local public on-line services and "re-engineering" administrative processes;
- Promoting the right to eSecurity for all EU citizens;
- Implementing eDemocracy through new forms of citizens' participation and community empowerment;
- Ensuring that all EU citizens are digitally literate and able to profit from the benefits of the knowledge society;
- Benchmarking and learning from the eStrategies of cities and their practical implementation.

(TeleCities 2002b)

There has been a strong emphasis upon the involvement of local government in the initiative and upon the engagement of individual citizens, both in decision making and through universal access to ICTs. From its inception, TeleCities has stressed that this means it is a democratic and representative network, encompassed in its vision of "eCitizenship for all" (TeleCities 2002a). Those involved with the TeleCities network argue that it provides a demonstration effect to allay the fears of non-users and at the same time helps to develop infrastructures which benefit a wide spectrum of the population. The initial aim was to provide "development from below" as a counterweight to the perceived "development from above" directed by the multinational corporate sector. By demonstration and examples, the TeleCities network hoped to overcome EU citizens' resistance to new technologies and dispel fears about privacy and employment impacts (Carter 1996). Projects in operation in 2002 are shown in Table 7.2. Some of the advantages to be gained for individual cities through demonstration projects were said to be:

access to both research findings and policy and decision making at levels which would not normally be possible to a city council nor to

Table 7.2 TeleCities projects in 2002

Project	Description
Clip Card	To test and implement a smart card-based system for the payment of traffic fines. It involves the installation of a network of recording terminals and payment terminals.
Muteis	To explain and understand functional and spatial diversity in Europe's digital economy at both macro and local levels. Aimed at improving knowledge of the macro impact of the digital economy and the origins and causes of local diversities.
PACE (Public administrations and e-commerce in Europe)	Improving public administration involvement in e-commerce markets, including e-commerce solutions for administrative problems.
e-CT (electronic calls for tenders)	Investigated possible public–private partnerships to access and use calls for tender for public works.
ODA (open digital administrations)	Providing citizens with the means to apply online for public services and track them through the delivery process.

Source: TeleCities 2002a.

most local agencies ... Cities are provided with a unique base, in terms of information, intelligence and contacts, from which to develop their strategies for economic regeneration and urban development and to maximize access to resources to finance this. Cities are now beginning to be able to influence the development of policy by European institutions through networks like TeleCities. This is the first time that local authorities have had a direct input into this policy arena as well as being able to (at least) try to represent the views of wider user and community interest.

(Carter 1996: 7).

Both TeleCities and the RISI/eris@ networks therefore act to promote cooperation and collaboration on a trans-European basis. They possess obvious advantages of gaining EU funding and providing a ready-made partnership network for further funding bids.[8] Another important aim is to influence EU policy making – as TeleCities (2002b: 4) states, "our goal is to influence aspects of EU policy development. This is achieved through maintaining a regular dialogue with the European institutions and producing policy contributions." These networks may therefore have increased the relative bargaining power of the regions and local governments involved, vis-à-vis both their national governments and EU institutions (Dai 1999). Moreover, the demonstration effect and lobbying power that the component projects constitute also provides the Commission with legitimation for its Information Society policies.

Conclusions: governance, networking and the Information Society

The previous section has provided evidence of the two main local and regional information society initiatives that operate in the EU. "These networks have been created, not least, with the goal of lobbying in Brussels, supporting a European RTD policy better adapted to regional needs, following a demand orientation rather than a technology-push approach" (Fuchs and Wolf 1996: 17). Increasingly, the EC's promotion of the Information Society has acknowledged the importance of developing consensus and partnership among key regional players in implementation and a need to move away from individual project-led initiatives. Assisting regional actors with the development of specific regional strategies is thus receiving increasing attention from the EU. It has been argued that "such regional strategies are more likely to match the economic specialisation of the region and to build upon the strengths of its institutional system or, vice versa, to aim at rectifying specific deficits of the region" (Fuchs and Wolf 1996: 18).

However, such questions of agency and local policy have largely been ignored in wider debates around the information society, which often imply that local policy makers are "little more than irrelevant, even anachronistic, distractions in this exciting and epoch-making transformation" (Graham 1996: 3). This omission is problematic, because local policy experimentation has major practical implications for the future of local economic development policy and planning. While it is increasingly difficult for cities at the receiving end of corporate (usually multi-national) decision making over investment and services to influence the development of ICT infrastructures, policy makers may be able to make some gains through using planning powers and in working with traditional suppliers. For example, one of the key figures in the TeleCities Network has argued that "the 'anarchy of the market place' does at least provide space in which to manoeuvre and to create experimental areas of collective space to support social and cultural innovation and to provide real services on the public broadcasting/public service model" (Carter 1996: 8).

In policy terms it is argued that "meaningful 'enclosures' need to be socially constructed in what Castells (1989) calls the global 'space of flows' – the pan-global electronic spaces increasingly dominated by massive media corporations and their commodified, capitalised outputs and applications" (Graham 1996: 24). The effects of ICTs in localities can thus depend heavily on how they are socially and politically constructed. Such social and political construction is currently underway in the range of

European examples outlined in the previous section. Those involved are attempting to create electronic networks through active policy making on a democratic and accountable basis, for example through the activities of local authorities, community organizations, trade unions, consumer groups and individuals, rather than being created solely by corporate business interests and central governments. Carter (1996: 8) states:

> The alliances which are beginning to emerge between social forces and (at least) some representative structures (including local authorities) working in this area, which could be broadly termed "socially useful cyberspace," may not be able to transform the forces of global capitalism but they are not without power and influence. Their role in determining how questions of the "governance of cyberspace" are resolved should not be underestimated. The ability of small-scale initiatives in cities and regions to use the advantages of the technologies, to use "cyberspace," to create communication and activity networks free from the usual spatial and temporal constraints is a crucial element in providing a democratic counter-balance to other technological and global trends.

At the same time there is a strong link between the development of such information-society policy networks and the transnationalization of European governance in the information age. To a large extent both the eris@ and the TeleCities networks are associated with the EU's new political drive toward a more integrated Europe with a more efficient and effective governance structure by utilizing new ICTs. An important feature of the digital age is the ever-increasing volume and frequency of real time and trans-border communications facilitated by the fast expansion and integration of information and communications networks. The role of new ICTs lies in that they are "the tool which has allowed networks to blossom and to increase their efficiency" (CEC 2001b: 11). Based on this understanding, recent EU policy initiatives aimed at making Europe the most competitive and dynamic economy "have provided the political drive to re-think the way public administrations work and co-operate among themselves and interact with citizens and enterprises, in Member States as well as across Europe, through the use of Internet or Internet-based networks" (CEC 2001b: 11).

Both initiatives began from the premise that the information society is predominantly concerned with socio-economic processes as opposed to being solely technologically driven. Taking this approach, the information society is seen as being concerned with cultural change and institutional reorganization. The task for European cities and regions is to avoid the shaping of this information society solely by exogenous forces in a reactive manner and to engage with the issues in a pro-active fashion. To this end, the two networks are intended to be part of an active learning strategy to test the best policy options in developing the European Information Society. The TeleCities and eris@ networks have already made substantial inputs into the development of EU policy making, particularly in ensuring that information society issues have a high profile in regional policy funding.[9] As far as TeleCities is concerned, influencing the European information society agenda "to ensure that the interests of cities are taken into account in policy making" is one of the network's central objectives.[10] The network claims substantial success in influencing the form of EU research spending and policy frameworks. Thus intense lobbying in the run-up to the adoption of the EU's Sixth Framework Program (6FP) resulted in several of the network's main concerns being incorporated into the final 6FP work programs. Similarly, with regard to the EC's eEurope 2005 Action Plan, TeleCities claim that

> thanks to regular contacts and meetings with the EC, TeleCities has been clearly mentioned in this Action Plan, among the support networks through which the good practices at the regional and local dimension and the results of the project analysis will be disseminated. The European Commission is therefore recognising the important role cities' networks can play in key EU policies.
>
> (TeleCities 2002a: 5)

In addition to the obvious advantages of gaining EU funding and providing a ready-made partnership network for further funding bids, both the TeleCities and eris@ networks act as platforms to promote communication, cooperation and collaboration on a trans-European basis. This is achieved in three main ways. First, through the use of the technology – ICTs, in particular the World Wide Web and e-mail mailing lists, are heavily used by the two networks to disseminate information (EU information society policy information and network-specific information). This facilitates long-distance and across-border communication among network members and between the networks and the outside world. Second, thematic working groups, which are horizontally organized involving members from different European countries working on specific issues, constitute an important experiment by the two networks in policy learning and transfer of experience. Third, regular network conferences and seminars provide an additional platform for transnational networking and information dissemination among members of each network.

The demonstration effect and lobbying power that the two networks' ICT-based projects constitute provides the Commission with legitimation for its Information Society policies. Certainly it can be argued that the creation of policy networks has had some success judged purely in very narrow terms. Thus the participant cities and regions have received substantial funding for pilot projects. For the Commission, the networks have acted as a useful lobbying tool for its own policies on ICTs and the

Information Society. They can also act as an information network for EC problems. The Commission has developed new modes of formulating and implementing structural policies and new modes of directing the behavior of sub-national authorities, without possessing far-reaching powers and competencies (Dai 2000b). Certainly through such network development, "the EU is transforming politics and government at the European and national levels into a system of multi-level, non-hierarchical, deliberative and apolitical governance, via a complex web of public/private network and quasi-autonomous agencies" (Hix 1998: 54).

These networks are poised to increase the relative bargaining power of the regions and local governments involved, vis-à-vis both their national governments and EU institutions (Dai 2000a). From the outset of the TeleCities Network, the member cities have expressed their "willingness to collaborate with the European Commission in defining an overall stra- tegic plan for the concerted development of telematics in the urban environment."[11] In a similar way, eris@ members are also inspired to "give the regions a significant voice in defining just how the [European] Information Society [policies] will be interpreted at the local level."[12] Both the TeleCities Network and the eris@ have their coordination office in Brussels, which can be used for coordinating internal activities as well as liaising with the EU institutions and other bodies. It is also worth noting that officials from the EU institutions are often among the invited speak- ers at each of the conferences organized by eris@ and TeleCities. These conferences prove to be important occasions for EU policy makers and representatives of the networks to have face-to-face communication.

It could be argued that this could "shift the loyalties and political activ- ities of hitherto separate regions' policy makers towards a new centre" (Webber and Gore 2002: 98), such that attention becomes directed more toward the creation of networks of interest and their interaction with the EC than toward national policy makers. One of the unanswered questions in this, though, is how far the "significant voice" of networks such as eris@ and TeleCities reflects the minority view of a few technological champions within each region rather than a broader agreement upon the direction of policy. Furthermore, other research on networking activities suggests that the major beneficiaries at the local scale are those localities that are already economically successful (Chorianopoulos 2002).

In addition it is not clear what the importance of this policy network model is for; economic and social development more generally, or whether it really *is* helping to bring about the desired transformations in local and regional economic development (Garmise and Rees 1997; Webber and Gore 2002). As some argue, "just because sub-national actors bypass states and operate independently in Europe does not necessarily imply that they have the power to shape outcomes. In other words, mobilisation and influence are not necessarily synonymous" (Jordan 2001: 201). New modes of governance, such as multi-level governance and networked governance, may have been established but exactly how *effective* these are remains open to question. While multi-level governance structures may represent a means of integrating the concerns of localities and regions into policy formation, it is not clear whether it leads to more effective policy making or whether for the localities concerned it simply involves the creation of "grant coalitions", adept at drawing down EU funding (Peck and Tickell 1994; Webber and Gore 2002).

A key question remains the relative influence of the various actors in the information society. While sub-national representatives in conjunction with the EC may seek to effectively rescale the governance of ICTs to the local and regional level, the major corporate players increasingly operate at a global scale. Graham (2002) argues that the dynamic between place and ICTs is serving to increase both the power of the already powerful and uneven development. Moreover, the new knowledge economy and information society remains a heavily metropolitan phenomenon despite continued predictions of the "end of geography." The success of peripheral regions and local areas (i.e. predominantly those involved in policy networks) in attracting and developing new economy activities remains limited (Gillespie *et al.* 2001). The impact and benefits of transnational policy networks in the e-Society thus need to be demonstrated rather than simply assumed and one of the weaknesses of research to date has been its emphasis on description at the expense of explanation. The European Commission acknowledges that "we are only at the start of the learning curve with respect to the use of networks as tools for public policies" (CEC 2000: iv). Finally, despite the emphasis upon the social contexts of technology use and adoption, it can still be argued that EU policy retains a view of ICTs that is strongly deterministic and predicated upon a number of unproven value-laden assumptions about the value of ICTs in addressing issues of economic development, social exclusion and regeneration (Southern 2002). As Grimes and Collins (2002: 972) comment, "it is clear that the European political programme of the IS continues to be driven more by theoretical and policy discourses rather than by empirically proven realities."

Notes

1 This proposal was not approved or put into practice by member states.
2 These documents essentially set out the priority areas for project development and thus areas of expenditure for regional development funds.
3 For example through the INFO2000 program (see CEC 1995b). On the issue of jobs, CEC (1996b: 5) states "as regards the crucial issue of job creation, *a significant number of new employment opportunities will result from developments in the services and content sectors*, in particular through new business activities such as electronic commerce and multimedia content creation" (emphasis in original).
4 The 22 regions are Steiermark (Austria), Liege (Belgium), West Finland, North

Karelia (Finland), Midi-Pyrénées, Limousin, Poitou-Charentes (France), Bremen, Brandenburg, Schleswig-Holstein (Germany), Central Macedonia, Epirus (Greece), South West, Shannon (Ireland), Calabria (Italy), Murcia, Extremadura (Spain), Vasterbotten, Blekinge County (Sweden), Wales, North of England, Yorkshire and the Humber (UK).

5 As with TeleCities, the list of priorities largely derives from the Bangemann Report (1994).
6 See eris@ Memorandum of Understanding, December 1997. Available at: http://www.erisa.be/ (accessed November 24, 2003).
7 TeleCities has 125 members – 113 local authorities, 7 business members and 5 members from other organizations.
8 TeleCities and eris@ have increasingly worked together, for example in joint lobbying on the content of the eEurope Action Plan and the Sixth Framework Program for Research and Technological Development.
9 In fact, the predecessors of the eris@ network, i.e., IRISI and RISI, were the outcome of substantial EU funding through the Structural Funds. Member cities of TeleCities have also received substantial sums of EU funding toward their information society projects in recent years. For more details see Dai (2000a), Chapter 3.
10 See TeleCities' own statement at: http://eurocities.poptel.org.uk/telecities/aboutTC/index.htm (accessed November 24, 2003).
11 See TeleCities' foundation document Declaration of Manchester, signed during the launching seminar of the network in Manchester, October 7–8, 1993. Available at: http://eurocities.poptel.org.uk/telecities/library/index.htm (accessed 24 November 2003).
12 *N.W. England IRISI News*, 14 April 1997. Available at: http://www.u-net.com/northwest/irisi/news.htm (accessed November 24, 2003).

Bibliography

Amin, A. and Thrift, N. (1995) "Institutional Issues for the European Regions: From Markets and Plans to Socioeconomics and Powers of Association," *Economy and Society* 24(1): 41–66.

Bangemann, M. (1994) *Europe and the Global Information Society: Recommendations to the European Council*, Brussels: European Commission.

Bennington, J. and Harvey, J. (1998) "Transnational Local Authority Networking within the EU: Passing Fashion or New Paradigm," in Marsh, D. (ed.) *Comparing Policy Networks*, Buckingham: Open University Press.

Benz, A. and Eberlein, B. (1999) "The Europeanisation of Regional Policies: Patterns of Multi-Level Governance," *Journal of European Public Policy* 6(2): 329–348.

Benz, A. and Fürst, D. (2002) "Policy Learning in Regional Networks," *European Urban and Regional Studies* 9(1): 21–35.

Carter, D. (1996) *"Digital Democracy" or "Information Aristocracy" – Economic Regeneration and the Information Economy*, Manchester: Manchester City Council.

Castells, M. (1989) *The Informational City*, Oxford: Blackwell.

Chorianopoulos, I. (2002) "Commenting on the Effectiveness and Future Challenges of the EU Local Authority Networks," *Regional Studies* 26(8): 933–939.

Commission of the European Communities (1993) *White Paper on Growth*

Competitiveness and Employment: The Challenges and Ways Forward into the 21st Century, Brussels: CEC.

—— (1994) *Europe's Way to the Information Society: An Action Plan*, Brussels: CEC.

—— (1995a) *A Working Document on the Social and Societal Aspects of the Information Society: The High Level Group of Experts*, Brussels: CEC.

—— (1995b) *Programme to Stimulate the Development of an EU Multimedia Content Industry and Encourage Use of Multimedia Content in the Emerging Information Society*, Brussels: CEC.

—— (1996a) *The Implications of the Information Society for European Union Policies: Preparing the Next Steps*, Brussels: CEC.

—— (1996b) *Europe at the Forefront of the Global Information Society: Rolling Action Plan*, Brussels: CEC.

—— (1996c) *Proposal for a Council Decision: Adopting a Multi-Annual Community Programme to Stimulate the Establishment of the Information Society in Europe*, Brussels: CEC.

—— (1996d) *Building the European Information Society for Us All: First Reflections of the High Level Group of Experts*, Brussels: CEC.

—— (1996e) *Learning in the Information Society*, Brussels: CEC.

—— (2000) *Europe 2002: An Information Society for All, Action Plan*, Brussels: CEC.

—— (2001a) *Networking People for a Good Governance in Europe*, Brussels: CEC.

—— (2001b) *European Governance, a White Paper*, Brussels: CEC.

Dai, X. (1999) *Networked Governance and European Regions in the Digital Age*, Paper presented to the CSGR annual conference "After the Global Crisis: What Next for Regionalism?" University of Warwick, September 16–18.

—— (2000a) *The Digital Revolution and Governance*, Aldershot: Ashgate.

—— (2000b) "Policy Push for European Integration: Implications of the Information Society," in Shahin, J. and Wintle, M. (eds) *The Idea of a United Europe*, Basingstoke: Macmillan.

Fuchs, G. and Wolf, H.-G. (1996) *Regional Rejuvenation with the Help of Information and Communication Technologies? The EU's Concept of the Information Society*, paper presented to the European Urban and Regional Studies Conference, Exeter, April.

Garmise, S. and Rees, G. (1997) "The Role of Institutional Networks in Local Economic Development: A New Model of Governance," *Local Economy* 12(2): 104–118.

Gibbs, D. (2001) "Harnessing the Information Society? European Union Policy and Information and Communication Technologies," *European Urban and Regional Studies* 8(1): 73–84.

Gillespie, A., Richardson, R. and Cornford, J. (2001) "Regional Development and the New Economy," *European Investment Bank Papers* 6(1): 109–131.

Graham, S. (1996) *Towards Urban Cyberspace Planning: Grounding the Global Through Urban Telematics Policy and Planning*, Paper presented to the workshop on "Exploring Electronic Space," Hikone, Japan, May 16–22.

—— (2002) "Bridging Urban Digital Divides? Urban Polarization and Information and Communication Technologies," *Urban Studies* 39(1): 33–56.

Grimes, S. and Collins, P. (2002) "The Role of Telematics in Integrating Ireland into Europe's Information Society," *European Planning Studies* 10(8): 971–986.

Hix, S. (1998) "The Study of the Eu Ii," *Journal of European Public Policy* 5(1): 38–65.

Jessop, B. (1994) "Post-Fordism and the State," in Amin, A. (ed.) *Post-Fordism: A Reader*, Oxford: Blackwell.

Jordan, A. (2001) "The European Union: An Evolving System of Multi-Level Governance ... or Government?," *Polity and Politics* 29(2): 193–208.

Lloyd, P. and Meegan, R. (1996) "Contested Governance: European Exposure in the English Regions," *European Planning Studies* 4(1): 75–97.

MacLeod, G. and Goodwin, M. (1999) "Space, Scale and State Strategy: Rethinking Urban and Regional Governance," *Progress in Human Geography* 23(4): 503–527.

McQuaid, R. (2002) "Entrepreneurship and Ict Industries: Support from Regional and Local Policies," *Regional Studies* 36(8): 909–919.

Mintrom, M. and Vergari, S. (1998) "Policy Networks and Innovation Diffusion: The Case of State Education Reforms," *The Journal of Politics* 60(1): 126–148.

OECD (2001) *Cities and Regions in the New Learning Economy*, Paris: OECD.

Peck, J. and Tickell, A. (1994) "Too Many Partners ... the Future for Regeneration Partnerships," *Local Economy* 9(3): 251–265.

Peters, B.G. and Pierre, J. (2001) "Developments in Intergovernmental Relations: Towards Multi-Level Governance," *Policy and Politics* 29(2): 131–135.

Peterson, J. (1997) "States, Societies and the European Union," *West European Politics* 20(4): 1–23.

Richardson, J. (1996) *European Union: Power and Policy Making*, London: Routledge.

Sidjanski, D. (1997) *Networks of European Pressure Groups*, Geneva: Institut Européen de l'Université de Genève.

Southern, A. (2000) "The Political Salience of the Space of Flows: Information and Communication Technologies and the Restructuring City," in Wheeler, J.O., Aoyama, Y. and Warf, B. (eds) *Fractured Geographies: Cities in the Telecommunications Age*, New York: Routledge.

—— (2002) "Can Information and Communication Technologies Support Regeneration?" *Regional Studies* 36(6): 697–702.

Swyngedouw, E. (2000) "Authoritarian Governance, Power and the Politics of Rescaling," *Environment and Planning D: Society and Space* 18: 63–76.

TeleCities (2002a) *Annual Activity Report*, Sienna: TeleCities.

—— (2002b) *Workprogramme 2003*, Sienne: TeleCities.

Tömmel, I. (1998) "Transformation of Governance: The European Commission's Strategy for Creating a 'Europe of the Regions'," *Regional and Federal Studies* 8(2): 52–80.

Webber, D.J. and Gore, T. (2002) "Dematerializing Local Economies: A Case for Ad Hoc Governance," *Local Economy* 17(2): 96–110.

Part III
Spaces of innovation

8 Urban governance, interspatial competition and the political geographies of the *new economy*

Reflections on the western European case

Neil Brenner

Introduction: myths of the new economy

The concept of the new economy has been deployed widely during the last decade to refer to a variety of putative technological and institutional transformations in contemporary capitalism. The notion is hardly coherent, however, for it is used in significantly divergent ways in different contexts, whether journalistic, political or academic. Nonetheless, discourses on the new economy generally refer to one or more among five key purported developments (Martin 2002).

1   *Technological transformations.* In some uses, the notion of the new economy refers to the rise and increasing structural importance of various new information and communication technologies (ICTs). These knowledge-driven technologies are said to provide the foundations for a new round of worldwide capitalist expansion that is also referred to as the "third industrial revolution."

2   *A new growth model.* Relatedly, the notion of a new economy is frequently used to describe a new macroeconomic growth model, based upon low inflation and low unemployment that supposedly resolved the economic bottlenecks of the 1980s. This new growth regime is usually said to have underpinned the "long Clinton boom" of the 1990s in the USA and to be, in principle, transferable to other national economies as well.

3   *The death of distance.* In many popular and policy oriented discussions, the notion of the new economy serves as a shorthand reference to the purported organizational flexibility and hypermobility of capitalist firms based upon ICTs and oriented toward a globalized, knowledge-driven economy. In this view, new economy industries are no longer tied to particular places, because they are not subject to traditional geographical constraints such as the need for physical proximity or localized agglomeration economies.

4   *A new phase of capitalism.* Building in varying degrees upon the

aforementioned assumptions, some authors have characterized the new economy as the technological and institutional basis for an entirely new phase of capitalism based upon globalized production, knowledge-driven industries, the extensive use of ICTs, increasingly flexible forms of work/production organization, a restructured macro-economic regime and transformed modes of political-economic regulation. A particularly prominent exponent of this view is Manuel Castells, whose three-volume book on *The Information Age* (1996, 1997, 1998) has provoked extensive discussion of ICTs, their political-economic context(s) and their medium- and long-term social and spatial implications.

5   *The transformation of governance.* Finally, many discussions of the new economy postulate the decline of traditional, hierarchical-bureaucratic forms of (national) state regulation and the consequent rise of new, highly flexible modes of economic governance based upon "networked" interconnections among a variety of entrepreneurial public agencies and private or semi-private actors. In this view, the rise of the new economy signals the growing obsolescence not only of old economy manufacturing industries but also of inherited forms of national state power.

This analysis rejects each of these widely prevalent, deeply ideological assumptions regarding the putative new economy. As numerous critically minded scholars have argued, the discourse of the new economy generates a seriously oversimplified characterization of contemporary technological, institutional and social transformations. As a result, it harmonizes the intense political-economic contradictions and social conflicts they generate and thoroughly distorts their deeply uneven, often highly polarizing effects upon populations and territories around the world. In particular, it can be argued that the notion of the new economy (a) exaggerates the obsolescence of old economy manufacturing industries; (b) overestimates the stability, coherence and interterritorial generalizability of the 1990s "Clinton boom;" (c) brackets the embeddedness of ICTs within non-substitutable, place-specific conditions of production and governance; (d) overstates the decline of national state institutions; and (e) ignores the ways in which ICTs have intensified, rather than alleviated, social and spatial inequalities throughout the capitalist political-economic landscape at all geographical scales.

Yet, despite these deeply problematic aspects of the discourse on the new economy, the widespread use of this catchphrase to characterize diverse trends within contemporary capitalism is arguably indicative of deeper structural changes in economic, political and social life at the dawn of the twenty-first century. As such, the notion of the new economy should not be dismissed as a purely ideological fantasy. Indeed, much like neoliberalism, the notion of the new economy represents what

Bourdieu has termed a "strong discourse" insofar as it "has behind it the powers of a world of power relations which it helps to make as it is, in particular by orienting the economic choices of those who dominate economic relations and so adding its own [...] force to those power relations" (Bourdieu 1998: 95). From this perspective, a key task for critical studies of the new economy is to decipher the determinate "political operations" (Bourdieu 1998: 95) through which its core ideological and institutional components are being promulgated in diverse political-economic contexts.

The term new economy is therefore used in this chapter not to describe a transparent or self-evident empirical reality, but rather to characterize a variety of emergent, often deeply contradictory *projects* of technological, institutional and geographical transformation that have proliferated under contemporary globalizing/neoliberal capitalism. More specifically, the trends that are frequently characterized under the rubric of the new economy will be interpreted here as key ideological elements within historically specific accumulation strategies (Jessop 1990) by means of which state institutions across the world economy are attempting to promote ICT-led growth and a variety of associated institutional transformations at once at local, national and supranational scales.[1]

In developing this thesis, I shall focus upon the distinctively geographical dimensions of these new economy projects and accumulation strategies. Like other contributions to this book (see, in particular, the chapter by Stefan Krätke), I contend that the proliferation of new economy strategies has not entailed the death of distance, the end of geography or the homogenization of industrial landscapes. On the contrary, such strategies have contributed, in crucial ways, to the formation of new urban and regional industrial clusters specialized in various forms of high-technology production (for instance, global cities, technopoles, new industrial districts, growth corridors and so forth). Moreover, the emergence of such "new industrial spaces" (Scott 1988) has been inextricably linked to the systemic decline and/or restructuring of traditional Fordist manufacturing regions. Consequently, along with regulatory projects oriented toward globalization (McMichael 1996) and neoliberalization (Peck and Tickell 2002), new economy accumulation strategies must be viewed as significant catalysts in generating the new global, continental, national and local mosaics of uneven spatial development and territorial inequality that have crystallized around the world during the last thirty years.

A vast, increasingly sophisticated literature has emerged in recent years to map these new geographies of industrial growth, decline and uneven spatial development (Lee and Wills 1997). Building upon these important contributions, this chapter will examine some of the distinctive *political geographies* that have been forged through new economy accumulation strategies during the last two decades. As indicated, much contemporary discourse on the new economy posits the dissolution or erosion of national states and the consolidation of new decentralized or "networked" forms of governance in the information age (see, for instance, Castells 1998). Against such arguments, I argue here that state institutions and policies have in fact played an important role in promoting ICT development at various geographical scales within each territorial economy. Just as crucially, this chapter suggests that the proliferation of strategies to promote high-technology growth and the clustering of ICTs has also been linked to a major transformation in the character of state regulation throughout the older capitalist world. Increasingly, the goal of promoting ICT development – and, more generally, post-Fordist industrialization – within national and local territories has been embraced not only by corporate elites but also by a variety of national, regional and local politicians and policy makers. This reorientation of political-economic governance away from the traditional Keynesian focus on full employment, social welfare, demand management and territorial equalization has underpinned a wide range of institutional and policy shifts since the 1980s. These include programs of deregulation, privatization, intergovernmental decentralization, fiscal retrenchment and local economic development.

As a result, I shall argue, the socially and spatially redistributive Keynesian welfare national states of the Fordist–Keynesian era have been tendentially superseded by what I shall term *glocalizing competition state regimes* (GCSRs). These newly emergent post-Keynesian state forms are oriented toward a geographical reconcentration of productive capacities and economic assets within strategic urban regions and industrial districts rather than the traditional goal of alleviating territorial disparities on a national scale. This *rescaling* of state regulation is arguably at once a major political medium through which new economy accumulation strategies have been mobilized and one of their most essential institutional-geographical consequences (Brenner 2004; Swyngedouw 1997). While my focus here is on the territorial economies of western Europe, the forms of state rescaling discussed in this chapter have arguably been apparent in North America and East Asia as well, albeit in contextually specific forms (Peck and Tickell 2002; Bunnell 2002).

The chapter is organized as follows. The next section discusses the endemic problem of uneven spatial development under capitalism and the changing role of national states in confronting it. On this basis, I consider the dominant strategies through which European national states attempted to regulate uneven development on a national scale during the "golden age" of Fordist–Keynesian capitalism up through the late 1970s. Subsequent sections outline the unraveling of such strategies, the severe curtailment of compensatory regional policies and the subsequent proliferation of projects to promote ICTs and other post-Fordist industrial specializations within strategic cities and regions. In this context, I emphasize not only the changing institutional context of economic governance and territorial regulation, but also the shifting geographical scales on which they are organized. A concluding section summarizes the implications of this analysis for scholarly debates on the new economy.

Urbanization, capitalist territorial organization and the regulation of uneven development

The geography of capitalism is complex, multifaceted and multiscalar, but the process of urbanization is arguably one of its key expressions and products. For, since the large-scale industrialization of capital during the course of the nineteenth century, capitalist growth has been premised fundamentally upon the production and continual transformation of urban spaces throughout the world (Lefebvre 2003 [1968]). Across the world economy, the process of capitalist urbanization has been profoundly uneven: it has not entailed a linear expansion of urban centers, but rather a "highly disequilibrated form of growth" (Storper and Walker 1989: 8) characterized by continual flux in the fortunes of places, regions and territories as industries emerge, expand, mature and decline.

While major propulsive industries have generally clustered together within specialized local and regional economies, they have also tended to disperse away from these territorial clusters as they have matured. More-over, many new industries have emerged away from established agglomeration economies, often in previously marginalized locations that provide fresh opportunities for innovative activities (Storper and Walker 1989: 70–99). Processes of industrial restructuring and technological change therefore reverberate in powerful and often destructive ways across urban and regional economies. As industries are restructured, so too are cities, regions and the broader spatial divisions of labor in which they are embedded. In this sense, the evolution of capitalism through successive regimes of accumulation involves not only changing industrial specializations but also a variety of geographical transformations in which (a) the propulsive centers of industrial dynamism are periodically shifted across territories and scales and (b) places, cities and regions are continually restructured in relation to changing macroeconomic conditions within the larger spatial division of labor (Storper and Walker 1989). In short, the urbanization process lies at the heart of the "continuous reshaping of geographical land-scapes" (Harvey 1989a: 192) that is endemic to capitalism as an historical system.

It is apparent, then, that the dynamics of industrial urbanization and the concomitant tendencies of territorial restructuring figure crucially in the process of uneven spatial development under capitalism. In general terms, uneven development refers to the circumstance that social, political and economic processes under capitalism are not distributed uniformly or homogenously across the earth's surface or among geographical scales, but are always organized within distinctive socio-spatial configurations. These include urban agglomerations, regional clusters, rural or underdeveloped zones, national territories, supranational economic blocs and so forth. These are in turn characterized by quite divergent economic conditions, developmental capacities and institutional arrangements.

Thus, within a capitalist political-economic system, inequalities are not only expressed socially, in the form of class and income polarization, but also spatially, through the polarization of development among different territories, places and scales. While these socially produced patterns of core-periphery polarization are always articulated in historically and geographically specific forms, they necessarily entail the systematic concentration of advanced socioeconomic assets and developmental capacities within certain core zones and, concomitantly, the chronic marginalization or peripheralization of other, less developed places and territories (Storper and Walker 1989).

The investigation of uneven development has long been one of the foundational concerns of critical geographical political economy. As Smith (1990) has argued in his seminal work on the topic, patterns of uneven geographical development under capitalism are not merely the accidental, contingent byproducts of pre-capitalist geographical differences or of individual-, household- or firm-level locational decisions. Rather, they represent *systemic* expressions of the endemic tension under capitalism between the drive to equalize capital investment across space and the pressure to differentiate such investment in order to exploit place-, territory- and scale-specific conditions for accumulation. On the one hand, the coercive forces of inter-capitalist competition pressure individual capitals to replicate one another's profit-making strategies in dispersed geographical locations and thus tend to equilibrate the conditions for capital accumulation across space. On the other hand, the forces of inter-capitalist competition engender an equally powerful process of geographical differentiation in which individual capitals continually seek out place-specific locational assets and territorially-specific conditions of production. These may enable them to protect, maintain or enhance their competitive advantages.

Consequently, as Smith (1990) indicates, each phase of capitalism is grounded upon historically specific patterns of uneven geographical development in which the contradictory interplay of equalization and differentiation is articulated. These patterns of socio-spatial polarization crystallize not only horizontally, among different types of places and territories across the world system, but also vertically, among different geographical scales stretching from the local, the regional and the national to the continental and the global. The contours of this uneven geography are thus never inscribed permanently onto the institutional landscape of capitalism, but are reworked continually through capital's restless developmental dynamic and through successive strategies to subject the latter to some measure of state regulatory control (Harvey 1982).

Most crucially here, each historical pattern of uneven geographical development is intertwined with certain basic regulatory dilemmas: for the uneven development of capital serves not only as a *basis* for the accumulation process but may also, under certain conditions, become a serious *barrier* to the latter (Harvey 1982). Uneven development, in other words, is not merely an aggregate geographical effect of differential patterns of capital investment, but generates a variety of endemic regulatory problems, both within and beyond the circuit of capital, that may severely destabilize the accumulation process (Peck and Tickell 1995). For instance, the polarization of territorial development between dynamic urban cores and peripheralized regions may enable certain individual capitals to reap the benefits of scale economies and other externalities, but it may also generate dysfunctional political-economic effects that destabilize the space economy as a whole.

An erosion of national industrial capacities may ensue as peripheralized regional economies are constrained to adopt cost-based or defensive strategies of adjustment, leading in turn to a premature downgrading of local infrastructures and to worsening life conditions for many local inhabitants (Leborgne and Lipietz 1992). Moreover, even within the most powerful urban agglomerations, the problem of uneven development may also "come home to roost" (Harvey 1989a: 144) as social polarization, overproduction, the perennial threat of capital flight and various negative externalities (such as severe infrastructural stress, housing shortages, traffic congestion and environmental destruction) unsettle established patterns of local industrial development.

And finally, if patterns of socio-spatial inequality are not maintained within politically acceptable limits, disruptive sociopolitical conflicts – between classes, class fractions, growth coalitions and other place-based alliances – may arise within a (national or local) territory and the state may find itself confronted with severe legitimation crises (Hudson 2001). Uneven geographical development may thus be associated not only with new profit-making opportunities for capital but also with potentially destabilizing, disruptive effects that, in the absence of effective regulatory intervention, can significantly erode the socio-territorial preconditions for sustainable capital accumulation.

While most studies of uneven geographical development have focused upon the interplay between capital investment patterns and the evolution of territorial inequalities, my concern here is to underscore the essential role of state institutions, at various scales, in mediating and regulating these processes (Brenner 2004). Such an inquiry is of considerable importance because, particularly since the consolidation of organized capitalism during the early twentieth century, national states have mobilized a variety of spatial policies designed precisely to influence the geographies of capital investment and, thereby, to manage uneven development within their territorial boundaries (Hudson 2001).

Strategies of territorial redistribution and other compensatory regional policies have frequently been mobilized in order to promote the equalization of industry across the national territory and thus to alleviate the more pernicious, polarizing effects of intra-national uneven development. In most western European countries, this managerial, redistributive and cohesion-oriented regulatory strategy was first mobilized by national states during the 1930s and reached its historical highpoint during the mid-1970s, just as the Fordist regime of accumulation was being dismantled throughout the North Atlantic zone. Subsequently, however, national strategies of territorial development and place-promotion have been deployed in order to channel socioeconomic capacities and infrastructural investments into the most globally competitive locations within each national territory. Since the late 1970s, this entrepreneurial, competitiveness-driven and growth-oriented approach to spatial regulation has superseded previously dominant forms of spatial Keynesianism and has significantly intensified intra-national spatial differentiation and territorial inequality across western Europe (Harvey 1989b).

It is against this background, I believe, that we can begin to analyze the interplay between new economy accumulation strategies and changing forms of state regulation in contemporary western Europe. In what follows, I shall trace the changing political strategies through which western European national states attempted to regulate the problem of uneven development within their territories since the late 1950s. Since the era of high Fordism, I argue, four successive approaches to the regulation of uneven spatial development have crystallized in western Europe, each of which has in turn been premised upon historically specific forms of urban and regional governance. As I will illustrate, the rescaling of national state power during the last two decades has been closely intertwined not only with the development of new approaches to the regulation of uneven spatial development but also with the mobilization of a variety of accumulation strategies intended to promote ICT development and other new economy industries in strategic urban and regional spaces.

Geographies of territorial regulation at the high point of spatial Keynesianism

The economic geography of post-war Fordism in western Europe was composed of a dispersed, yet hierarchical topology in which a functional division of space was imposed at various geographical scales (Lipietz 1994). Spatial divisions of labor emerged within each national territory in the form of hierarchical relationships between large-scale metropolitan regions, in which the lead firms within the major, propulsive Fordist industries were clustered and smaller cities, towns and peripheral zones, in which branch plants, input and service providers and other subordinate economic functions were located. In the western European context, the geographical heartlands of the Fordist accumulation regime stretched from the Industrial Triangle of northern Italy through the German Ruhr district to northern France and the English Midlands; but each of these regional production complexes was in turn embedded within a nationally specific system of production. Throughout the post-war period, these and many other major European urban regions and their surrounding industrial satellites were characterized by consistent demographic growth and industrial expansion. As the Fordist accumulation regime reached maturity, a major decentralization of capital investment unfolded as large firms began more extensively to relocate branch plants from core regions into peripheral spaces (Rodriguez-Pose 1995). Under these conditions, urban and regional governance was increasingly nationalized as western European states attempted to construct centralized bureaucratic hierarchies, to establish nationally standardized frameworks for capitalist production and collective consumption, to underwrite urban and regional growth and to alleviate uneven spatial development throughout their national territories.

First, in order to standardize the provision of welfare services and to coordinate national economic policies, national states centralized the instruments for regulating urban development, thereby transforming local states into mere transmission belts for centrally determined policy regimes (Mayer 1992). Within this managerial framework of urban governance, the state's overarching function at the urban scale was the reproduction of the labor force through public investments in housing, transportation, social services and other public goods, all of which were intended to replicate certain minimum standards of social welfare and infrastructure provision across the national territory (Castells 1977). In this manner, local states were instrumentalized in order "to carry out a national strategy based on a commitment to regional balance and even growth" (Goodwin and Painter 1996: 646). Insofar as the national economy was viewed as the primary terrain for state action, local and regional economies were treated as mere subunits of relatively autocentric national economic spaces dominated by large-scale corporations. These centrally financed local welfare policies also provided important elements of the social wage and thus contributed significantly to the generalization of the mass consumption practices upon which Fordist growth was contingent (Goodwin and Painter 1996: 641). As theorists of the dual state subsequently recognized, the pervasive localization of the state's collective consumption functions during the postwar period was a key institutional feature within a broader scalar division of regulation in which production-oriented state policies were organized at a national scale (Saunders 1979). Accordingly, throughout this period, state strategies to promote economic development, including urban economic development, were mobilized primarily at a national scale rather than through autonomous regional or local initiatives. In this context, a range of national social and economic policy initiatives – including demand-management policies, nationalized ownership of key industries (coal, shipbuilding, power, aerospace), the expansion of public sector employment, military spending and major expenditures on housing, transportation and public utilities – served directly or indirectly to underwrite the growth of major urban and regional economies (Martin and Sunley 1997: 280).

Second, even though major cities and metropolitan regions received the bulk of large-scale public infrastructure investments and welfare services during the Fordist–Keynesian epoch due to their high population densities, such city-centric national state initiatives were counterbalanced extensively through a variety of state expenditures, loans programs and compensatory regional aid policies designed to spread growth into under-developed regions and rural peripheries across the national territory. From the Italian Mezzogiorno and Spanish Andalusia to western and southern France, the agricultural peripheries and border zones of West Germany, the Limburg coal-mining district of northern Belgium, the Dutch northeastern peripheries, the northwestern regions and islands of Denmark, the Scandinavian North, western Ireland and the declining industrial zones of the English North, South Wales, parts of Scotland and much of Northern Ireland, each European country had its so-called "problem areas" or "lagging regions." These were generally composed of economic zones which had been marginalized during previous rounds of industrial development or which were locked into obsolete technological-industrial infrastructures (Clout 1981).

Accordingly, throughout the postwar period until the late 1970s, a broad range of regional and spatial policies were introduced across western Europe that explicitly targeted such peripheralized spaces. Generally justified in the name of "balanced national development" and "spatial equalization," these redistributive regional and spatial policies entailed the introduction of various forms of financial aid, locational incentives and transfer payments to promote industrial growth and economic regeneration outside the dominant city cores. Additionally, they often channeled major public infrastructural investments into such locations. As Dunford and Perrons (1994) indicate, such interregional resource transfers had a significant impact upon the intra-national geographies of uneven development during the post-war period, contributing to an unprecedented convergence of per capita disposable income within most western European states. This nationally oriented project of industrial decentralization, urban deconcentration and spatial equalization was arguably the political lynchpin of spatial Keynesianism, the system of state territorial regulation that prevailed throughout the Fordist–Keynesian period of capitalist development (Martin and Sunley 1997).

Third, it is worth noting that, within this nationalized system of urban governance, metropolitan political institutions acquired a crucially important mediating role between managerial local states and centrally organized, redistributive forms of spatial planning. Above all between the mid-1960s and the early 1970s, diverse types of consolidated metropolitan institutions were established in many major western European city-regions (Keating 1997). These metropolitan or region-wide administrative bodies were widely viewed as mechanisms for rationalizing welfare service provision and for reducing administrative inefficiencies within expanding urban agglomerations. In this sense, metropolitan institutions served as a key, coordinating administrative tier within the centralized hierarchies of intergovernmental relations that prevailed within the Keynesian welfare state apparatus. As suburbanization and industrial decentralization proceeded apace, metropolitan political institutions were increasingly justified as a means to establish a closer spatial correspondence between governmental jurisdictions and functional territories (Lefèvre 1998). By the early 1970s, metropolitan authorities had acquired important roles in guiding industrial expansion, infrastructural investment and population settlement beyond traditional city cores into suburban fringes, primarily through the deployment of comprehensive land-use plans and other mechanisms to influence intra-metropolitan locational patterns. In this sense, metropolitan institutions appear to have significantly influenced the geographies of urbanization during the era of high Fordism.

In sum, spatial Keynesianism is best understood as a broad constellation of national state strategies designed to promote capitalist industrial growth by alleviating or overcoming uneven geographical development within each national space-economy. Spatial Keynesianism intensified the nationalization of state space in two senses: first, it entailed the establishment of a complex system of subnational institutions for the territorial regulation of urban development; and second, it entailed the embedding of major local and regional economies within a hierarchically configured, nationally focused political and economic geography. Accordingly, throughout the post-war period, local governments were subsumed within nationally organized institutional matrices defined by relatively centralized control over local social and economic policies, technocratic frameworks of metropolitan governance, extensive interregional resource transfers and redistributive forms of national spatial planning. Taken together, such policies and institutions attempted to promote a structured coherence for capitalist growth by (a) transforming cities and regions into the localized building blocks for national economic development and (b) spreading urbanization as evenly as possible across the national territory (see Figure 8.1).

By the early 1970s, however, it had become apparent that the fantasy of transcending uneven spatial development through the promotion of balanced urbanization within a relatively closed national economy was as short lived as the Fordist accumulation regime upon which it was grounded.

Geoeconomic and geopolitical context:
- 1960s to early 1970s: high Fordism
- Differentiation of global economic activity among distinct national economic systems under "embedded liberalism"

Privileged spatial target(s):
- National economy

Major goals:
- Deconcentration of population, industry and infrastructure investment from major urban centers into rural peripheries and "underdeveloped" zones
- Replication of standardized economic assets, investments and public goods across the entire surface of the national territory
- Establishment of a nationally standardized system of infrastructural facilities throughout the national economy
- Alleviation of uneven development within national economies: uneven spatial development is seen as a *limit* or *barrier* to stabilized industrial growth

Dominant policy mechanisms:
- Locational subsidies to large firms
- Local social welfare policies and collective consumption investments
- Redistributive regional policies
- National spatial planning systems and public infrastructural investments

---

Figure 8.1 Spatial Keynesianism and the political regulation of uneven development.

Crisis-management and the new politics of endogenous growth in the 1970s

New approaches to the political regulation of uneven spatial development gradually began to crystallize in the early 1970s, as the Fordist developmental regime entered a phase of systemic, crisis-induced restructuring on a world scale (Lipietz 1994). A number of geo-economic shifts occurred during this era that decentered the predominant role of the national scale as a locus of economic and political coordination. These developments led to the transfer of new regulatory responsibilities and burdens both upwards to supranational institutional forms such as the EU and downwards to the regional and local levels.

These rescalings of state space were mediated through a range of relatively *ad hoc*, trial-and-error regulatory responses, crisis-management strategies and political experiments. On a national scale, diverse political alliances mobilized strategies of crisis-management in order to defend the institutional infrastructures of the Fordist–Keynesian order. From the first oil shock of 1973 until around 1979, traditional recipes of national demand-management prevailed throughout the OECD zone as central governments tried desperately to recreate the conditions for a Fordist virtuous circle of growth. However, as Jessop (1989: 269) remarks of the

British case, such countercyclical tactics ultimately amounted to no more than an "eleventh hour, state-sponsored Fordist modernisation," for they were incapable of solving, simultaneously, the dual problems of escalating inflation and mass unemployment. Meanwhile, as the boom regions of Fordism experienced sustained economic crises, the policy framework of spatial Keynesianism was further differentiated to include deindustrializing, distressed cities and manufacturing centers as geographical targets for various forms of state assistance and financial aid. In contrast to traditional Keynesian forms of spatial policy, which had focused almost exclusively upon underdeveloped regions and peripheral zones, national *urban* policies were now introduced in several western European states to address the specific socioeconomic problems of large cities, such as mass unemployment, deskilling, capital flight and infrastructural decay.

In this manner, many of the redistributive policy relays associated with spatial Keynesianism were significantly expanded during the 1970s. Crucially, however, even though the spatial targets of regional policies were now differentiated to include urban areas as key recipients of state aid, the state's underlying commitment to the project of spatial equalization at a national scale was maintained and even reinforced throughout this decade.

Yet, even as these new forms of state support for urban development were extended, a range of nationally imposed policy initiatives and intergovernmental realignments unsettled the entrenched, managerial-welfarist framework that had prevailed throughout the post-war period. As of the late 1970s, the national scale likewise became an important institutional locus for restructuring-oriented political projects that aimed to dismantle many of the policy relays associated with the Keynesian welfare national state. During the post-1970s recession, as national governments were pressured increasingly to rationalize government expenditures, national grants to sub-national administrative levels, including both regions and localities, were generally reduced. These new forms of fiscal austerity caused local governments throughout western Europe to become more dependent upon locally collected taxes and non-tax revenues such as charges and user fees (Mouritzen 1992).

In the immediate aftermath of these shifts, many western European local governments attempted to adjust to the new fiscal conditions by delaying capital expenditures, drawing upon liquid assets and engaging in deficit spending, but these proved to be no more than short-term stopgap measures. Subsequently, additional local revenues were sought in, among other sources, economic development projects (Fox Przeworski 1986). Whereas the new national urban policies introduced during this period enabled many cities to capture supplementary public resources, most local governments were nonetheless confronted with major new budgetary constraints due to the dual impact of national fiscal retrenchment and intensifying local socioeconomic problems. One of the most significant institutional outcomes of the national fiscal squeeze of the

1970s, therefore, was to pressure localities to seek new sources of revenue through a proactive mobilization of local economic development projects and inward investment strategies (Mayer 1994).

Under these conditions, a variety of "bootstraps" strategies intended to promote economic growth from below, without extensive reliance upon national subsidies, proliferated in many major western European cities and regions (Bullmann 1991). In contrast to their earlier focus on welfarist redistribution, local governments now began to introduce a range of strategies to rejuvenate local economies, beginning with land-assembly programs and land-use planning schemes and subsequently expanding to diverse firm-based, area-based, sectoral and job-creation measures (Eisenschitz and Gough 1993; Hall and Hubbard 1998). Although this new politics of urban economic development would subsequently be diffused in diverse political forms throughout the western European city-system, during the 1970s it remained most prevalent within manufacturing-based cities and regions of the so-called old economy in which industrial restructuring had generated particularly devastating socioeconomic problems (Parkinson 1991).

Thus, even as national governments continued to promote economic integration and territorial equalization at a national scale, neo-corporatist alliances between state institutions, trade unions and other local organizations within rustbelt cities and regions from the German Ruhr district to the English Midlands elaborated regionally-specific sectoral, technological and employment policies in order to promote what was popularly labeled "endogenous growth" (Hahne 1985; Stöhr and Taylor 1981). Throughout the 1970s, the goal of these leftist, neo-corporatist and social democratic alliances was to establish negotiated strategies of industrial restructuring in which economic regeneration was linked directly to social priorities such as intra-regional redistribution, job creation, vocational retraining initiatives and class compromise. Under these conditions, the basic Fordist–Keynesian priorities of social redistribution, territorial equalization and class compromise were maintained, albeit within the more geographically bounded parameters of regional and/or local economies rather than as a project to be generalized throughout the entire national territory.

In sum, the 1970s are best viewed as a transitional period characterized by intense interscalar struggles between political alliances concerned to preserve the nationalized institutional infrastructures of spatial Keynesianism and other, newly formed political coalitions concerned to introduce more decentralized frameworks for the regulation of capitalist territorial development. Although the new regulatory frameworks sought by such modernizing coalitions remained relatively inchoate, such coalitions shared a broad commitment to the goal of endogenous growth and a more or less explicit rejection of nationally encompassing models of territorial development. In this sense, the proliferation of local and regional regulatory experiments, fueled by political coalitions oriented toward place-specific trajectories of socioeconomic development, articulated qualitatively new regulatory projects. These had markedly destabilized the nationalizing approach to the regulation of uneven spatial development that had prevailed during the post-war golden age. While central governments generally continued during the 1970s to promote such nationalizing, spatially redistributive agendas, the diffusion of this new bootstraps strategy during the same decade appears, retrospectively, to have entailed a major *de facto* modification of the inherited institutional framework of spatial Keynesianism. It also opened up a politico-institutional space in which (national, regional *and* local) states could mobilize accumulation strategies oriented toward the cultivation and territorialization of ICTs and other new economy industries within their most strategically positioned cities, regions and industrial districts.

The rise of glocalization strategies and the quest for a new economy

The crisis of the Fordist developmental model intensified during the 1980s. This led to a new phase of industrial transformation, territorial reconfiguration and state spatial restructuring throughout western Europe. The strategies of crisis-management introduced during the 1970s had neither restored the conditions for a new growth cycle nor successfully resolved the deepening problems of economic stagnation, rising unemployment and industrial decline within major western European cities and regions. Consequently, during the course of the 1980s, most European national governments abandoned traditional Keynesian macroeconomic policies in favor of monetarism. Thus, a competitive balance of payments subsequently replaced full employment as the overarching goal of monetary and fiscal policy (Scharpf 1991). By the late 1980s, neoliberal political agendas such as welfare state retrenchment, trade liberalization, privatization and deregulation had been adopted not only in the United Kingdom under Thatcher and in West Germany under Kohl, but also in more socially moderate or hybrid forms in many traditionally social democratic or social/christian democratic countries such as the Netherlands, Belgium, France, Spain, Denmark and even Sweden (Rhodes 1995).

This geopolitical sea-change resulted in the imposition of additional fiscal constraints upon most municipal and metropolitan governments, whose revenues had already been significantly reduced during the preceding decade. Political support for large-scale strategic planning projects waned and welfare state bureaucracies were increasingly dismantled, downsized or restructured, not least at metropolitan and municipal levels. In the wake of these political realignments, during the mid-1980s, major metropolitan institutions such as the Greater London Council and the *Rijnmond* in Rotterdam were summarily abolished. Elsewhere within western Europe, metropolitan institutions were formally preserved but significantly weakened in practice due to centrally imposed budgetary pressures and enhanced competition between city cores and suburban peripheries for capital investment and state subsidies (Barlow 1991). The fiscal squeeze upon public expenditure in cities and regions and the dissolution or weakening of metropolitan governance were thus among the important localized expressions of the processes of welfare state retrenchment that began to unfold throughout western Europe during the 1980s. As of this decade, the national preconditions for municipal Keynesianism were being systematically eroded as local and metropolitan governments were increasingly forced to "fend for themselves" in securing a fiscal base for their regulatory activities (Mayer 1994).

During this same period, a new mosaic of urban and regional development began to crystallize throughout the western European city-system. Across western Europe, the crisis of North Atlantic Fordism triggered the tumultuous decline of many large-scale manufacturing regions that had been grounded primarily upon Fordist mass production industries and, concomitantly, the transformation of numerous erstwhile lagging regions into attractive locations for ICT investment and flexible production systems (Scott and Storper 1992). At the same time, established metropolitan cores such as London, Amsterdam, Paris, Frankfurt, Milan and Zürich were being transformed into strategic nodal points within global and European financial networks. As Veltz (1993) explains, the post-1970s period has witnessed the consolidation of an "archipelago economy" in which corporate headquarters, major decision-making centers and most high value-added economic activities have been concentrated within the most powerful metropolitan nodes in a worldwide inter-urban network.

For Veltz (2000), this trend toward "metropolitanization" represents an important expression of a marked intensification of territorial inequalities that has been unfolding at all scales within post-1970s western Europe. This includes an intra-European divide between "winning" and "losing" regions; various intra-national divides between booming, ICT-based urban cores and declining manufacturing zones or depressed rural peripheries; intra-regional divides between central city cores and their surrounding hinterlands; and intra-metropolitan divides between wealthy or gentrified areas and disadvantaged, impoverished neighborhoods. Figure 8.2, based upon Krätke's (1993, 1995) pioneering research on the rescaling of European urban systems, provides one particularly useful representation of how these metropolitanization tendencies have transformed the European urban hierarchy since the crisis of the Fordist–Keynesian system (see Figure 8.2).

Krätke's model describes contemporary transformations of the European urban hierarchy with reference to two structural criteria: the industrial structure of the city's productive base (Fordist vs. post-Fordist) and the spatial scale of its command and control functions (global, European, national, regional, non-existent). The arrows in the figure indicate various

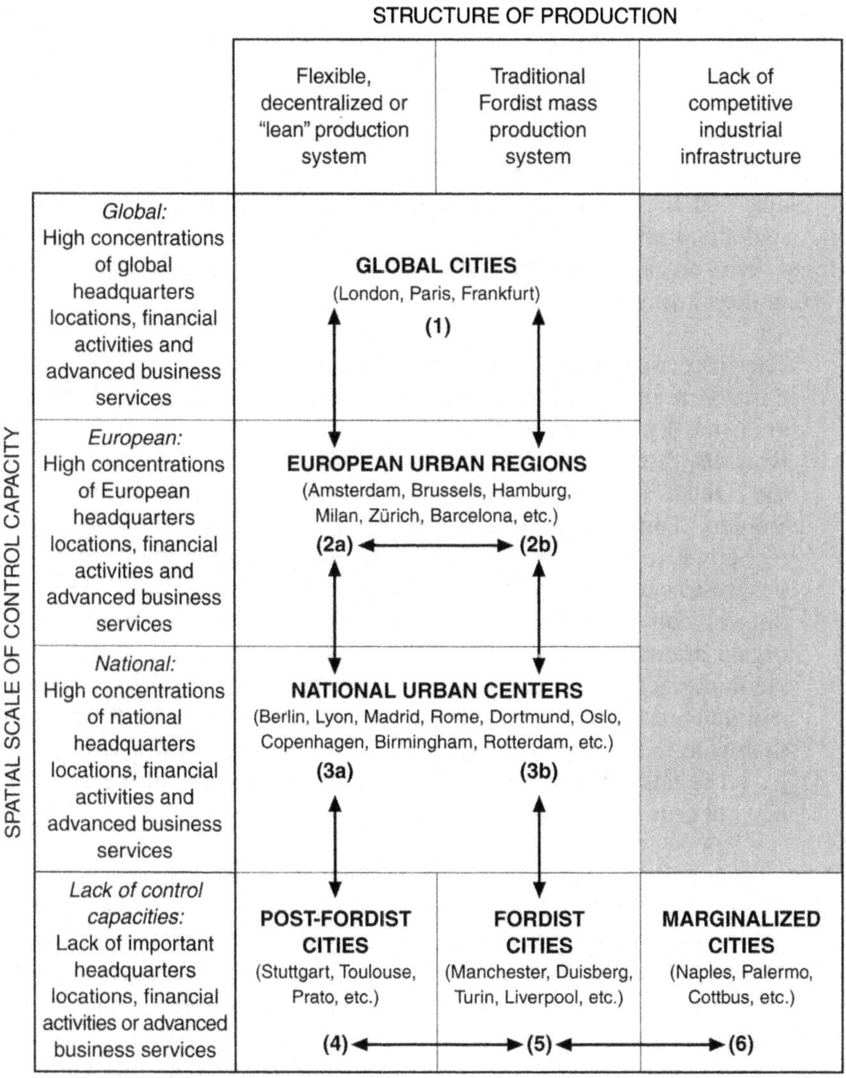

STRUCTURE OF PRODUCTION

	Flexible, decentralized or "lean" production system	Traditional Fordist mass production system	Lack of competitive industrial infrastructure
Global: High concentrations of global headquarters locations, financial activities and advanced business services	**GLOBAL CITIES** (London, Paris, Frankfurt) ↑ **(1)** ↑		
European: High concentrations of European headquarters locations, financial activities and advanced business services	**EUROPEAN URBAN REGIONS** (Amsterdam, Brussels, Hamburg, Milan, Zürich, Barcelona, etc.) **(2a)** ◄────► **(2b)** ↑ ↑		
National: High concentrations of national headquarters locations, financial activities and advanced business services	**NATIONAL URBAN CENTERS** (Berlin, Lyon, Madrid, Rome, Dortmund, Oslo, Copenhagen, Birmingham, Rotterdam, etc.) **(3a)** **(3b)** ↑ ↑		
Lack of control capacities: Lack of important headquarters locations, financial activities or advanced business services	**POST-FORDIST CITIES** (Stuttgart, Toulouse, Prato, etc.) **(4)** ◄────	**FORDIST CITIES** (Manchester, Duisberg, Turin, Liverpool, etc.) ────► **(5)** ◄────	**MARGINALIZED CITIES** (Naples, Palermo, Cottbus, etc.) ────► **(6)**

(Left axis label: SPATIAL SCALE OF CONTROL CAPACITY)

Figure 8.2 The changing European urban hierarchy (based on Kräkte 1995: 141).

possible changes in position among cities within the European urban hierarchy. Various cities have been listed to exemplify each of these levels.

Particularly since the 1980s, the new territorial inequalities depicted
within Figure 8.2 have been still further exacerbated. This is due to the
dual processes of economic globalization and European integration, both
of which have massively reinforced the strategic positions of the most
powerful urban and regional economies. Additionally, they contribute

significantly to the further marginalization of the less developed or peripheralized zones of the European economy (Dunford and Perrons 1994). As Petrella (2000: 70) argues, the last two decades have witnessed the establishment of an "Archipelago Europe" characterized by an increasing concentration of technological, financial, economic and political capacities within "a restricted number of 'islands' of wealth and innovation, surrounded by a sea of 'peripheries.'" Moreover, Petrella (2000: 70–71) explains that these "islands" are composed of Europe's major metropolitan agglomerations, the heartlands of ICT growth that have been increasingly delinked from their hinterlands and other peripheralized locations within their host states:

> The 'core islands' of Archipelago Europe already have a name: the Parisian region; London East Anglia; the new Edinburgh, Glasgow area; the Frankfurt, Stuttgart and Munich regions; the new Berlin; Brussels 'district'; Rotterdam and Antwerp, together with the rest of the Dutch Randstad; Denmark; Stockholm, Lombardia, the new Veneto, Torino, Madrid, Barcelona. The most aggressive financial resources will be 'available' in these cities/regions, the 'best' universities, research centres and scientific institutions, the 'greatest' theatres, operas, concert houses and musea, headquarters of multinational organisations and networks of the most dynamic SMEs [small- and medium-sized enterprises]. The 'core islands' will tend to establish, maintain and strengthen tighter flows and linkages among themselves than with the rest of 'their' national, European and global peripheries [. . .] The linkage between the core islands of the Archipelago and the rest are growing increasingly weaker.

Following the consolidation of the Single European Market and the launching of the euro during the 1990s, these polarizing tendencies have been still further entrenched both at national and European scales (Taylor and Hoyler 2000). Under these circumstances, economic activities, technological capacities and advanced infrastructural investments have been increasingly concentrated within a "vital axis" stretching from the South East of England, Brussels and the Dutch Randstad through the German Rhinelands southwards to Zürich and the northern Italian Industrial Triangle surrounding Milan (Dunford and Perrons 1994).

In a now-famous report prepared for the French spatial planning agency DATAR shortly prior to the consolidation of the Single European Market, Brunet (1989) famously described this core European urban zone as a "blue banana" whose strategic importance would be further enhanced as geo-economic and European economic integration proceeded (Figure 8.3).

Notably, Brunet's famous representation of western Europe's urbanized boom zone represented a nearly exact inversion of the geography of

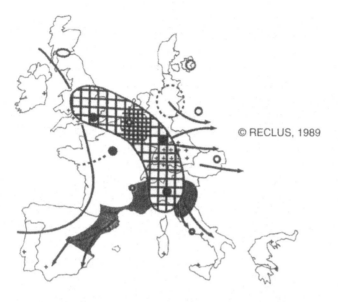

© RECLUS, 1989

Figure 8.3 Brunet's blue banana (source: DATA 1989).

development zones that had been promoted during the era of spatial Key-nesianism. In stark contrast to the notions of cumulative causation upon which earlier spatial and regional policies had been based, in which the spatial diffusion of growth potentials was seen to benefit both cores and peripheries, Brunet's model implied that winning cities and regions would form a powerful, densely interlinked and increasingly autonomous urban network. This network would be dominated by advanced infrastructural facilities, high value-added activities and new economy industries, leaving other regions essentially to fend for themselves or risk being marginalized still further in the new geo-economic context.

As Brunet's model dramatically illustrated, the tumultuous economic transformations of the 1980s were causing the economic geography of post-war spatial Keynesianism to be turned inside-out. As of this decade, growth was no longer being spread outwards from developed urban cores into the underdeveloped peripheries of each national economy. Rather, it was instead being systematically reconcentrated into the most powerful agglomerations situated within Europe-wide and global spatial divisions of labor. And, most crucially here, Brunet's map depicted these urban cores as the geographical heartlands of new economy industries based upon ICTs and other high technology sectors. These were surrounded by, but increasingly delinked from, outlying peripheries that were seen to be locked in to old economy technologies, industries and institutional forms.

Despite its serious limitations as a social-scientific depiction of contemporary European political-economic space (Krätke *et al.* 1997), the remarkably wide influence of Brunet's model of the European blue banana was symptomatic of a major, state-led reorientation of political-economic governance that began to unfold throughout western Europe during the course of the 1980s. As urban economic restructuring intensified in conjunction with processes of global and European integration, western European central governments began more explicitly to target major cities and city-regions as the locational keys to national economic competitiveness (Leitner and Sheppard 1998). In the "Europe of regions" – a catchphrase that became increasingly important in national policy discussions during this period – cities were no longer seen merely as containers of declining industries and socioeconomic problems, but were now viewed as dynamic growth engines through which ICTs and other knowledge-based industries could be fostered and territorialized. This view of cities as incubators for the new economy, and thus as essential national economic assets, became increasingly dominant in mainstream policy circles by the late 1980s, as national and local governments prepared for the introduction of the Single European Market.

As western European states attempted to transform their most economically powerful cities, city-regions and industrial districts into the growth engines for ICT development and post-Fordist growth, they also developed radically new approaches to the institutional mediation of uneven spatial development within their territories. Initially, with the ascendancy of neoliberalism and the imposition of new forms of fiscal austerity in many western European states, inherited programs of territorial redistribution were scaled back, thereby exposing local and regional economies more directly to the pressures of Europe-wide and even global economic competition (Martin and Sunley 1997). Such policy initiatives were aimed primarily at reducing public expenditures and at undermining traditional forms of *dirigiste*, centralized economic management (Ansell 2000).

As illustrated above, the local economic initiatives of the 1970s emerged in a politico-institutional context in which central governments remained broadly committed to the Fordist–Keynesian project of promoting national spatial equalization and socio-spatial redistribution. In stark contrast, however, the local economic initiatives of the 1980s were articulated under supralocal conditions in which neoliberal policy orthodoxies were acquiring an unprecedented influence, leading in turn to a marginalization or even abandonment of traditional national compensatory regional policies in most western European states (Brenner and Theodore 2002). In this transformed political context, the goal of equalizing economic development capacities across the national territory was increasingly seen to be incompatible with the new priority of promoting place-specific locational assets and endogenous ICT development within cities and city-regions. Accordingly, in addition to their efforts to undercut traditional redistributive regional policy relays, national governments mobilized a number of institutional and economic restructuring strategies during the course of the 1980s in order to establish a new, competitive infrastructure for various forms of high-technology economic development within their territories:

- Local governments were granted new revenue-raising powers and an increased level of authority in determining local tax rates and user fees, even as national fiscal transfers to sub-national levels were diminished (Fox Przeworski 1986; Mayer 1994). Such fiscally retrenched and institutionally streamlined local state apparatuses were widely viewed as a key precondition for the creation of the political-economic environment in which new economy industries would cluster.
- New responsibilities for planning, economic development, social services and spatial planning were devolved or decentralized downwards to sub-national (regional and local) governments (Harding 1994). This new framework of regionalized and localized policy capacities was frequently justified as an important means to foster the place-specific conditions of production and regulation required by ICTs and other new economy industries.
- National spatial planning systems were redefined. Economic priorities such as promoting structural competitiveness – particularly in ICTs – superseded traditional welfarist, redistributive priorities such as equity and spatial equalization. Meanwhile, in many European countries, the most globally competitive urban regions and industrial districts frequently replaced the national economy as the privileged target for major spatial planning initiatives and infrastructural investments (Brenner 1998). Although many peripheralized cities and regions likewise attempted to attract high-technology investment, most national policy makers believed that clusters of new economy industries should be promoted above all in those regions that were already well endowed with advanced infrastructural facilities, dynamic labor markets and a significant legacy of investment by high-technology firms.
- National, regional and local governments introduced new, territory- and place-specific institutions and policies. These ranged from enterprise zones, urban development corporations and airport development agencies to training and enterprise councils, inward investment agencies and development planning boards. They were designed to reconcentrate or enhance advanced socioeconomic assets within cities and to position them strategically in supranational and global circuits of capital (Hall and Hubbard 1998; Harding 1994, 1997). Such measures were viewed as an important means through which to accelerate the development of new economy clusters and to poach ICT investment away from other potential locations both within and beyond western Europe.

- The forms and functions of local states were systematically redefined. Whereas post-war western European local governments had been devoted primarily to various forms of welfare service delivery, these institutions were transformed during the 1980s into entrepreneurial agencies. Above all, they were oriented toward the promotion of economic development and a "good business environment" within their jurisdictions (Mayer 1992; Harvey 1989b). Even though they frequently entailed significant tax concessions and other financial incentives to transnational capital, these highly localized strategies of economic development were frequently justified as a necessary basis for establishing and maintaining the unique types of "untraded interdependencies" (Storper 1996) upon which high-technology industrialization is generally thought to be contingent.

Taken together, then, these wide-ranging rescalings of the Fordist–Keynesian regulatory architecture were widely seen as a means to establish a new "lean and mean" framework of state regulation oriented toward mobilizing and coordinating local socioeconomic assets and inter-firm networks, not least within ICTs and other high-technology sectors (Swyngedouw 1997).[2] At the same time, they entailed a dramatic intensification of *state-led* interlocality competition in which municipal governments across Europe devised new institutional and policy strategies through which to lure high-technology investments into their territorial jurisdictions.

In stark contrast to the standardized geographies of state space under Fordism, in which national states attempted to maintain minimum levels of service provision throughout the national territory, the establishment of an entrepreneurial, competitiveness-oriented institutional infrastructure for political-economic governance during the 1980s has entailed an increasing differentiation and fragmentation of state regulatory activities at various spatial scales.

On the one hand, the consolidation of entrepreneurial forms of urban governance (Harvey 1989b) has been premised upon the establishment of new sub-national layers of state and para-state institutions through which cities can be marketed as customized, competitive locations for ICTs and other strategic economic functions within global and European spatial divisions of labor. On the other hand, the devolutionary and decentralizing initiatives mentioned above have fundamentally reconfigured entrenched intergovernmental hierarchies and scalar divisions of regulation. These impose powerful new pressures upon sub-national administrative units to fend for themselves in an increasingly uncertain geopolitical and geo-economic environment (MacLeod 2000). In this manner, within the intensely polarized economic geographies of Archipelago Europe, a "parallel mosaic of differentiated spaces of regulation" (Goodwin and Painter 1996: 646) has been established through ongoing processes of state rescaling and urban policy reform.

In the face of these combined institutional realignments, inherited local and supralocal frameworks for the political regulation of uneven development have been thoroughly reconfigured: the *nationalizing* approach to the regulation of territorial inequalities that had underpinned the Fordist–Keynesian system has been superseded by what might be termed a *glocalizing* political strategy. Its central goal is to position strategic local (and/or regional) spaces competitively within continent-wide or global circuits of capital accumulation. In contrast to post-war strategies of spatial Keynesianism, which had contributed to a marked alleviation of intranational uneven development across western Europe, these glocalization strategies have actively intensified the latter (a) by promoting a systematic reconcentration of advanced high-technology industries within each national territory's most competitive locations; (b) by encouraging increasingly divergent, place-specific forms of economic governance, welfare provision and territorial administration within different local and regional economies and (c) by institutionalizing highly competitive relations, whether for public subsidies or for private investments, among major subnational administrative units. The declared goal of national and local spatial policies is thus no longer to alleviate uneven geographical development but actively to *intensify* it through policies intended to strengthen the unique, place-specific socioeconomic assets of strategic, globally competitive urban regions as locations for high-technology clustering.[3] The basic elements of these newly consolidated glocalization strategies are summarized in Figure 8.4.

To be sure, the crystallization of these glocalization strategies has resulted from a variety of economic, political and geographical dynamics during the last thirty years. These glocalization strategies may be articulated in a variety of neoliberal, social democratic or hybrid forms (Eisenschitz and Gough 1993; Brenner and Theodore 2002). In the present context, the key point is that such strategies have served as an essentially important medium through which accumulation strategies oriented toward the establishment and territorialization of new economy industries have been mobilized within major European cities and city-regions. As this discussion indicates, by means of glocalization strategies, national and local states have played key roles in promoting and anchoring new economy industries and ICTs within strategic locations inside their territories. The deployment of such glocalization strategies has, in turn, been indicative of a broader reorientation within the politics of uneven spatial development across western European territorial economies.

The rescaled formation of national and local state power that has crystallized through these transformations may be provisionally characterized as a "glocalizing competition state regime" (GCSR). It can be described as *glocalizing* because it rests upon concerted (national and local) political strategies to position diverse sub-national spaces (localities, cities, regions, industrial districts) within supranational (European or global) circuits of

---

Geoeconomic and geopolitical context:
- Late 1970s – present: ongoing processes of regulatory experimentation in the wake of the crisis of North Atlantic Fordism
- New global–local tensions: global economic integration proceeds in tandem with an increasing dependence of large corporations on localized agglomeration economies
- The search for a new institutional fix proceeds at all spatial scales in a geoeconomic context defined by US-led neoliberal dominance

Privileged spatial target(s):
- Major urban and regional economies situated within supranational and/or global circuits of capital

Major goals:
- Reconcentration of population, industry and infrastructure investment into strategic urban and regional economies
- *Differentiation* of national economic space into increasingly specialized urban and regional economies
- Promotion of *customized*, place-specific forms of infrastructural investment oriented towards global and European economic flows
- Intensification of interspatial competition at all scales: uneven development is now seen as a *basis* for economic growth rather than as a limit or barrier to the latter

Dominant policy mechanisms:
- Deregulation and welfare state retrenchment
- Decentralization of intergovernmental arrangements, socioeconomic policies and fiscal responsibilities
- Spatially selective investments in advanced infrastructures, generally within strategic cities, regions and industrial districts
- Place-specific regional and local industrial policies
- Local economic initiatives; proliferation of "place-marketing" strategies

Spatio-temporality of economic development:
- "Glocal developmentalism": fragmentation of national space into distinct urban/regional economies with their own place-specific locational features and developmental trajectories

---

Figure 8.4 Glocalization strategies and the new politics of uneven development.

economic activity. It is a *competition state* because it privileges the goals of structural competitiveness and organizational flexibility over traditional welfarist priorities such as equity and redistribution. And it is a *regime* because it represents an unstable, uncoordinated and continually evolving spatial mosaic of political strategies, institutional modifications and regulatory experiments rather than a fully consolidated or coherent state form.

The ambiguous resurgence of metropolitan regionalism in the 1990s

A number of commentators have emphasized the contradictory and chronically unstable character of ICT-based accumulation strategies. First, such accumulation strategies focus one-sidedly upon ICTs and other new economy sectors and thus neglect to cultivate or rejuvenate extant socio-economic assets within particular territories (Krätke and Borst 1999). Second, accumulation strategies oriented toward new economy industries tend to intensify uneven development, social exclusion and territorial disparities at all spatial scales within the territories in which they are deployed (Bunnell 2002). In this manner, they generate significant negative externalities and other social costs, thereby undermining the very socio-territorial conditions upon which sustainable capitalist growth is contingent. Third and more generally, while ICTs may successfully unleash short- and medium-term bursts of economic growth within certain "paradigmatic" local and regional economies – such as Silicon Valley or the Third Italy – the conditions underlying these paradigms are extremely difficult, if not impossible, to replicate in other socio-institutional contexts characterized by different industrial histories and regulatory arrangements.

These chronic limitations of new economy accumulation strategies have been significantly exacerbated during the 1990s in conjunction with the diffusion of GCSRs throughout western Europe. As indicated above, one of the major effects of glocalization strategies has been to enhance competitive pressures upon all sub-national administrative units and thus to intensify uneven geographical development still further within each national territory. While these institutional realignments may temporarily benefit a select number of powerful, globally competitive urban regions, where ICTs are disproportionately clustered, they generally inflict a logic of regulatory undercutting upon most local and regional economies, a trend which may seriously downgrade national economic performance in the medium- and long-term. At the same time, the increasing geographical differentiation of state regulatory activities induced through glocalization strategies is "as much a hindrance as a help to regulation" (Painter and Goodwin 1996: 646). For, in the absence of institutional mechanisms of meta-governance capable of coordinating subnational regulatory initiatives and competitive strategies, these ongoing rescaling processes may severely undermine the state's own organizational coherence and functional unity, leading in turn to serious governance failures and legitimation deficits (Jessop 1998; Hudson 2001).

The contradictory tendencies unleashed during the last two decades of industrial restructuring and state rescaling have arguably had important ramifications for the evolutionary trajectories of GCSRs. During the course of the 1990s, many glocalizing competition state regimes were faced with the increasingly pervasive regulatory deficits of their own predominant strategies of political-economic governance. As a result, they have been constrained in the way in which they engage in various forms of institutional restructuring through which to manage the disruptive, dysfunctional socioeconomic consequences of ICT-led growth and unfettered interlocality competition. Thus, whereas the rescaling of political-economic governance during the 1970s and 1980s was animated primarily through strategies to manage economic crisis, to rejuvenate industrial growth within major local and regional economies and to promote ICT-led reindustrialization, the rescaling projects of the 1990s have been mediated increasingly through strategies designed to manage the pervasive governance failures associated with the previous round of regulatory restructuring and state rescaling. In this manner, during the 1990s, a variety of political responses to what Offe (1984) once termed "the crisis of crisis-management" have been superimposed upon the local economic initiatives and crisis-management strategies that had been initially mobilized in western European cities and states following the demise of North Atlantic Fordism in the 1970s. Political strategies designed to manage this crisis of crisis-management have arguably played an essential role in reshaping the institutional and geographical architectures of GCSRs since the early 1990s, when the contradictions of first-wave glocalization strategies, entrepreneurial urban strategies and ICT-led growth became widely apparent throughout western Europe.

As of this period, glocalization strategies began increasingly to encompass not only new economy accumulation strategies but also a variety of local and supralocal "flanking mechanisms and supporting measures" (Jessop 1998: 97–98) intended to manage the diverse tensions, conflicts and contradictions generated by such strategies both within and beyond localities. Although these newly emergent strategies of crisis-management have not alleviated the limitations of ICT-led accumulation strategies, they have entailed the establishment of any number of institutional mechanisms through which the most disruptive political-economic consequences of such strategies may be monitored and managed.

It is in this context, I would argue, that the widespread proliferation of new *regionally* focused regulatory projects during the last decade must be understood (Brenner 2003). As indicated, the first wave of glocalization strategies focused predominantly upon the downscaling and decentralization of formerly nationalized administrative capacities and regulatory arrangements toward local tiers of state power. It was under these conditions that many of the metropolitan institutional forms that had been inherited from the Fordist–Keynesian period were abolished or downgraded. More recently, however, the metropolitan and regional scales have become strategically important sites for a new round of regulatory experiments and institutional shifts throughout western Europe.

From experiments in metropolitan institutional reform and decentralized regional industrial policy in Germany, Italy, France and the Netherlands to the Blairite project of establishing a patchwork of Regional Development Agencies (RDAs) throughout the United Kingdom, these developments have led many commentators to predict that a "new regionalism" is superseding both the geographies of spatial Keynesianism *and* the forms of local economic development that emerged immediately following the initial crisis of North Atlantic Fordism (MacLeod 2000). Against such arguments, however, the preceding discussion points toward a crisis-theoretical interpretation of these initiatives as an important *evolutionary modification* of GCSRs in conjunction with their own immanent contradictions. Although the politico-institutional content of contemporary regionalization strategies continues to be an object of intense contestation, they have been articulated thus far in at least two basic forms.

On the one hand, regionally focused strategies of state rescaling have frequently attempted to transpose ICT-based strategies of local economic development upwards onto a regional scale, leading in turn to a further intensification of uneven spatial development throughout each national territory. In this scenario, the contradictions of ICT-led growth are to be resolved through the upscaling of local economies into larger, regionally configured territorial units, which are in turn to be promoted as integrated, unified and competitive locations for globally competitive ICT investment. In this approach to regional state rescaling, the scalar configuration of GCSRs is modified in order to emphasize regions rather than localities. Nevertheless, the basic politics of ICT promotion, spatial reconcentration, unfettered interspatial competition and intensified uneven development is maintained unchecked.

On the other hand, many contemporary strategies of regionalization have attempted provisionally to countervail the dynamics of unfettered interlocality competition by promoting selected forms of social redistribution, social cohesion and spatial equalization *within* strategic regional institutional spaces. Although such initiatives generally do not significantly undermine uneven spatial development between regions, they can nonetheless be viewed as efforts to modify some of the most disruptive local and regional impacts of the ICT-based glocalization strategies that prevailed during the 1980s, particularly in the context of intensifying city-suburban conflicts and zero-sum intra-regional competition for high-technology investment.

Indeed, this aspect of regional state rescaling may be viewed as an attempt to reintroduce a downscaled form of spatial Keynesianism *within* the sub-national regulatory architecture of glocalizing states: the priority of promoting equalized, balanced growth is thus to be promoted at a regional scale, within delimited sub-national zones, rather than throughout the entire national territory.

Which mixture of these opposed glocalization strategies prevails within a given national, regional or local institutional environment – and the degree to which they privilege ICTs over other sectoral specializations and economic development strategies – hinges upon intense sociopolitical struggles in which diverse social forces strive to influence the geography of state regulatory activities and private investment toward particular political ends. Nonetheless, both of these new, rescaled forms of

crisis-management appear to represent significant evolutionary modifications within the GCSRs that were consolidated during the 1980s. In this
newest approach to the political regulation of uneven development in
western Europe, the priorities of ICT development, economic competitiveness and crisis-management are juxtaposed uneasily in an unstable,
continually shifting institutional matrix for urban and regional governance.
While there is little evidence at the present time to suggest that either of
these regionalized glocalization strategies will engender sustainable forms
of economic regeneration and ICT-led growth in the medium term, they
are nonetheless likely to continue to intensify the geographical differentiation of state power and the uneven development of capital throughout
western Europe into the foreseeable future.

Conclusion: new economy; new landscapes of regulation

> The old bugbear of uneven development refuses to go away despite
> the blurring of borders and extension of transnational corporations. It
> keeps coming back in new forms.
>
> (Walker 1997: 5)

This chapter has attempted to demonstrate how the rise of strategies to
promote ICT-based economic development in European cities and city-
regions has been intertwined with a broader rescaling of national state
spaces following the dismantling of spatial Keynesianism in the late 1970s.
Within this newly emergent, glocalized configuration of state power,
national governments have not simply transferred power downwards, but
have attempted to institutionalize competitive relations between major
sub-national administrative units as a means to position major local and
regional economies strategically within supranational (European and
global) circuits of capital. In this sense, even as traditional, nationally
focused regulatory arrangements have been decentered, national states
have attempted to retain control over major sub-national political-
economic spaces by integrating them within operationally rescaled, but
still nationally coordinated, accumulation strategies.

I have suggested that the discourse on the new economy has played a
key role in these newly emergent accumulation strategies, for it has
served, simultaneously (a) to naturalize the purported "constraints" of
contemporary globalization; (b) to justify the retrenchment of inherited,
Fordist–Keynesian state institutions and redistributive policy relays; (c) to
promote the channeling of public resources into particular sectors (above
all, ICTs and high-technology industries) and places (above all, global
cities and industrial districts) over and against others; and (d) to legitimate
the resultant forms of territorial inequality and sociospatial exclusion as
the necessary byproducts of globalized, knowledge-driven, informational
capitalism. I have argued, however, that the ICT-led accumulation strat-

egies are chronically unstable, for they perpetuate economic instability and uneven development at all geographical scales. It is in this context, I believe, that the production of new regionalized scales of state spatial regulation across western Europe during the 1990s can be understood. Such newly emergent, regionalized regulatory experiments operate both as upscaled institutional arenas for ICT-led growth strategies and as frameworks for crisis-management through which some of the contradictions associated with such strategies may be addressed – albeit in inchoate, deeply provisional ways (Brenner 2003). Figure 8.5 provides a schematic periodization summarizing the key stages of this argument.

In the context of this book, the overarching message of this chapter is

---

Spatial Keynesianism: late 1950s–early 1970s

National states promote economic development by spreading industry, population and infrastructural investment evenly across the national territory

Urban managerialism: local states and metropolitan authorities operate mainly as sites of welfare service provision and collective consumption

Fordism in crisis (transitional phase): early 1970s–early 1980s

A new politics of "endogenous" growth emerges in crisis-stricken industrial areas: goal is to mobilize customized policies to confront place-specific forms of economic decline and industrial restructuring

Meanwhile various national redistributive policy relays are retrenched, forcing subnational territorial administrations to "fend for themselves" under conditions of intensifying economic uncertainty and accelerating industrial restructuring

Glocalization strategies/Round I: 1980s

The mobilization of glocalization strategies: national states promote the reconcentration of economic capacities and infrastructure investments into the most globally competitive cities, regions and industrial districts within their territories

Decentralization of intergovernmental systems to enhance the capacity of subnational institutional levels to promote place- and jurisdiction-specific conditions for industrial development

Proliferation of local economic development strategies throughout the western European city-system in response to the new interspatial competition

Glocalization strategies/Round II: 1990s–present

The "metropolitanization" and/or regionalization of glocalization strategies: national states increasingly target large-scale metropolitan regions rather than cities or localities as the most appropriate scales for economic rejuvenation

Crystallization of competitive regionalism: metropolitan institutions are rejuvenated in conjunction with projects to promote interlocality cooperation and regional strategies of economic development

Metropolitan regions are increasingly viewed as a strategic institutional arena in which new regulatory experiments can be developed

---

Figure 8.5 State strategies and the political regulation of uneven development: a schematic periodization of the western European case, 1960–2000.

that the notion of the new economy is a fundamentally *political* concept: it is best understood less as a simple description of an unproblematic empirical reality, than as an ideologically refracted product of diverse political strategies oriented toward a specific vision of how contemporary capitalist economies and states should be (re)organized. As I have argued, the notion of the new economy has underpinned distinctive accumulation strategies through which the economic geographies and regulatory landscapes of western Europe have been fundamentally reworked during the last thirty years. From this point of view, the development of ICTs and other high-technology sectors in major urban agglomerations cannot be understood adequately without an examination of the matrices of national and local state power within which they are situated and the concerted political strategies through which they have been fostered. At the same time, I have suggested that the mobilization of new economy accumulation strategies has in turn been inextricably linked to major changes in the political geographies of statehood across western Europe. While this chapter has focused specifically upon the interplay between ICT development and the changing politics of uneven spatial development, it may be argued, more generally, that new economy accumulation strategies have played a key role in the creation of Schumpeterian workfare post-national regimes (Jessop 2000, 2002) across western Europe and beyond.

In light of this analysis, it seems clear that sub-national spaces such as cities, regions and industrial districts are key geographical sites in which new economy industries are being cultivated and territorialized. However, such subnational spaces are not only sites for the agglomeration of new economy firms (see the chapter by Krätke). They are also important institutional arenas in which a variety of regulatory experiments are being mobilized, both to promote industrial regeneration and to manage some of the market failures and governance failures associated with the latter. In my view, in the absence of viable solutions to these regulatory problems, it is highly unlikely that ICTs or other new economy industries will provide a stable foundation for sustainable capitalist growth at any geographical scale. By way of conclusion, therefore, it may be useful to enumerate some of the overarching regulatory problems that have been engendered through this pervasive localization (and regionalization) of economic development strategies during the last thirty years.

1   *Inter-sectoral coordination.* New economy accumulation strategies neglect to address the problems of traditional and/or revitalized manufacturing industries. As such, they bracket important sources of employment and industrial dynamism under contemporary capitalism based on the assumption that the new economy can, in itself, ground macroeconomic growth. However, such assumptions are deeply flawed (Martin 2002). In the absence of policy mechanisms designed to facilitate restructuring within manufacturing industries while articulating

them to the growth potentials associated with ICTs, it is unlikely that new economy sectors could provide a viable basis for sustained, generalized economic regeneration.

2   *Interscalar coordination.* New economy accumulation strategies have generally been associated with a fragmentation of regulatory arrangements among diverse jurisdictions and across various places and scales within each national territory. In this manner, they undermine the coherence of supralocal institutional arrangements and engender major problems of interscalar coordination among dispersed, increasingly disarticulated policy regimes. In the absence of such coordination, however, a variety of governance problems – including unfettered inter-locality competition; destructive, predatory bidding wars and poaching forays among regional and local states; and intense inter-territorial conflicts – may proliferate. Such problems may in turn seriously undermine the socio-territorial preconditions upon which industrial development both in new economy sectors and in other sectors depends.

3   *Territorial inequality and sociospatial exclusion.* Finally, as I have emphasized throughout this chapter, new economy accumulation strategies tend to channel investment and public goods not only toward particular sectors, but also toward particular places which are deemed to be optimal sites for the development of ICTs and other new economy industries. In this manner, new economy accumulation strategies reinforce and accelerate the tendencies of spatial reconcentration and metropolitanization that are already associated with the contemporary archipelago economy in western Europe (Veltz 1993). In this manner, new economy accumulation strategies significantly intensify uneven spatial development and socio-spatial exclusion, essentially abandoning marginalized regions and populations to fend for themselves in the global "space of flows" (Castells 1996). However, in the absence of institutional mechanisms through which to regulate such socio-territorial inequalities, the macroeconomic sustainability and political acceptability of ICT-led industrial development strategies may in turn be called into question.

Whether or not ICT-led growth can be promoted in a non-polarizing, politically negotiated and socially equitable form is a matter that remains to be fought out in and through political struggle in diverse institutional sites and at a variety of spatial scales.

Notes

1 Jessop (1990: 198) defines an accumulation strategy as "a specific economic 'growth model' complete with its various extra-economic preconditions and [...] a general strategy appropriate to its realization."
2 According to Veltz (1997: 79; italics added), the current round of economic

restructuring has qualitatively transformed the relationship between capital and territory: "Whereas in Taylorist–Fordist mass production, territory mainly appeared as a stock of generic resources (raw materials, labour), nowadays it increasingly underpins a process of *the creation of specialized resources*. Competitiveness among nations, regions and cities proceeds less from static endowments as in classical comparative-advantage theories, than from their ability *to produce new resources*, not necessarily material ones and *to set up efficient configurations* in terms of costs, quality of goods or services, velocity and innovation." The argument proposed here is that rescaled state institutions have come to play essential roles in the production, coordination and maintenance of the "specialized resources" and "efficient configurations" of political-economic organization upon which ICTs and other new economy industries depend. My claim, however, is not that policy makers possess some unique, privileged insight into the requirements of high-technology capital. My claim, rather, is that *speculative projects* to create such requirements – however they are understood – have played a significant role in a major reorientation of state power and state spatial strategies during the last thirty years (Brenner 2004).

3 Peck's (2002: 356) characterization of the uneven geographies of neoliberal workfarism can thus be applied as well to newly emergent patterns of spatial, regional and urban policy in western Europe: "Uneven geographic development is being established as an intentional, rather than merely incidental, feature of the delivery of workfare programs, while local experimentation and emulation are becoming seemingly permanent features of the policymaking process [...] In stark contrast to the aspirations to fair and equal treatment under welfare regimes, when spatial unevenness, local discretion and instances of atypical ... treatment were often constituted as policy problems in their own right, or at least anomalies, workfare makes a virtue of geographical differentiation, subnational competition and [...] circumstance-specific interventions [...] Although disorder and flux continue to reign, it is becoming increasingly clear that these changes – and the distinctive scalar dynamics that underpin them – are more than simply transitory, but are concerned with a far-reaching, if not systemic, reorganization of the regulatory regime."

Bibliography

Agnew, J. (2001) "How Many Europes? The European Union, Eastward Enlargement and Uneven Development," *European Urban and Regional Studies* 8(1): 29–38.

Ansell, C. (2000) "The Networked Polity: Regional Development in Western Europe," *Governance* 13(3): 303–333.

Barlow, M. (1991) *Metropolitan Government*, New York: Routledge.

Bourdieu, P. (1998) *Acts of Resistance: Against the Tyranny of the Market*, New York: The New York Press.

Brenner, N. (1998) "Global Cities, 'Glocal' States: Global City Formation and State Territorial Restructuring in Contemporary Europe," *Review of International Political Economy* 5(1): 1–37.

—— (2003) "Standortpolitik, State Rescaling and the New Metropolitan Governance in Western Europe," *DISP* 152: 15–25.

—— (2004) *New State Spaces: Urban Restructuring and State Rescaling in Western Europe*, Oxford: Oxford University Press.

Brenner, N. and Theodore, N. (eds) (2002) *Spaces of Neoliberalism*, Boston and Oxford: Blackwell.

Brunet, R. (1989) *Les Villes "Europeennes,"* Paris: DATAR.

Bullmann, U. (1991) *Kommunale Strategien gegen Massenarbeitslosigkeit: Ein Einstieg in die sozialökologische Erneuerung*, Opladen: Leske und Budrich.

Bunnell, T. (2002) "Multimedia Utopia? A Geographical Critique of High-Tech Development in Malaysia's Multimedia Super Corridor," *Antipode* 34(2): 265–295.

Castells, M. (1977 [1972]) *The Urban Question*, Cambridge, MA: MIT Press.

—— (1996) *The Rise of the Network Society*, Cambridge, MA: Blackwell.

—— (1997) *The Power of Identity*, Cambridge, MA: Blackwell.

—— (1998) *End of Millennium*, Cambridge, MA: Blackwell.

Clout, H. (ed.) (1981) *Regional Development in Western Europe*, 2nd edn, New York: John Wiley and Sons.

DATAR (1989) *Les villes "Europeennes,"* Paris: La Documentation Française.

Dunford, M. and Perrons, D. (1994) "Regional Inequality, Regimes of Accumulation and Economic Development in Contemporary Europe," *Transactions of the Institute of British Geographers* 192(2): 163–182.

Eisenschitz, A. and Gough, J. (1993) *The Politics of Local Economic Development*, New York: Macmillan.

Fox Przeworski, J. (1986) "Changing Intergovernmental Relations and Urban Economic Development," *Environment and Planning C: Government and Policy* 4(4): 423 –39.

Friedmann, J. (1986) "Regional Development in Industrialized Countries: Endogenous or Self-Reliant?," in Bassand, M., Brugger E.A., Bryden J.M., Friedman F. and Stuckey B. (eds) *Self-Reliant Development in Europe. Theory, Problems, Actions*, Brookfield, VT: Gower.

Goodwin, M. and Painter, J. (1996) "Local Governance, the Crises of Fordism and the Changing Geographies of Regulation," *Transactions of the Institute of British Geographers* 21(4): 635–648.

Hahne, U. (1985) *Regionalentwicklung Durch Aktivierung Intraregionaler Potentiale*, Munich: Florenz.

Hall, T. and Hubbard, P. (eds) (1998) *The Entrepreneurial City: Geographies of Politics, Regime and Representation*, London: Wiley.

Harding, A. (1994) "Urban Regimes and Growth Machines: Towards a Cross-National Research Agenda," *Urban Affairs Quarterly* 29(3): 356–382.

—— (1997) "Urban Regimes in a Europe of the Cities?" *European Urban and Regional Studies* 4(4): 291–314.

Harvey, D. (1982) *The Limits to Capital*, Chicago: University of Chicago Press.

—— (1989a) *The Urban Experience*, Baltimore: Johns Hopkins Press.

—— (1989b) "From Managerialism to Entrepreneurialism: The Transformation in Urban Governance in Late Capitalism," *Geografiska Annaler* B, 71(1): 3–18.

Hudson, R. (2001) *Producing Places*, New York: Guilford.

Jessop, B. (1989) "Conservative Regimes and the Transition to Post-Fordism: The Cases of Great Britain and West Germany," in Gottdiener, M. and Komninos, N. (eds) *Capitalist Development and Crisis Theory*, New York: St. Martin's Press.

—— (1990) *State Theory*, London: Polity.

—— (1998) "The Narrative of Enterprise and the Enterprise of Narrative: Place-Marketing and the Entrepreneurial City," in Hall, T. and Hubbard, P. (eds) *The Entrepreneurial City*, London: John Wiley & Sons.

—— (2000) "The Crisis of the National Spatio-Temporal Fix and the Ecological Dominance of Globalizing Capitalism," *International Journal of Urban and Regional Research* 24(2): 323–360.

—— (2002) *The Future of the Capitalist State*, New York and London: Polity.

Keating, M. (1997) "The Invention of Regions: Political Restructuring and Territorial Government in Western Europe," *Environment and Planning C: Government and Policy* 15(4): 383–398.

Krätke, S. (1993) "Stadtsystem Im internationalen Kontext und Vergleich," in Roth, R. and Wollmann, H. (eds) *Kommunalpolitik*, Opladen: Leske und Budrich.

—— (1995) *Stadt, Raum, Ökonomie*, Basel: Birkhäuser Verlag.

Krätke, S. and Borst, R. (1999) *Berlin: Metropole im Wandel*, Berlin: Leske und Budrich.

Krätke, S., Heeg, S. and Stein, R. (1997) *Regionen im Umbruch*, Frankfurt a.M.: Campus.

Leborgne, D. and Lipietz, A. (1992) "Two Social Strategies in the Production of New Industrial Spaces," in Benko, G. and Dunford, M. (eds) *Industrial Change and Regional Development: The Transformation of New Industrial Spaces*, London: Belhaven.

Lee, R. and Wills, J. (eds) (1997) *Geographies of Economies*, London: Arnold.

Lefebvre, H. (1978) *De L'état: Les Contradictions De L'état Moderne*, Paris: Union Générale d'Éditions.

—— (2003 [1968]) *The Urban Revolution*, Minneapolis: University of Minneapolis Press.

Lefèvre, C. (1998) "Metropolitan Government and Governance in Western Countries: A Critical Overview," *International Journal of Urban and Regional Research* 22(1): 9–25.

Leitner, H. and Sheppard, E. (1998) "Economic Uncertainty, Inter-Urban Competition and the Efficacy of Entrepreneurialism," in Hall, T. and Hubbard, P. (eds) *The Entrepreneurial City*, Chichester: Wiley.

Lipietz, A. (1994) "The National and the Regional: Their Autonomy Vis-à-Vis the Capitalist World Crisis," in Palan, R. and Gills, B. (eds) *Transcending the State-Global Divide*, Boulder: Lynne Rienner.

MacLeod, G. (2000) "The Learning Region in an Age of Austerity: Capitalizing on Knowledge, Entrepreneurialism and Reflexive Capitalism," *Geoforum* 31(2): 219–236.

—— (2001) "New Regionalism Reconsidered: Globalization, Regulation and the Recasting of Political Economic Space," *International Journal of Urban and Regional Research* 25(4): 804–829.

Martin, R. (2002) *From the Old Economy to the New Economy: Myths, Realities and Geographies*, Paper presented at the Regional Studies Association Conference on "Geographies of the New Economy." London, October 25. Available online at http:www.regional-studies-assoc.ac.uk/events/ronmartin.ppt (October 26, 2003).

Martin, R. and Sunley, P. (1997) "The Post-Keynesian State and the Space Economy," in Wills, J. (ed.) *Geographies and Economies*, London: Arnold.

Mayer, M. (1992) "The Shifting Local Political System in European Cities," in Dunford, M. and Kafkalas, G. (eds) *Cities and Regions in the New Europe*, New York: Belhaven Press.

—— (1994) "Post-Fordist City Politics," in Amin, A. (ed.) *Post-Fordisms: A Reader*, Cambridge, MA: Blackwell.

McMichael, P. (1996) *Development and Social Change*, London: Sage.

Mouritzen, P.E. (1992) *Managing Cities in Austerity*, London: Sage.

OECD (1976) *Regional Problems and Policies in OECD Countries*, Paris: OECD.

Offe, C. (1984) "'Crisis of Crisis Management': Elements of a Political Crisis Theory," in Keane, J. (ed.) *Contradictions of the Welfare State*, Cambridge, MA: MIT Press.

Painter, J. and Goodwin, M. (1996) "Local Governance and Concrete Research: Investigating the Uneven Development of Regulation," *Economy and Society* 24(3): 334–356.

Parkinson, M. (1991) "The Rise of the Entrepreneurial European City: Strategic Responses to Economic Changes in the 1980s," *Ekistics* 350: 299–307.

Peck, J. (2002) "Political Economies of Scale: Fast Policy, Interscalar Relations and Neoliberal Workfare," *Economic Geography* 78(3): 331–360.

Peck, J. and Tickell, A. (1994) "Searching for a New Institutional Fix," in Amin, A. (ed.) *Post-Fordism: A Reader*, Cambridge, MA: Blackwell.

—— (1995) "The Social Regulation of Uneven Development: 'Regulatory Deficit,' England's South East, and the Collapse of Thatcherism," *Environment and Planning* A, 27: 15–40.

—— (2002) "Neoliberalizing Space," in Brenner, N. and Theodore, N. (eds) *Spaces of Neoliberalism*, Boston and Oxford: Blackwell.

Petrella, R. (2000) "The Future of Regions: Why the Competitiveness Imperative Should Not Prevail over Solidarity, Sustainability and Democracy," *Geografiska Annaler* B, 82(2): 67–72.

Rhodes, M. (1995) "'Subversive Liberalism': Market Integration, Globalization and the European Welfare State," *Journal of European Policy* 2(3): 384–406.

Rodriguez-Pose, A. (1995) *The Dynamics of Regional Growth in Europe*, Oxford: Clarendon Press.

Saunders, P. (1979) *Urban Politics: A Sociological Interpretation*, London: Heinemann.

Scharpf, F. (1991) *Crisis and Choice in European Social Democracy*, Ithaca: Cornell University Press.

Scott, A.J. (1988) *New Industrial Spaces*, Berkeley and Los Angeles: University of California Press.

Scott, A.J. and Storper, M. (1992) "Industrialization and Regional Development," in Scott, A.J. and Storper, M. (eds) *Pathways to Industrialization and Regional Development*, New York: Routledge.

Sharpe, L.J. (1995) "The Future of Metropolitan Government," in Sharpe, L.J. (ed.) *The Government of World Cities: The Future of the Metro Model*, New York: John Wiley and Sons.

Smith, N. (1990) *Uneven Development*, Cambridge, MA: Blackwell.

Stöhr, W. and Taylor, D.R. (1981) *Development from above or Below? The Dialectics of Regional Planning in Developing Countries*, New York: Wiley.

Storper, M. (1996) *The Regional World*, New York: Guilford.

Storper, M. and Walker, R. (1989) *The Capitalist Imperative*, Cambridge, MA: Blackwell.

Swyngedouw, E. (1997) "Neither Global nor Local: 'Glocalization' and the Politics of Scale," in Cox, K. (ed.) *Spaces of Globalization*, New York: Guilford Press.

Taylor, P.J. and Hoyler, M. (2000) "The Spatial Order of European Cities under Conditions of Contemporary Globalization," *Tijdschrift voor Economische en Sociale Geografie* 91(2): 176–189.

Veltz, P. (1993) *Mondialisation, villes et territoires: L'économie d'archipel*, Paris: Presses Universitaires de France.

—— (1997) "The Dynamics of Production Systems, Territories and Cities," in Moulaert, F. and Scott, A.J. (eds) *Cities, Enterprises and Society on the Eve of the 21st Century*, London: Pinter.

—— (2000) "European Cities in the World Economy," in Bagnasco, A. and Le Galés, P. (eds) *Cities in Contemporary Europe*, New York: Cambridge University Press, pp. 33–47.

Walker, R. (1997) "California Rages: Regional Capitalism and the Politics of Renewal," in Lee, R. and Wills, J. (eds) *Geographies of Economies*, London: Arnold.

Do regional systems of innovation matter?

Michael Fritsch

The real questions

Scholars engaged in research in the field of regional economics or economic geography have little doubt that regions do matter for research and development (R&D). For these experts, the real questions are deeper and concern issues like the relative importance of the impact of location, the ways in which the influence of location comes into effect and how regional conditions for innovation activity can be improved. This chapter deals with these questions. Its starting point is a brief overview of empirical findings about the spatial distribution of innovation activity. The following sections represent an attempt to explain this evidence based on the notion of labor division in the field of innovation. The main characteristics of such a division of innovative labor have significant implications for the spatial organization of innovation activity as well as for the analysis. The concept of regional innovation systems and the role of different actors in such a regional system are explained followed by an overview of results of recent research concerning regional innovation systems. Finally, an exposition of basic policy options is given and some important issues for further research are specified.

Empirical evidence for the role of location for R&D

With regards to the "death of distance" that is implied by ongoing improvements of telecommunication techniques, the clustering of economic activity found in many empirical studies may be regarded as surprising.[1] These results clearly show that location matters for production, particularly for innovation. Moreover, it seems that under the conditions of globalization, the regional environment is becoming even more relevant. A simple reason for this tendency toward "glocalization" is that spatially-rooted factors gain in relative importance as the accessibility of other factors becomes easier or cheaper. Clustering suggests that there are agglomeration advantages at work that stimulate certain types of activity (Baptista 1998; Porter 1998). Among the most important of these agglomeration advantages are a relatively high potential for face-to-face contacts, the presence of positive external effects, easy access to research institutions and differentiated input markets such as the labor market and the market for specialized innovation related services. All these factors may facilitate the generation and transfer of knowledge which constitutes a key element of innovation activity (Antonelli 2002: chapter 3).[2]

There are clear indications that the quality of regional innovation systems may differ considerably and that only some part of such differences can be attributed to the degree of agglomeration or clustering (Fritsch 2000, 2002, 2004). Agglomeration economies in clusters may stimulate the competitiveness of the firms involved. However, they explain only a fraction of the differences in the efficiency and the success of their R&D activity. Obviously, regional factors matter for innovation processes, but it is hard to make a more general judgment on the strength of the regional impact as compared to other causes like industry-specific factors or influences that are effective on the national level (Howells 1999). At least in some regions the impact of location appears to be rather strong. In this regard one might ask, for example, if the US computer industry would have gained the same strength and competitiveness if the Silicon Valley Cluster had not emerged. Regional factors have been rather important in this particular example. But is it not also true that the development of Silicon Valley was significantly stimulated by the characteristics of the industry and the national innovation system? Could the same phenomenon have occurred in other industries or in other countries such as Germany, for instance? Apparently, the different levels are not discrete but instead are mutually dependent (Scott 1996).

Problems of a division of innovative labor

Numerous studies on the genesis and development of certain innovations have shown that there are diverse actors involved (Jewkes *et al.* 1969). Many innovation processes are characterized by a high degree of labor division. Further, there are indications that the intensity of labor division has increased considerably in the last few decades (Arora and Gambardella 1994; Hagedoorn 2002). Yet, if the division of innovative labor plays such a prominent role, it would be inappropriate for this analysis to solely focus on a single actor, thereby neglecting the contributions of other actors. To take all relevant relationships into account, a more comprehensive approach to a system of innovation needs to be applied (see section on regional systems of innovation in a globalizing economy). There are some characteristics of innovation activity which imply a number of specific problems of labor division as compared to "normal" production processes. These special features can considerably affect the organization and the spatial distribution of R&D.

A first key problem that may severely impede a division of innovative labor is that, by its very nature, the result of an innovation process is unknown in advance and can not be predicted with certainty. Thus, it is not possible to completely specify a respective contract in advance. The resulting incomplete contracts leave room for opportunistic behavior by the contractual parties, i.e., self-serving interpretation of the terms of the contract to the disadvantage of other contract parties. Due to this danger of opportunistic behavior, economic actors may avoid contracting out certain tasks of the innovation process.

A second problem for a division of innovative labor may arise because R&D processes often require very special inputs that are not commonly traded in large markets. This rareness of suitable inputs is in many cases a result of the novelty inherent in innovation. Because of this novelty, markets for skills and resources that are important for an innovation process may not be readily available. In this case, the respective markets are rather "thin," i.e. there are only very few suppliers and transactions take place rather infrequently. Because suppliers are rare, this may require an immense amount of search costs to identify a suitable transaction partner. Moreover, if only few transactions take place, a clear market price may not exist so that negotiations about the price and further conditions of an exchange tend to be rather costly.

A third problem for a division of innovative labor is the potential of asymmetric information to severely hamper the trading of knowledge on markets. Because knowledge is the key input and output of innovation activity, a transfer of knowledge constitutes a necessary precondition for any division of labor in the field of R&D. Asymmetric information with regard to trading of knowledge means that the supplier possesses better information about the subject to be traded than his counterpart on the demand side. As a reaction to the risks involved in having this kind of incomplete information, rational customers will offer less than they would if they had been provided full information. For the supplier, describing the characteristics of the information offered may in many cases imply a more or less complete disclosure. Yet, once a potential customer possesses the information, he has no reason to purchase it. Therefore, information that is intended to be sold cannot be completely disclosed. Due to this asymmetry, the level of transactions on the market may be rather low and adverse selection processes may result in a poor quality of supply.

A fourth possible difficulty concerns the transfer of information or knowledge as such.[3] One obstacle to the transmission may be that the knowledge is "tacit," i.e., it is not completely codified so that it can only be communicated face-to-face or through a transfer of the person that possesses that knowledge. Moreover, the identification and the use of relevant information may require a certain "absorptive capacity" (Cohen and Levinthal 1989). This means that the recipient must already possess some knowledge – such as basic skills or a shared language – in order to be able to assess the economic value of new information and to assimilate and then apply it to his own commercial ends. Another potential problem in regard to information transfer is the danger of uncontrolled knowledge flows, i.e., the possibility of the transaction partner obtaining valuable information without adequate compensation.

As a result of these problems, many contributions to innovation processes cannot be easily traded on anonymous "spot markets." A division of innovative labor between different organizations may, therefore, require incompletely specified, long-term agreements ("relational contracting") that imply a considerable degree of cooperative spirit and trust.[4] Thus, a cooperative relationship may be regarded as one of the main characteristics of a division of labor in innovation processes. In addition to the role of cooperative relationships in the division of innovative labor, the literature suggests some further potential benefits of cooperation on R&D. One of these issues is that, as far as cooperative relationships are characterized by relatively "open" exchange of information, such flows of knowledge or information may be stimulating for innovation activity.[5] Many authors emphasize that not only formal cooperative relationships, such as joint ventures or contract research, are important for knowledge flows, but that informal relationships like "information trading" (reciprocal exchanges of information between personnel of competing firms) may also play a significant stimulating role for innovation activity (e.g. von Hippel 1987; Saxenian 1994).

In a division of innovative labor, spatial proximity can be conducive for at least two reasons. First, if the establishment and management of incomplete contracts as well as the transfer of knowledge require face-to-face contact, large geographic distance between partners may act as a severe impediment. Second, spatial proximity to other establishments in the same industry can constitute a prerequisite for benefiting from certain resources in the region. These include the labor market, research institutes, infrastructure and the presence of specialized suppliers. These issues may at least partly explain why innovation activity tends to be clustered in space and why flows of new knowledge are concentrated within the environment close to the source.

Regional systems of innovation in a globalizing economy

The concept

One great advantage of the "system of innovation" approach is that the analysis can explicitly account for division of innovative labor between individuals and organizations (Freeman 1987; Lundvall 1992a; Nelson 1993; for an overview Edquist 1997). The important issue of labor division is largely neglected when the innovation activity of particular individuals or organizations lies, more or less exclusively, at the center of attention.

Innovation systems consist of innovative agents, the relationships between these agents, as well as the rules and institutions influencing the generation of innovation and the relevant selection mechanisms.[6]

With regard to the spatial definition of an innovation system, many authors deal with whole nations. They thus, implicitly or explicitly, assume that the similarities of institutions, language and culture form a "natural" geographical frontier (Lundvall 1992a: 3). However, there is no need to limit the innovation-system approach to nations. While for some issues (e.g., markets for goods in global technological competition) it may be more suitable to choose a higher level of aggregation and to investigate the international division of innovative labor on a world-wide scale (Lundvall 1992a: 3f.), other questions may be analyzed more appropriately on a lower aggregation level, e.g., regions within nations. Such a regional focus is particularly appropriate when the local environment is important and short-distance interaction plays a significant role (Cooke *et al.* 1997: 488f.; Cooke 1998; Howells 1999; Lagendijk 2001).

In this context, the regional system should not only be regarded as a down-scaled sub-category of the national innovation system where certain characteristics deviate from the national average. Rather, such a top-down perspective may be quite inappropriate when the regional dimension is dominant and location-specific factors are much more important than issues at the national level. Empirical research has indeed provided considerable evidence for the significance of face-to-face contact, localized patterns of communication, knowledge sharing and searching, etc. that may well result in diverging innovation performance.[7] Therefore, the national innovation system can also be regarded as the aggregate of rather different regional systems in the sense of a bottom-up approach. According to this view, the region-specific factors have a stronger impact than they do in a top-down approach. In any case, the different dimensions of the innovation system – region, nation, world, industry – are connected and interact (Scott 1996).

A role model of regional innovation systems

Our knowledge about how regional innovation systems work is still rather limited. The simple role model illustrated in Figure 9.1 may be helpful as a conceptual framework for assessing the main issues of our current understanding. This model includes three types of actors in a region:

- *Public institutions for research, education and other forms of knowledge transfer* generate, accumulate and distribute information. Included under this heading are mainly universities, other public research institutions as well as transfer agencies. One of the main tasks of these institutions is to absorb and store the relevant knowledge that has been generated elsewhere in order to be able to spread

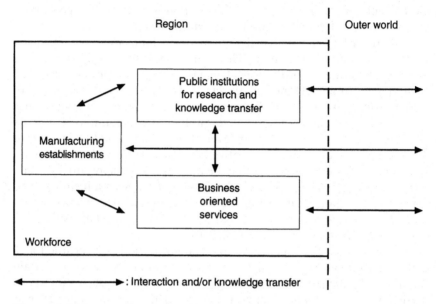

Figure 9.1 Main actors in a regional innovation system.

it to other actors in the region. In this sense, the public research institutes take on the role of an "antenna" for innovation activity in a
region (Fritsch and Schwirten 1999, 2002). Particularly through the
provision of education and by collaborating with private sector firms
they supply the regional system with important inputs for innovation
activity (Varga 2000).

- *Manufacturing establishments* act as final producers in the regional
innovation system. Their role is to commercialize the available knowledge by incorporating it into marketable goods and then selling these
goods to customers inside and outside the region. In fulfilling this role
they need to be able to absorb the relevant knowledge – in most cases
this will require them to perform some R&D activity as well (Cohen
and Levinthal 1989). The competitiveness of the manufacturing establishments in an innovation system is of crucial importance for its economic success. If the manufacturing establishments do not perform
well and are not competitive on a world wide scale, the public institutions for research, education and other forms of knowledge transfer
may remain largely ineffective. This is, for example, a problem in
many eastern European regions that were governed by a socialist
regime, an example being the states of the former German Democratic Republic.
- *Suppliers of business-oriented services* support innovation activities
in public research institutions and manufacturing establishments.

Business-oriented services include support in the fields of engineering and planning, tax preparation and legal services, market research, advertising, engineering and planning as well as business consulting and financial services, such as the provision of venture capital.[8] The presence of high-quality specialized services may allow for a relatively high degree of labor division that in turn results in a high efficiency of regional innovation activity.

The regional workforce with its qualification and knowledge constitutes an additional main element of a regional innovation system. In particular, it is an important source for all kinds of entrepreneurship in both long established and newly founded firms.

It is important to recognize that these elements only constitute a framework for regional innovation activity. Because of the dynamic character of innovation processes, the elements of the innovation system are subject to permanent change. Innovation systems are "learning systems" in which communication among agents is one of the main sources of the creation of new knowledge (Antonelli 2002: chapter 3). Accordingly, diverse empirical examples show that the interaction of the elements in a regional innovation system and their relationships to the outer world are of key importance for the system's performance. This is a principal hypothesis in the literature on industrial districts (Porter 1998 and the contributions in Pyke *et al.* 1990), of the network approach to the analysis of innovation activity (Camagni 1991a; Saxenian 1994) as well as of the concept of "innovative milieux" (Aydalot and Keeble 1988; Crevoisier and Maillat 1991). The emphasis on the interaction of an innovation system's elements corresponds to a basic hypothesis in economic science, which states that division of labor will result in efficiency gains. One may therefore expect a relatively high regional level of interaction on R&D to lead to correspondingly high productivity in innovation processes. These relationships, particularly if they are cooperative in nature, are also frequently regarded as an important medium of transferring relevant knowledge.

Because a significant part of the knowledge that is relevant for innovation processes is not codified but tacit, it remains with the respective individuals. It is, therefore, localized. Moreover, this knowledge may be specific to the conditions in a particular market, establishment or region. Path-dependencies, indivisibilities and external effects (e.g. agglomeration economies) in the creation of knowledge lead to a regional embeddedness of innovation activity. For this reason, each regional innovation system is characterized by a specific knowledge stock that makes the system unique and distinguishes it from that of other regions (Antonelli 2002: chapter 3; Maskell and Malmberg 1999).

In many well-functioning regional innovation systems, new innovative firms and entrepreneurship play an important role.[9] The regional dimension is of considerable relevance for new firm formation processes because most founders of new businesses are regionally embedded and come from the same region in which they start their businesses (Johnson and Cathcart 1979). Entrepreneurs tend to "spin-off" from regional firms and research institutions. Their entry into the market presents a challenge to the incumbent firms, which may induce them to change their product program and their general economic behavior. This is particularly true for innovative entry. The example of the "new economy" shows that new innovative firms can be important agents of change. To the founder, setting up a new firm presents a way of commercializing his knowledge. To set up a new firm can be understood as a means for the founder to commercialize his knowledge (Audretsch 1995: 47–55).

One main reason for this is that innovative ideas as such can hardly be traded on a market – be it because of their vagueness, because of market imperfections (see the section on problems of a division of innovative labor) or because incumbent firms are focused on drawing profits from their established product program and are not interested in implementing new ideas that may require radical changes. Moreover, in quite a number of cases starting a firm may represent the one and only chance of putting an idea into practice (Audretsch 1995: 54f.).

As the section on problems of a division of innovative labor showed, a division of innovative labor requires transfer of knowledge between the parties involved. Such transfers of knowledge are termed "spillovers" (Breschi and Lissoni 2001; Feldman 1999; Karlsson and Manduchi 2001). There are diverse ways in which such knowledge spillovers may become effective. These include market transactions, cooperative relationship, publication of R&D results, flow of innovative goods and mobility of personnel including spin-offs from private-sector firms and public research institutions. Independent of the specific means of such knowledge transfers, one can expect that intensive division of labor and interaction is associated with a correspondingly high level of spillovers. Thus, due to the efficiency gains of labor division, pronounced spillovers should be one of the chief characteristics of an efficiently functioning innovation system.

How regional innovation systems work: evidence from recent research

Reviewing the recent empirical research on the regional dimension of innovation activity, four main topics can be identified:

- regional differences in the extent of R&D activity and innovation performance;
- the significance of regional knowledge spillovers, their role in innovation processes and the way in which these spillovers become effective;
- the role of R&D cooperation in regional innovation systems;
- the formation of new innovative firms in a regional context.

With regard to the first topic, there can be no doubt that innovation activity is not spread evenly but instead is clustered in space (see the section on empirical evidence for the role of location for R&D). However, attempts to empirically detect a clear impact of location on the innovation behavior of economic actors have been largely unsuccessful (see Fritsch 2000, for a brief review of the evidence). Recent empirical analyses of innovation activity in a number of European regions (for the project design, see Sternberg 2000) have been successful in identifying such inter-regional differences of innovation behavior (Fritsch 2000). Taking the efficiency of R&D expenditure as a measure of the quality of a regional innovation system (Fritsch 2002), there is significant variation showing some correspondence to a center-periphery hypothesis that suggests better conditions for innovation activity in the center as compared to more remote areas or regions that are characterized by a relatively low degree of agglomeration (the periphery). An analysis of the German regions in the sample shows that the interregional differences in the efficiency of their respective innovation activity can, to a considerable degree, be explained by the differences in the amount of regional knowledge spillovers (Fritsch and Franke 2003). This result supports the hypothesis that the interaction of the elements of a regional innovation system is of crucial importance for its performance.

Empirical research has found that the spread of new knowledge tends to be heavily concentrated around its source.[10] Obviously, spatial proximity is of significant importance for such information flows. However, the relative importance of the different spillover channels is unclear. A quite popular hypothesis suggests that R&D cooperation may play an important role in this respect, particularly for the flow of "tacit" knowledge, which is not completely codified. Analyses of R&D cooperation in the European regions mentioned above have shown that R&D cooperation is a rather widespread phenomenon (Fritsch and Schwirten 1999, 2002; Fritsch 2001, 2003). A particular regional focus could be found for R&D cooperation between manufacturing establishments and public research institutes as well as for horizontal cooperation among manufacturing establishment in the same industry and for relationships with providers of business services. This highlights the importance of spatial proximity for these types of interaction.

The spatial pattern of the R&D cooperation with suppliers and customers seems to correspond largely to the regional dimension of the respective markets. Cooperative relationships between research institutes tended to be interregional on a world wide scale (Fritsch and Schwirten 2002). The analysis of this data also revealed significant differences in cooperation behavior between regions (Fritsch 2001, 2003, 2004). Quite surprisingly, the propensity to cooperate on R&D was below average in establishments located in highly urbanized areas with a rich supply of cooperation partners. Contrary to the popular assumption, R&D

cooperation was not found to be a strong medium for knowledge spillovers. Additionally, there was no significant positive relationship between the propensity for R&D cooperation and the efficiency of regional innovation activity.

A number of examples clearly demonstrated that new firms and entrepreneurship can constitute a powerful driving force for the specific regional innovation system (Bresnahan *et al.* 2001; Feldman 2001). They are a particularly important explanatory factor for cluster formation (Klepper 2001; Cooke 2002). The empirical evidence suggests that once new firm formation processes in a cluster have taken off and passed a certain threshold, the development of the cluster benefits from self-reinforcing effects. Therefore, studying well-developed clusters with a rich supply of supporting services and institutions may not tell us about the beginning stages of new firms' cluster building processes. Thus, one important question that remains to be answered is: "What are the important factors in the initial stage of cluster formation?" The answer to this question is particularly relevant for a policy designed to stimulate the development of regional innovation systems.

Policy options

As this analysis has shown, innovation processes are characterized by an intensive division of labor that has a pronounced spatial dimension. The available empirical evidence clearly demonstrates that regional conditions are highly relevant for innovation processes. Further, there is good reason to assume that the quality of the regional innovation system is of particular importance for relatively new industries like the "new economy" (Audretsch and Feldman 1996b; Cooke 2002: chapter 6). If the current trend continues, we should expect a further increase in labor division, regional specialization and clustering of innovation activity in the future. The emerging spatial pattern will then be characterized by only a few regional centers of excellence throughout the world for each technological field in which the main market players have to be present in order to monitor technological developments and absorb relevant knowledge (Patel and Vega 1999; Pearce 1999). There are two general conclusions that can be drawn from the recognition that regions do matter for R&D activity. First, innovation policy should take into account the spatial dimension of innovation processes and the importance of regional conditions. This implies that regional institutions should at least participate in the design and operation of technology policy measures by contributing their expertise about local conditions. Second, the local level could be an appropriate starting point for a policy designed to initiate and stimulate innovation activity. In many cases, innovation policy at the regional level may well prove to be more promising than on a national scale.

When outlining possible strategies of a regional innovation policy, it is helpful to distinguish between different types of regions. One category comprises regions where the innovation system is underdeveloped or largely missing as is the case in many peripheral, sparsely-populated areas or in less-developed countries. Under these conditions, the main task for innovation policy is to create the basic prerequisites for R&D and initiate innovation processes. A second category comprises regions that possess a well-developed innovation system that is equipped with public research institutions, a supply of innovation-related services and qualified labor. If the innovation system in such a region is well functioning, policy may try to safeguard this development and keep the system intact. In case the regional innovation system is not working satisfactorily, the problem is how to revitalize it.

The regional endowment with public institutions for research and education is obviously a well suited means for building up a new innovation system because it is subject to direct political control. The existence of public research facilities may constitute an important source and necessary precondition for private-sector R&D. However, while the lack of public research institutions can be a severe impediment for regional innovation activity, the presence of appropriate public institutions as such constitutes only a necessary condition of a well-functioning regional innovation system. With regards to complementary private sector activity, experience shows that attempts to directly create certain technological clusters or to steer innovation activity in a certain field are quite likely to fail. Thus, policy should abstain from such endeavors (Cooke 2002). Additionally, it is rather difficult to promote interaction among the actors both within and outside the regional innovation system and to stimulate the emergence of an "innovation culture." Empirical examples show that many of the well-functioning high-tech innovation systems benefited from massive external impulses during their early stages and that development required considerable time, often several decades (Bresnahan *et al.* 2001; Sternberg 1996).

Theoretical concepts as well as empirical evidence suggest that once the development of an innovation system has "taken off," the main bottleneck for the system's performance tends to be deficient interaction, a lack of absorptive capacity and the absence of a productive innovation culture. This may particularly hold true for "older" innovation systems with a well-developed institutional infrastructure. There are a number of well-documented examples in which the performance of such mature innovation systems is severely blocked by the "lock-in" effects of long-established ties as well as by inadequate institutions (Grabher 1993).[11] In these cases, the main task for policy is to re-launch the system, in order to overcome the existing impediments and spur new development.

Whatever the circumstance, a productive innovation culture constitutes an important ingredient of a successful regional innovation system. There are, however, no simple recipes for the creation of a culture that leads to guaranteed success. Nevertheless, one can provide some guidelines.

Generally, a policy of stimulating interaction and division of innovative labor should provide sufficient opportunities and incentives for contact and information exchange in a region. It may also be helpful and promising to publicly provide information about potential partners for R&D cooperation as well as management advice with regard to organizing such cooperative relationships. In order to ensure appropriate interaction between public research and private-sector firms, the institutional setting should provide incentives for public research institutions and pay attention to the needs of the region's private economy. Additionally, policy should not hamper labor mobility between institutions as this is an important medium for knowledge transfer. This particularly pertains to spin-offs from public research institutions and private-sector firms.

Stimulating entrepreneurship can be an effective means for promoting further development and overcoming blockages. As mentioned earlier, the connection of a regional innovation system to the outer world is of immense importance for its performance. Policy should, therefore, avoid everything that might hinder this connection and instead seek to stimulate external contact.[12] Because a large part of relevant new knowledge is tacit in its nature and can only be communicated face-to-face, the exchange of personnel with outside institutions is of particular importance. Promoting such exchanges may be an important line of action for regional innovation policy. Policy could also safeguard a sufficient level of absorptive capacity for external knowledge in the region. This may be a matter of providing basic skills or the creation and support of institutions which monitor technological developments and make the results available to the actors in the innovation system.

The main issues for further research

This chapter has discussed how regions matter for R&D and the opportunities for policy to improve the quality of regional innovation systems. There are, however, numerous open questions that deserve further investigation. The following three areas of research about regional innovation systems are more or less direct results of the analysis:

- One set of questions concerns the ways in which knowledge spillovers become effective (Breschi and Lissoni 2001). What is the role of cooperation, labor mobility, trade of goods and other forms of interaction for the transfer of knowledge? How could and should policy stimulate such spillovers? If absorptive capacity is a bottleneck for knowledge spillovers, in what way can policy lead to improved capabilities?
- Little is known about the early development stages of regional innovation systems (Bresnahan *et al.* 2001). Why do some regions experience a quick acceleration that leads to rapid development while others remain static? Which factors spur self-enforcing growth processes and

what are the main impediments for such a development? What is the role of public research institutions in initiating self-reinforced development?

- Furthermore, we should know more about promising policy options, in particular, what kind of policies might be used to stimulate the division of innovative labor and the emergence of a productive innovation culture? What instruments could help to build up productive innovation networks? In which way could the regional system be appropriately linked to the outer world? How can obstacles in old systems be overcome?

For all three research areas, new firm formation processes and entrepreneurship may play an important role. Given the large contribution of R&D to economic growth, regional innovation policy may be a highly effective strategy for promoting development. It is therefore of great importance to learn more about the regional dimension of innovation activity and the possibilities for improving the efficiency of regional innovation systems. One should, however, not forget that regions are embedded in national systems. Thus, nation-wide regulations and conditions may have severe implications for regional innovation activity. Finally, if one considers the relationship between the regional and the national system as an appropriate starting point for policy measures, this may constitute the subject of important further research.

Notes

1 For empirical evidence see Audretsch and Feldman (1996a), Cooke (2002: 130–156), Baptista and Swann (1998), Feldman (1994), Porter (1998), Prevezer (1998), Scott (1996), Shohet (1998), and Swann (1998).
2 The body of literature does not provide a standard definition of knowledge. Knowledge is more than just information because it also comprises the ability to assess its usefulness as well as to interpret and to apply it. In contrast to information, knowledge is often context-dependent. "Information is the medium in which knowledge is processed, stored and communicated. Knowledge is the content." (Chichilnisky 1999, 9).
3 For a comprehensive treatment of problems of information transfer see von Hippel (1994).
4 See MacNeil (1978) for a detailed characterization of the different types of agreements.
5 See, for example, Axelsson (1992), Lundvall (1992b) and Powell (1990).
6 "A [...] system of innovation is that set of distinct institutions which jointly and individually contributes to the development and diffusion of new technologies and which provides the framework within which governments form and implement policies to influence the innovation process. As such it is a system of interconnected institutions to create, store and transfer the knowledge, skills and artifacts which define new technologies" (Metcalfe 1995: 462f.).
7 For an overview see Howells (1999: 77–84).
8 These kinds of activities are often summarized as "knowledge intensive business services" (KIBS).

9 Examples are the Silicon Valley (Saxenian 1994), the US Capitol region (Feldman 2001), Munich (Sternberg and Tamasy 1999), Cambridge (Wicksteed 1985) and many others. For an overview see Bresnahan *et al.* (2001).
10 Acs *et al.* (1992), Jaffe *et al.* (1993), Anselin *et al.* (1997). For an overview see Karlsson and Manduchi (2001).
11 Examples can be found in many old-industrialized regions of North America and western Europe as well as in many parts of the former socialist countries of eastern Europe (see the contributions in Fritsch and Brezinski 1999).
12 This concerns, for example, any rules (e.g. in public policy programs) that discriminate against cooperation with partners that are located outside the region or abroad.

Bibliography

Acs, Z.J., Audretsch, D.B. and Feldman, M.P. (1992) "The Real Effects of Academic Research: Comment," *American Economic Review* 82: 363–367.

Anselin, L., Varga, A. and Acs, Z.J. (1997) "Local Geographic Spillovers Between University Research and High Technology Innovation," *Journal of Urban Economics* 42: 422–448.

Antonelli, C. (2002) *The Microeconomics of Technological Systems*, Oxford: Oxford University Press.

Arora, A. and Gambardella, A. (1994) "The Changing Technology of Technological Change: General and Abstract Knowledge and the Division of Innovative Labour," *Research Policy* 23(5): 523–532.

Audretsch, D.B. (1995) *Innovation and Industry Evolution*, Cambridge, MA: MIT Press.

Audretsch, D.B. and Feldman, M.P. (1996a) "Knowledge Spillovers and the Geography of Innovation and Production," *American Economic Review* 86(3): 630–640.

—— (1996b) "Innovative Clusters and the Industry Life Cycle," *Review of Industrial Organization* 11(2): 253–273.

Axelsson, B. (1992) "Corporate Strategy Models and Networks – Diverging Perspectives," in Axelsson, B. (ed.) *Industrial Networks: A New View of Reality,* London: Routledge.

Aydalot, P. and Keeble, D. (eds) (1988) *High Technology and Innovative Environments: The European Experience*, London: Routledge.

Baptista, R. (1998) "Clusters, Innovation, and Growth: A Survey of the Literature," in Swann, P., Prevezer, M. and Stout, D. (eds) *The Dynamics of Industrial Clusters: A Comparative Study of Computing and Biotechnology*, Oxford: Oxford University Press.

Baptista, R. and Swann, P. (1998) "Clustering Dynamics in the UK Computer Industries: A Comparison with the USA," in Swann, P., Prevezer, M. and Stout, D. (eds) *The Dynamics of Industrial Clusters: A Comparative Study of Computing and Biotechnology*, Oxford: Oxford University Press.

Breschi, S. and Lissoni, F. (2001) "Knowledge Spillovers and Local Innovation Systems: A Critical Survey," *Industrial and Corporate Change* 10(4): 975–1005.

Bresnahan, T., Gambardella, A. and Saxenian, A. (2001) " 'Old Economy' Inputs for 'New Economy' Outcomes: Cluster Formation in the New Silicon Valleys," *Corporate and Industrial Change* 10(4): 835–860.

Camagni, R. (1991a) "Local 'Milieu,' Uncertainty and Innovation Networks: Toward a New Dynamic Theory of Economic Space," in Camagni, R. (ed.) *Innovation Networks*, London: Belhaven.

—— (ed.) (1991b) *Innovation Networks: Spatial Perspectives*, London: Belhaven.

Chichilnisky, G. (1999) "Introduction," in Chichilnisky, G. (ed.) *Markets, Information, and Uncertainty*, Cambridge: Cambridge University Press.

Cohen, W. and Levinthal, D.A. (1989) "Innovation and Learning: The Two Faces of R&D – Implications for the Analysis of R&D Investment," *Economic Journal* 99(397): 569–596.

Cooke, P. (1998) "Global Clustering and Regional Innovation – Systemic Integration in Wales," in Braczyk, H.-J., Cooke, P. and Heidenreich, M. (eds) *Regional Innovation Systems – the Role of Governances in a Globalised World*, London: UCL Press.

—— (2002) *Knowledge Economies – Clusters, Learning and Cooperative Advantage*, London: Routledge.

Cooke, P., Uranga, M.G. and Etxebarria, G. (1997) "Regional Innovation Systems: Institutional and Organisational Dimensions," *Research Policy* 26(4–5): 475–491.

Crevoisier, O. and Maillat, D. (1991) "Milieu, Industrial Organization and Territorial Production System – Towards a New Theory of Spatial Development," in Camagni, R. (ed.) *Innovation Networks: Spatial Perspectives*, London: Belhaven.

Edquist, C. (1997) "Systems of Innovation Approaches – Their Emergence and Characteristics," in Edquist, C. (ed.) *Systems of Innovation – Technologies, Institutions and Organizations*, London: Pinter.

Feldman, M.P. (1994) *The Geography of Innovation*, Boston: Kluwer.

—— (1999) "The New Economics of Innovation, Spillovers and Agglomeration: A Review of Empirical Studies," *Economics of Innovation and New Technology* 8(1–2): 5–25.

—— (2001) "The Entrepreneurial Event Revisited: Firm Formation in a Regional Context," *Industrial and Corporate Change* 10(4): 861–891.

Freeman, C. (1987) *Technology Policy and Economic Performance: Lessons from Japan*, London: Pinter.

Fritsch, M. (2000) "Interregional Differences in R&D Activities – an Empirical Investigation," *European Planning Studies* 8(4): 409–427.

—— (2001) "Cooperation in Regional Innovation Systems," *Regional Studies* 35(4): 297–307.

—— (2002) "Measuring the Quality of Regional Innovation Systems – a Knowledge Production Function Approach," *International Regional Science Review* 25(1): 86–101.

—— (2003) "Does Cooperation Behavior Differ between Regions?," *Industry and Innovation* 10(1): 25–39.

—— (2004) "R&D-Cooperation and the Efficiency of Regional Innovation Activities," *Cambridge Journal of Economics* 28: 829–846.

Fritsch, M. and Brezinski, H. (eds) (1999) *Innovation and Technological Change in Eastern Europe Pathways to Industrial Recovery*, Cheltenham: Edward Elgar Publishers.

Fritsch, M. and Franke, G. (2003) "Innovation, Regional Knowledge Spillovers and R&D," *Research Policy* 32: 245–255.

Fritsch, M. and Schwirten, C. (eds) (1999) "Enterprise-University Co-Operation and the Role of Public Research Institutions in Regional Innovation Systems," *Industry and Innovation* 6(1): 69 83.

—— (2002) "R&D Cooperation between Public Research Institutions – Magnitude, Motives and Spatial Dimension," in Schätzl, L. and Revilla Diez, J. (eds) *Technological Change and Regional Development in Europe*, Heidelberg: Physica.

Grabher, G. (1993) "The Weakness of Strong Ties: The Lock-in of Regional Developments in the Ruhr Area," in Grabher, G. (ed.) *The Embedded Firm – On the Socioeconomics of Industrial Networks*, London: Routledge.

Hagedoorn, J. (2002) "Inter-Firm R&D Partnerships: An Overview of Major Trends and Patterns since 1960," *Research Policy* 31(4): 477–492.

Howells, J. (1999) "Regional Systems of Innovation," in Archibugi, D., Howells, J. and Michie, J. (eds) *Innovation Policy in a Global Economy*, Cambridge: Cambridge University Press.

Jaffe, A.B., Trajtenberg, M. and Henderson, R. (1993) "Geographic Localization of Knowledge Spillovers as Evidenced by Patent Citations," *Quarterly Journal of Economics* 108(3): 576–598.

Jewkes, J., Sawers, D. and Stillermann, R. (1969) *The Sources of Invention*, 2nd revised and enlarged edn, London: Macmillan.

Johnson, P.S. and Cathcart, D.G. (1979) "New Manufacturing Firms and Regional Development: Some Evidence from the Northern Region," *Regional Studies* 13: 269–280.

Karlsson, C. and Manduchi, A. (2001) "Knowledge Spillovers in a Spatial Context – a Critical Review," in Fischer, M.M. and Fröhlich, J. (eds) *Knowledge, Complexity and Innovation Systems*, Heidelberg: Springer.

Klepper, S. (2001) *The Evolution of the U.S. Automobile Industry and Detroit as Its "Capital,"* Carnegie Mellon University (mimeo).

Lagendijk, A. (2001) "Scaling Knowledge Production: How Significant Is the Region?," in Fischer, M.M. and Fröhlich, J. (eds) *Knowledge, Complexity and Innovation Systems*, Heidelberg: Springer.

Lundvall, B.-Å. (1992a) "Introduction," in Lundvall, B.-Å. (ed.) *National Systems of Innovation and Interactive Learning*, London and New York: Pinter.

—— (1992b) "User-Producer Relationships, National Systems of Innovation and Internationalisation," in Lundvall, B.-Å. (ed.) *National Systems of Innovation and Interactive Learning*, London and New York: Pinter.

MacNeil, I.R. (1978) "Contracts: Adjustment of Long-Term Economic Relations under Classical, Neoclassical and Relational Contract Law," *Northwestern University Law Review* 72(6): 854–905.

Maskell, P. and Malmberg, A. (1999) "Localized Learning and Industrial Competitiveness," *Cambridge Journal of Economics* 23: 167–185.

Metcalfe, J.S. (1995) "The Economic Foundations of Technology Policy: Equilibrium and Evolutionary Perspectives," in Stoneman, P. (ed.) *Handbook of the Economics of Innovation and Technological Change*, Oxford: Blackwell.

Nelson, R.R. (ed.) (1993) *National Innovation Systems – a Comparative Analysis*, New York: Oxford University Press.

Patel, P. and Vega, M. (1999) "Pattern of Internationalisation of Corporate Technology: Location vs. Home Country Advantages," *Research Policy* 28(2–3): 145–155.

Pearce, R.D. (1999) "Decentralized R&D and Strategic Competitiveness: Globalised Approaches to Generation and Use of Technology in Multinational Enterprises," *Research Policy* 28(2–3): 157–178.

Porter, M. (1998) "Clusters and the New Economics of Competition," *Harvard Business Review* November–December: 77–90.

Powell, W.W. (1990) "Neither Market nor Hierarchy: Network Forms of Organization," *Research in Organizational Behavior* 12: 295–336.

Prevezer, M. (1998) "Clustering and UK Biotechnology," in Swann, P., Prevezer, M. and Stout, D. (eds) *The Dynamics of Industrial Clusters: A Comparative Study of Computing and Biotechnology*, Oxford: Oxford University Press.

Pyke, F., Becattini, G. and Sengenberger, W. (eds) (1990) *Industrial Districts and Inter-Firm Cooperation in Italy*, Geneva: International Institute for Labor Studies.

Saxenian, A. (1994) *Regional Advantage*, Cambridge, MA: Harvard University Press.

Scott, A.J. (1996) "Regional Motors of the Global Economy," *Futures* 28(5): 391–411.

Shohet, S. (1998) "Clustering and UK Biotechnology," in Swann, P., Prevezer, M. and Stout, D. (eds) *The Dynamics of Industrial Clusters: A Comparative Study of Computing and Biotechnology*, Oxford: Oxford University Press.

Sternberg, R. (1996) "Technology Policies and the Growth of Regions: Evidence from Four Countries," *Small Business Economics* 8(2): 75–86.

—— (2000) "Innovation Networks and Regional Development – Evidence from the European Regional Innovation Survey (ERIS): Theoretical Concepts, Methodological Approach, Empirical Basis and Introduction to the Theme Issue," *European Planning Studies* 8(4): 389–407.

Sternberg, R. and Tamasy, C. (1999) "Munich as Germany's No. 1 High Technology Region: Empirical Evidence," *Regional Studies* 33(4): 367–377.

Swann, P. (1998) "Clusters in the US Computing Industry," in Swann, P., Prevezer, M. and Stout, D. (eds) *The Dynamics of Industrial Clusters: A Comparative Study of Computing and Biotechnology*, Oxford: Oxford University Press.

Swann, P., Prevezer, M. and Stout, D. (eds) (1998) *The Dynamics of Industrial Clusters: A Comparative Study of Computing and Biotechnology*, Oxford: Oxford University Press.

Varga, A. (2000) "Universities in Local Innovation Systems," in Acs, Z.J. (ed.) *Regional Innovation, Knowledge and Global Change*, London: Pinter.

von Hippel, E. (1987) "Cooperation Between Rivals: Informal Know-How Trading," *Research Policy* 16(6): 291–302.

—— (1994) " 'Sticky Information' and the Locus of Problem Solving: Implications for Innovations," *Management Science* 40(4): 429–439.

Wicksteed, S.Q. (1985) *The Cambridge Phenomenon – the Growth of High Technology Industry in a University Town*, London: Segal Quince Wicksteed.

10 Internet-based electronic business

A sociology of discontinuities and failures of new companies in the fields of entertainment and technology in California*

Gerhard Krauss

Introduction

The second half of the nineties was characterized by a boom of start-up activity in sectors making use of the Internet technology, such as electronic commerce. Many of those newly founded companies, however, later on failed and only very few succeeded in surviving the critical years of 2000 and 2001. Perhaps one merit of this mass phenomenon of disbandings might have been to contribute to a less emphatic picture of start-up firms and to make us aware of a quite usual phenomenon in emerging industries and in fields of highly innovative activity, but to a high degree dissimulated as such: the phenomenon of *failure*.[1] Failure as part of the innovation process has rarely been put in the center of economic or sociological analysis regarding the study of entrepreneurship and start-up firms. The theoretical approaches that took into account the role of disbandings and unsuccessful entrepreneurial activity, studying both founding and disbanding rates of populations or the role of entry and exit in industrial demography (see Aldrich 1999; Audretsch 1995), were often based on quantitative methods, mobilizing large data pools and still applied a somewhat static view.

In contrast to the mainstream research on newly emerging fields and entrepreneurial activity, a process-oriented approach using essentially qualitative methods (in combination with secondary analysis of statistical data as far as these might be available) seems to be an interesting alternative, not at least because of the lack of reliable quantitative data and the rapid, highly dynamic change characterizing these domains. Finally, the focus on the *process* of innovation is susceptible to opening up new perspectives for a deeper comprehension of the course of start-up activities in pioneering fields.

While the critique of linear models of the innovation process has already been widely accepted and assimilated by research, now viewing the course of the innovation process as rather non-linear and even somewhat chaotic and disorderly, very little research really focused on failure as an essential characteristic of newly emerging technological fields. This might seem somewhat surprising since, in reality, especially in newly emerging knowledge-based or high technology fields, many (more or less important) failures or half-failures appear in the course of the innovation process, facing economic and innovation actors to many problems of a very different nature with which they have to cope in their everyday business life.

This chapter is interested in a quite small part of newly emerging activity, related to an innovative use of Internet technology: the field of knowledge-based and service-oriented Internet start-ups selling services or products via the Internet. It is based on a study of young firms in these fields, focusing on their concrete strategies and innovation projects while relating them to their institutional environments. These environments in such young, dynamic and still emerging fields where themselves changing, but there were also some invariants specific to the given innovation space. It was very attractive to study these new developments in places pioneering Internet-technology-based business models; we therefore decided to concentrate this work on the pioneering phase of the development of electronic commerce in California. However, while taking into account the institutional specifics of innovative districts in California and the mechanisms supporting and guiding the innovative behavior of economic actors, we should avoid exaggerating an institutional determinism, since – as this chapter will show – it is not a mere issue of institutional forces alone that might explain the concrete destiny of young firms, but rather a complex interplay of institutional, industry or task-specific and action-specific elements.

For the purpose of this study, we have examined selected, typical development patterns of young e-commerce companies in California. The region has played a leading role for the expansion of electronic commerce, as well as for the development of the related necessary technological basis. On the one hand, in this domain numerous innovation projects and firm foundings occurred. On the other hand many failures, collapses and development breaks of young companies happened, which could be attributed to the fact that the development and diffusion of this new form of economic transaction was still at the early beginning. The initial uncertainties about sustainable business models and possible development scenarios were so important that the failures of young start-up companies during this early phase were more representative than the later success of a few, finally successful companies. This addresses the question if this is to be seen as a typical characteristic of newly emerging, and in the long run lasting sectors, failure initiating substantial learning processes and therefore preparing the emergence and evolution of those new sectors, or if failure is rather the result of a somewhat "too irrational" economic behavior, being in contradiction either with a superior economic rationality or with the forces of institutional isomorphism, working in a given institutional context of a regional innovation system or economic branch.

This chapter focuses on this pioneering phase of the development of electronic commerce in California by studying essentially firms which had been created by the end of the 1990s. In the center will be the question about the development patterns, as well as the development breaks of the firms, in a highly turbulent environment, characterized, at that time, by still rather unclear and uncertain development perspectives. In particular, we were concerned by the question of what kind of problems the companies and their founders or managers were faced with while realizing their e-commerce projects, whether those problems were overcome, and finally what role the regional embeddedness of the firms played.

Consequently, particular attention will be paid to the interplay of the individual strategies of economic actors, on the one hand, and the institutional context in which the companies are operating, on the other hand. More generally, we will study simultaneously as well the "social embeddedness" of the firms, as their particular individual strategies and innovation projects. Both dimensions are closely interrelated, while leaving still a certain margin of liberty to the creative forces of human action.

The presentation of this chapter's case studies will make clear that this relationship is relatively complex and contains manifold aspects. Whereas the innovation efforts may be guided and supported by the given institutional structures, it is the innovation project itself – requiring a coordination of innovation efforts and the accomplishment of related tasks – which is at the center of the preoccupation and the actions of the economic actors. In view of the high pressure on innovation actors to accomplish concrete tasks and to cope with problems related to the innovation process, the institutional structures are – contrary to the classical view of Durkheim – not completely "external" to the social agent. Rather, they are closely intertwined with the reality of social action and, as would say Anthony Giddens, exist only through the recurrent actions of social actors. While they guide economic action and innovation behavior, institutions do not predetermine human strategies and action, and above all, not in a mechanistic manner. Institutions and institutionalized rules may be mobilized by actors as a kind of resource in a politicized exchange, which especially seems to be a typical feature of newly emerging (and in a certain way pioneering) industries.

According to this interpretation of the role of institutional structures, the theory leaves an important margin to the creative aspects of the strategies of actors who are faced with concrete problems they have to resolve *together*, in order to be able to realize innovations as a *collective* product or process. To accomplish their tasks, the innovation agents may mobilize institutional support as well as resources accumulated during their own biographical history. But there remains an important impact of the innovation actor: the way in which he or she is able to profit from available resources and institutional structures, and in what way he or she is able to escape from institutionally or socially deterministic forces.

The hypothesis is that the resources available to actors are very much provided by the regional context and therefore it is important to study companies in relation with their regional environment. The discussions about high technology districts and industrial clusters show that the spatial dimension plays a role and that the decisive competencies are to a high degree concentrated in local or regional spaces of social interaction. However, this does not exclude that at the same time another typical feature of contemporary high-technology or knowledge-based industries is their international openness toward global markets and competition. With regard to electronic commerce, the regional context is important insofar as electronic commerce cannot be simply reduced to the mere technical dimension, but is embedded into a certain social, institutional and organizational context. This is true not only for the user-side of electronic commerce, but also for the developer-side and the offering of e-commerce solutions by young, specialized e-commerce firms. Frequent face-to-face communication in the regional or local interaction space is, in fact, very important. Through such permanent interactions the economic actors become "socialized" acquire a spontaneous knowledge about the context surrounding them and develop a context-specific, practical intelligence which helps them to operate "intelligently" (varying according to their particular position) in the respective economic domain.

Regional innovation regimes in California

California represents an important economic engine for the United States. The economic power of the region may be measured in terms of important export numbers, high standards of income, as well as a highly developed R&D infrastructure with a large pool of specialized service providers and suppliers who are adapted to the needs of the knowledge- and technology-intensive industries. In the past, the Californian economy has created an important part of jobs for highly qualified specialists and is characterized by a flexibilized labor market with a high rate of self-employment and firm foundations.

An important characteristic of the Californian economy is its strong positioning in the global market place. California has higher export numbers than any other state in the US. In 2001, California's share of the total US exports was about 16 percent. The three most important sectors were electronic products and computers (47 percent of Californian exports), industrial machines (11 percent) and electronic equipments and parts (2.9 percent). These numbers may vary according to the state of the international economy. In this respect, for example, the general crisis of the international economy recently has led to a significant reduction of high-tech exports and to California's exports in general, amplifying temporarily the economic problems of California's high-technology districts, such as Silicon Valley.

The development of exports and investments reflects the important change of the Californian economy during the last decades. The contemporary Californian economy is to a much higher degree linked with international networks than some decades ago. In the past, important exports of high-tech products on the one hand enabled the regional economy to realize growth rates above the US average. However, the strong dependence on high-technology exports, on the other hand, appeared to have a negative impact on the regional economy during periods of economic crisis and consequently led to growth rates below average during those times (or even to negative growth rates). Statistically, the success in the high-technology sector contributed to an economic standard above average of the Californian population, which had to be paid, however, at the price of extremely high prize standards and significant income differences.

The economic force of California is partly a result of a certain kind of "social openness," allowing the integration of immigrant labor and a permanent influx of human capital from foreign countries and in sum is based on a large pool of qualified labor. In this respect, the region may profit from its geostrategic position and its traditional role as an arrival region for an important part of immigrants and foreign workers. Compared to the rest of the United States, the population of California is younger, is expanding more rapidly and is much more heterogeneous concerning its ethnic structure. Whereas the part of whites is around 15 percent below the US average, the part of people with Asian origins is three times higher than in the US in general. In addition, there is also a higher proportion of people with multiple ethnic origins. Since the mid-1960s, the immigration from Asia has grown steadily, especially the influx of qualified labor. As a consequence, in 1990 for example, around a quarter of the engineers and researchers employed by California's technology-intensive industries were of foreign origin, a percentage twice as high as those of other highly industrialized US states, such as Massachusetts or Texas (cf. Saxenian 1994: 249).

Another typical feature is the institution of a highly flexibilized labor market, which is of a particular importance especially in the high-technology sectors. Highly qualified specialists and managers move easily and often between companies: changing the company seems to be an important mechanism of career advancement for these groups. Consequently, in periods of economic boom, the companies have to compete for highly qualified labor. To a high extent, the knowledge- and research-intensive industries in California need qualified personnel, especially for research and development activities.

The importance of the knowledge-based and high-technology industries is a central element of the strong economic power of the region. In this respect, research and development activities play a decisive role. California concentrates the highest number of engineers and scientists of all US states; several worldwide highly reputed institutions of scientific research competence are located here. In 1999, the total expenditures in R&D in California reached almost 50 billion dollars, which represents 3.9 percent of the Californian GDP (National Science Board 2002: Appendix Table 4–23). This leading position is also reflected by patent statistics (cf. US PTO 2000). In 1999, California ranked first among all US states, having almost 19,000 new patents which represent 20 percent of all new US patents. Nevertheless this leading position is somewhat relativized if the number of patents is reported to the number of inhabitants: in this case, California looses its first rank, but still remains among a leading group of US states (Zucker and Darby 1999).

Among the influential actors of the innovation process are, on the one hand, internationally renowned companies from Silicon Valley such as Hewlett Packard (Palo Alto), Advance Micro Devices (AMD) in Sunnyvale or Intel with its headquarters in Santa Clara. On the other hand, there are academic or research institutions such as the research-based Californian universities (for example, the different locations of the University of California, Stanford University in Silicon Valley) and other highly reputed institutions (for example the California Institute of Technology in Pasadena near Los Angeles, etc.).

The innovation region lives from its great social and technological diversity and heterogeneity; the social foundations of its technological dynamics are based upon a large range of highly skilled and specialized workers (including an important ethnic diversity) and upon a permanent influx of foreign workers or immigrants bringing various skills with them. Those immigrant workers often readily accept the harder living conditions, typical for high-technology districts such as Silicon Valley. Certain ethnic groups, for example East Indians, are reputed for their particular skills in the domain of software engineering or even in e-commerce (and more generally for their particular culture in mathematics and natural sciences), while other Asian or Hispanic immigrants often have lower skills and are thus more often employed for easier tasks.

As diverse as the regional ecology of the economic and technological innovation actors might be, as flexible and permanently changing are the relationships between actors. On the one hand, in the high-tech economy, which is characterized by a division of work between highly specialized firms, new configurations of interorganizational relationships emerge and reemerge permanently. On the other hand, we find a kind of "flexible recycling" (Bahrami and Evans 2000), which may result in new reconfigurations of knowledge and competencies and which opens the possibility to give rise to new successful firms out of the rests of failed companies.

A characteristic element of the institutional context in Silicon Valley is the phenomenon to stimulate risk taking, to give continuous rise to found-ings of new technology firms and to show a relatively high tolerance regarding the phenomenon of "failure" of young technology firms (cf. Sax-enian 1994: 38; Kenney 2000: 9). Paradoxically, the foundations of the Silicon Valley model were not founded by pure market-economy forces, but were very much a result of state intervention in the form of the mili-tary contract research and supply policy. Eventually, this played a decisive role for the evolution of the local technology-oriented business culture: financially powerful clients created secured sales markets for the techno-logy firms and in fact carried an important part of the costs related to the technological risks (Leslie 2000: 49).

One of Silicon Valley's current central characteristics is the extremely high firm dynamics: as in virtually no other region, new start-up companies emerge steadily and, at the same time, replace the numerous market exits of disbanding firms. Those companies may take advantage from a rich infrastructure of supporting organizations, composed of a large and diver-sified range of specialized service providers: first-class law firms, special-ized in the particular needs of high technology companies, consulting firms, head hunters, venture capital firms, marketing firms, accounting firms, industrial real estate firms, as well as further intermediary organi-zations and diverse specialized service firms (Kenney 2000; Lee *et al.* 2000: part III). The rapid development of new knowledge-intensive industries and technologies would not be possible without such an environment of supporting institutions, suited to the needs of knowledge-intensive indus-tries and high-technology fields. And it would not be possible either without those highly flexible economic structures, characterized by dynamic firm founding processes, many young technology companies and a strong entrepreneurial culture as well as rapidly changing fluid networks and firm populations.

Among others, the powerful and prestigious law firms of Silicon Valley are of particular importance. These include Wilson Sonsini Goodrich & Rosati in Palo Alto, Brobeck Phleger & Harrison in San Francisco or Cooley Godward in Palo Alto. Their importance and size is reflected by their turnover: for example, in 2001, the ten largest law firms of the Bay Area had a turnover of about 3.5 billion dollars (*Daily Journal San Fran-cisco* 7.1.2002: 2). These numerous experts for certain high quality services represent an essential element of Silicon Valley's social ecology. Even for the disbanding of failed technology companies and for the sale of their equipment several specialized service companies have established them-selves in the region (Kenney 2000: 228).

More generally, the technology-based industries in California seem to be very much embedded in a highly developed and highly diversified service economy. This might indicate that, in fact, there exist strong inter-dependencies between technological innovations and social innovations. Interestingly enough, while California is one of the worldwide leading technology regions, at the same time its service sector is particularly developed and differentiated.[2] As is true for specialized high-technology industries, those intermediary service providers tend to form spatially concentrated clusters. In Silicon Valley, for example, in proximity to the campus of Stanford University we find clusters of venture capital firms (along Sand Hill Road in Menlo Park, or in Palo Alto), of law firms (on Page Mill Road in Palo Alto, with some of the largest law firms of Silicon Valley) and of consultant firms (in Menlo Park and Palo Alto). Finally, most of the large accounting firms are located in San Jose. In the Valley, there are also different technology clusters: for example, software and Internet firms – the kind of firms this chapter is interested in – tend to cluster around Palo Alto, Mountain View and Sunnyvale (Lee *et al.* 2000: 271–273).

The high firm dynamics and fluctuation are reflected in the statistics of foundings and disbandings. In 2000, the firm foundation rate of California of 18.4 percent was significantly above the US average of 10.8 percent. On the one hand, in absolute numbers, most start-up firms are located in California; around one fourth to one third of all newly founded companies in the US are located there. On the other hand, there are equally high numbers of disbandings, but many of them occur outside California, especially in Delaware because of its business friendly corporate law.[3] Apart from this firm fluctuation above average, California has a relatively high share of small firms; more than half of the companies of manufacturing industries have less than ten employees. In addition, California has the highest share of self-employed or "one-man-firms" among all US states.

However, Silicon Valley is not the only high-tech region in California. Apart from Silicon Valley, there is an equally high concentration of knowledge- and technology-intensive industries in South California. Here, particular competencies exist in the domain of the information and communication technology, new media, as well as medical equipments and biotechnology.

Over many decades, South California has evolved toward a center of different high-tech complexes, especially in aeronautics and electronics (see Scott 1993; Numark 1999). The latter were to a high degree dependent on large military contracts. In the meantime, the dramatic reduction of these contracts since the mid-1990s led to a profound transformation and restructuring of the regional economy during a relatively short period of time (cf. Numark 1999). This was one of the reasons for the above average unemployment rates in the 1990s (besides the problems of other technology sectors, in particular, in the San Francisco Bay Area), which contrasted with the low unemployment figures during the Reagan era when a relatively high level of defense spending was of great benefit to the Californian economy. In May 2002, the unemployment rate of California (6.3 percent) was above the US average (5.8 percent) which is, however, compared to international standards, still rather low (Dickerson 2002). During the last 15 years, California has lost about 310,000 jobs in the aeronautics and military-related sectors (Center for Continuing Study of the California Economy 2001: 5–45). In 2000, these sectors now represented only around 8 percent of all jobs in the manufacturing industries, in contrast to 26 percent in 1960. Despite these dramatic changes, South California has succeeded in keeping its position beside Silicon Valley as one of the leading high-technology regions in the world.

However, South California has also further strong sectors; of particular relevance are, for example, the media and entertainment industries. The center of the film industry is located in the Los Angeles area (Hollywood), around which has emerged a large sector of different media firms, specialized service providers and investors. More generally, South California is home to an important firm population of the media industry. The companies cover a large field of services and products between technology and content. As a consequence, Internet-related business models in this area focus in particular on applications of the Internet technology in the new media and entertainment sectors. This applies, for example, to the new technological possibilities in the online distribution of film products, to video-on-demand, video games as well as to specific information services.

In particular, during the last few years, the region developed toward a leading center of the video games industry (Pham 2001). A certain number of worldwide leading firms have their headquarters in South California, essentially in the Los Angeles region. Others have at least their principal publishing studios here. Many of them are located in the western Los Angeles area and in Santa Monica (for example THQ, Electronic Arts, Activision, Disney Interactive, TDK Mediactive, Fox Interactive, Sammy Entertainment, Interplay Entertainment Corp., Infogrames, Vivendi Universal Games etc.). The reason for this development is that for the new media companies the spatial proximity to the strong entertainment industry in Los Angeles and Hollywood becomes more and more important.[4]

On the other side, since the mid-1990s, the major film studios began to create their own departments for "interactive entertainment," in order to develop video games based on film contents.

Finally, an important feature of the regional innovation regime is the existence of a highly developed and differentiated venture capital industry. Venture capital firms offer high quality services to their client companies. Their function is not limited to the mere financial aspects, i.e. the access to venture capital, but in addition applies to further knowledge-intensive services. These are oriented toward the particular technological and industrial branch, such as counseling and gate-keeping, or different kinds of support for important business decisions. Thanks to their close contact to the companies, as well as to their specialization, the venture capitalists dispose of a detailed knowledge of the given technology sector. In addition, many venture capitalists dispose of experts who themselves come from the given technology sector; several venture capital funds have even been created or are managed by former entrepreneurs or managers of technology companies.

The regional concentration of venture capital firms, particularly in the San Francisco Bay area, including Silicon Valley, and in South California is unique worldwide. During the last two decades, the Bay area alone concentrated the highest raise of venture capital in the world. At the same time, most venture capital investments worldwide occurred here (Kenney and Florida 2000: 98). For example, during the first quarter of 2002, more than one third of all American venture capital investments went to technology firms in Silicon Valley (PricewaterhouseCoopers 2002). Two further Californian regions also figure among the first five ranks: these are Los Angeles and Orange County (third rank or 6.9 percent of all venture capital investments in the United States) and San Diego (fifth rank or 6.2 percent). A fourth Californian region (Sacramento, North California) ranks fifteenth.

Together, these four regions represent half of all American venture capital. Regarding the sector of services related to information technology, there is an impressing dominance of Silicon Valley which concentrated almost half of all American venture capital investments of this sector during the first quarter of 2002. In addition, the remaining Californian regions concentrated 8 percent of those investments. The regional differentiation of the venture capital investments reflects the very strong concentration of the technological competencies in this field in Silicon Valley.

Development of Internet-based business in California

Historically, important steps in the development of Internet technology were realized in California, especially in Southern California. The particular role of Southern California in the development of the network technologies, which later on should become the base of the Internet, can be explained by the traditionally high importance of military contracts and the particular relationships of the defense industry to academic and research institutions in the region.[5] Southern California historically was very much closed to a particular kind of world, which is the defense world, and the world of government contracting, while keeping a quite diverse economic base. This contrasts with Northern California which stands for the historical origins of the semiconductor revolution and an industry that is much more geared toward a broader dissemination of technology to a larger audience of people, with numerous spin-offs and start-up companies. If government funding from the Department of Defense played an important role in Silicon Valley, too, its importance for Southern California was even higher.

The creation of Netscape in Silicon Valley represented a further important step toward larger applications of the Internet. Technology firms like Netscape contributed to the formation of a base for the further development of Internet applications and electronic commerce. The environment in Silicon Valley, in this respect, favored a technology-driven strategy, i.e. an embedding of the companies in technology-driven networks. The leading companies providing the technological means for Internet-based electronic business were, to a high extent, located in Silicon Valley. Those companies, in addition, represented a large reservoir of potential start-up founders for Internet applications, such as electronic commerce. However, while many Internet start-ups were realized in Silicon Valley, there were only a few places in California developing their own social identity of the sector, based on intense relationships in a local space of social interaction. Probably the most prominent example for such a phenomenon was the case of the Internet firms in San Francisco. With the rise of the Internet, many dot.coms started to locate in South of Market (SoMa), a socially very dynamic and heterogeneous neighborhood in downtown San Francisco. This neighborhood was characterized by an important service sector, a strong profile in multimedia, design, apparel and printing, as well as a dynamic arts scene (essentially photographers, film makers and other artists), bars, clubs and restaurants.

The choice of the location by those dot.coms essentially was due to the lifestyle aspirations and to the social characteristics of their entrepreneurs or founders and staff, in combination with the availability of affordable office space in proximity to high speed network access. The urban character of San Francisco, i.e. a town with a real city center and public transportation system, in the perception of this staff, differed significantly from the sterile, nevertheless quite expensive and dispersed agglomerations of Silicon Valley. These neither represented countryside nor town and have no clear geographical center, while their everyday life is marked by an intensive social use of individual, private transportation (automobile). Instead of living in a small town or agglomeration in Silicon Valley, the remarkably young staff of the San Francisco Internet start-ups, which comprised an important share of college drop-outs and above average high-school students, liked to live in downtown San Francisco and to work in a socially heterogeneous downtown quarter, where they could live their bohemian-hedonistic urban lifestyle. San Francisco seemed to provide these companies with a certain aura and world openness. A particularity of San Francisco Internet firms, compared to those of Silicon Valley or Southern California, was their stronger specialization on market niches in the hope of being able to dominate those niches worldwide. This strategy was based on the assumption of an increasing differentiation and fragmentation of the Internet which would be profitable to globally oriented start-up firms. The objective, therefore, was to create numerous niches with a corresponding worldwide public (which, later on, appeared to be much more difficult in practice than it seemed to be in theory, leading to the failure of a number of firms).

The social ecology in which companies are embedded thus plays a decisive role. This is also true for the other regions. In Silicon Valley, it is the strong technology base which influences the business of the firm, whereas in the Los Angeles region, the economic profile in the Internet field is rather a combination of technology and content coming from the highly developed entertainment and media industry. And in both regions, too, a number of companies failed and went bankrupt. During the early boom of the Internet start-ups, for example, many new media companies, marketing and diffusing content over the web (e.g. films or music online), had been created in the major media locations west of Los Angeles close to Hollywood, such as Santa Monica. These companies faced similar problems as the San Francisco start-ups, the combination of Internet technology and creative content being much more difficult in practice than estimated, in addition to the problems of opening up a sufficiently large public of user-clients. After the Internet bubble burst, the firm population here changed profoundly. Many of the failed companies increasingly got replaced by yet another type of firm, which also profited from the spatial proximity to the entertainment industry – the publishing firms of online video games.

Institutional logics and social exchange relationships of actors

During the last two decades, and especially since the 1990s, research began to focus more extensively on the role of collective institutions in innovation and production, as well as on the sectoral level of industries and on different spatial levels (national, regional, local). Peter Hall and David Soskice subsume these different works under the category of the social production system approach (Hall and Soskice 2001: 3). Studying different national institutional contexts, Hall and Soskice themselves have identified essentially two ideal-type patterns: *coordinated market economies*, on the one hand, and *liberal market economies*, on the other hand. Their thesis is that liberal market economies favor better radical innovations, whereas coordinated market economies are better suited to support incremental innovations. Similarly, the institutional dimension was also taken into account by the recent research on regional innovation systems, mostly analyzing *institutionalized* regional innovation systems (cf. Cooke *et al.* 2004). For some time, major works of the neoinstitutionalist school had focused on the idea of the legitimacy of organizational practice, distinguishing different forms of isomorphism in order to conceptualize the influence of the institutional and social environment on organizations (cf. DiMaggio and Powell 1991). Neoinstitutionalist arguments have further been used by sociologists studying entrepreneurship, for example, by combining arguments of the population ecology and neoinstitutionalist schools, focusing on institutional learning and legitimacy (see Aldrich 1999).

This chapter's study of Internet companies in California seems to suggest that a mere institutional perspective may be somewhat too narrow if we want to interpret the particular evolution and destiny of start-up companies. However, it may at first be useful, if one also takes into consideration the actors' capacity to act against institutional forces. But even a pure institutionalist perspective would not necessarily imply that the institutional context represented an "iron cage." Rather, they are reproduced in a dynamic and non-identical way through practice. Using neoinstitutionalist arguments, the failure of start-up companies in newly emerging fields may be interpreted as an indicator for non-isomorphism or, in other words, for a too high degree of non-conformism with established innovation patterns. However, whereas the diagnosis may be true on a general level, conformism may also imply a risk of failure in the case when it reduces the possibilities of the actors to open up alternative paths (e.g. completely new economic or technological fields, or deviant business strategies etc.). That means that failure in innovation may result from conformism as well. As a consequence, it is important to take into account two aspects. First, the efforts of the actors to impose their ideas against contradicting institutional structures while mobilizing resources and power in their exchange with other innovation actors, and second, the concrete issue of innovation (nature of the problems, tasks etc.).

The failure of start-up companies in the *new economy* occurs in different forms, varying across technological fields, industries and times. For example, in the Internet sector, a very common form of failure is bankruptcy, a phenomenon which was of major importance during its pioneering phase and after the burst of the Internet bubble. But in practice, there exist also numerous minor or less important forms of failure, starting with companies' inability to cope with everyday problems. Often, when problems occur and failure becomes likely, companies can adopt counterstrategies. These may result, for example, in the closing down of a particular project, program, department, location and so on. They may also cause the company to dismiss parts of the staff in order to avoid bankruptcy. Another possibility is to sell the company (or parts of it) in time, often to another competing company.

For the present chapter, we have selected a few contrasting examples from the case studies, of which we will analyze two more thoroughly. The first represents a typical, fast-growing Silicon Valley e-commerce company of the 1990s, specializing in the sale of software online, which went bankrupt in early 2002. The second was a small business, located in Hollywood and offering online knowledge-intensive services to investors in the film industry, which, for some time, was close to bankruptcy. Other cases we will implicitly refer to are Internet start-up companies from

Silicon Valley and from the entertainment and media clusters of the Los Angeles region.

Our first case study represents an example for a very early Internet start-up, before the boom of the Internet started. The institutional context at that point was neither very much supportive nor particularly reluctant toward Internet start-ups. While Internet applications, translated into businesses, seemed to possess considerable potential, it was rather unclear and uncertain at that time what realistic development scenarios could look like.

At its origins, the company had been founded as one of the first Internet shops in the world (as a spin-off from another company located in the San Francisco Bay area). The objective was to distribute software via the Internet and to deliver it to the clients digitally with a proprietary download technology. For this purpose, the location of the company in Silicon Valley in close proximity to the major software houses seemed to be quite advantageous. The company already went public in 1998, just at the early beginning of the Internet boom. During its first years it grew rapidly into a leading Internet-based retailer for consumer software, owning the products itself (instead of just operating as a broker), thus being able to determine the price structure of its products on its own. For a long time, the company was considered a model for a young, rising and promising e-commerce company, realizing a high and rapid growth (for example, for several years, the company figured among the ten most rapidly growing companies in Silicon Valley, with a peak of 400 employees in 1999).

The company went bankrupt in early 2002. The failure reflected the complex interdependencies between, on the one hand, changing institutional environments, and on the other hand, the concrete business decisions that the management needed to make under conditions of high insecurity. In fact, under these conditions the selection of a business strategy and its implementation was rather uncertain and could be evaluated only in retrospect because of the lack of prior experience and unclear development scenarios. At the same time, business decisions at the top of the firm were the result of a kind of bargaining or collective exchange process between different actors, in particular between the management and investors, or control bodies of the firm.

While the institutional context and the technology culture in Silicon Valley in general was rather favorable to unconventional innovations, the support of the social environment for the kind of business model of the company was not at all certain during the very early pioneering phase of the Internet sector. In this respect, it seems obvious that the company itself, together with its investors, had a stake in contributing to increase the legitimacy of this kind of business activity in general, and the firm's concrete business model in particular. This meant that the company contributed itself to shaping its institutional environments while using the existing infrastructure (e.g. the largely diversified, highly specialized, high quality services for new technology firms), instead of being merely an object of institutional influences.

In the case of this company, the innovation represented not merely a technological one, but consisted of a business model for a new (theoretically cost-efficient) form of software distribution, using a particular technology as an instrument. At the time of the IPO, there were theoretically different possibilities for the selection of a business strategy and a long-term organizational development plan for the firm. The selection of an offensive business strategy, oriented toward a rapid growth, was a political decision taken very much by the founders and investors. The model they had in mind was the early successes of Amazon, still one of the very few examples of a successful e-commerce firm. The objective was to replicate the success story of Amazon in the field of software. This implied a specialization on the electronic commerce of consumer software, a business development perspective oriented toward rapid growth. The choice finally was stressed by hiring a management team with large experience in electronic business to consumer commerce.

This strategy finally failed due to different reasons. On the one hand, in software retail, the margins were not very high. In this respect the company wanted to reduce the costs by distributing and selling software online (instead of the more expensive form of physical distribution). However, in practice, it was very difficult to get the products for electronic online distribution. It was impossible to obtain all software products that could be offered to be downloaded by consumers. Apart from technical reasons hindering online distribution, a major issue was the very problematic relationship with the established physical distribution systems. Successfully realizing an innovation in the form of a new kind of software distribution would, in practice, have meant getting support from the field's major powerful actors in order to be able to profit from introducing this new practice.

Due to the particular structure of the established innovation systems in software publishing at that time, this young company in fact did not have access to products of the big software houses. While the software available on the web theoretically should have been cheaper than in the store (because there is no cost of packaging, no cost of printed manual etc.), in reality the company did not succeed in selling the software products cheaper, because the manufacturers did not give them a good price. The problem was the existence of already highly developed physical distribution systems, in which the manufacturers themselves had invested a lot, giving the manufacturers enormous power in distribution:

> The problem was to convince the manufacturers of that time [...] to have their products downloaded was actually difficult, because they had been fighting for the past decade of getting distribution through CompUSA, or on the PCs with Dell, or Gateway, or Compaq, or

Hewlett Packard. And they have been paying all these people for the distribution! So, at the end of the day, most of the consumer software companies – there was only about ten that mattered – had won the distribution war! And now all of a sudden this new distribution system came out called the Internet! So, they said [...] you know we spent the last ten or fifteen years killing our competitors and winning the distribution. And now we have a brand new distribution area over here? You want us to support that, even though we put all our money into building the physical channel? It's like no! I own this channel, I don't want to share with anybody! Why should I support the online channel which would kill me?

So, we were much more successful in the people who did not have the big distribution. So it is all their competitors like to go online and download.... But the biggest names, the biggest products, they had their own distribution. They didn't want to do it online.

So this was a little hindrance – and this even happens today – was a little of a hindrance of getting software downloaded online! Even though, all the studies (Forrester, Jupiter etc.) everybody said number one should be software and number two would be music!

(anonymous)

Apart from these basic problems and the fundamental decision, what kind of market to enter, the company, in addition, did not succeed in coping with the problems related to its rapid growth and its internal organization structure. The company was composed of different divisions, competing with each other for resources and setting their own agendas. Additionally, it had grown in a more or less uncoordinated way. Given the lack of legitimacy of the consumer-based business model of the company and the problems in increasing its legitimacy, it was virtually impossible to develop a coherent overall vision or to mobilize all internal actors in the same direction.

Consequently, it was equally difficult to prioritize resources and to create an efficient internal organization in order to reduce operational costs. The failure became apparent already two years before the company's bankruptcy, leading to a radical restructuring and change of the business strategy with priority given to the business and government markets. However, the change came too late and the enormous costs run up in the preceding years finally killed the company.

Interestingly enough, according to other case studies, companies were also faced with the problem of deciding what kind of strategy to develop as a new actor, in order to become part of existing innovation systems. This seemed also to be a typical feature, for example, for the complex of the entertainment industry in the Los Angeles area. In one case, a young start-up located in close proximity to Hollywood was developing a business model and technology for Internet-based video-on-demand distribution (by streaming technology). In contrast to other companies active in the field of Internet-based video-on-demand that often merely give priority to the technology, the company in question explicitly specialized in high quality, culturally valuable content. The founders, essentially coming from the entertainment business themselves, disposed of important relationships with the major film studies, which theoretically should have been an advantage for getting high quality content from the film studios. Nevertheless, in practice it seemed to be very difficult to obtain the content even for those founders having close relationships to the studios.

The reasons for these difficulties are rather complex, but it seems that there might be a potential competition with the planned expansion of similar services of the film industry in the future, making the studios rather reluctant to give valuable content out of their control. As a consequence, the company had to shutter its video-on-demand online services and reduce its staff to a handful of employees, in order to avoid bankruptcy in the short term (while in its best times it had up to 80 employees), which in fact is an indicator for the failure of the business model.

Another, rather contrasting, example was a small-sized company located in Hollywood providing knowledge-intensive services to investors in the film industry. In contrast to the first type of development, at the time of its founding it did not really enter into competition with either powerful economic actors nor established business activities. Rather, it contributed to the creation of a niche for a new kind of specialized, knowledge-based service which was especially of interest to the large film studios. In addition, its small size contrasted with the typical growth-orientation of most venture capital financed Internet start-ups of the late 1990s. Due to its small size, the company was marked by the social biography of its founder.

This case is interesting as it shows a completely different development pattern, with ups and downs, and sometimes very critical situations during times of economic and institutional change. It differs from other cases insofar as it is based on a longer previous development history. The knowledge, on which the Internet-based service was essentially based, was nothing completely new that had only been invented in the 1990s. Rather, it was the assimilation of Internet technology by an almost ten year old, highly specialized small service firm; the use of the Internet being a logical consequence of the nature of the service offered. With the emergence of the Internet, a knowledge and information selling firm of this kind could hardly have avoided using this technology, at least in the long term, in its relationships with customers.

The service offered by the company consisted of providing detailed information about films (or new film projects), being of high value for investors, traders, national and international distribution companies, production companies or film festivals. The high value of the knowledge held by the company explained the high price level of the services offered. This also reflected a fundamental difference to the common Internet start-up, insofar as the service of the company was based on a large stock of knowledge, accumulated over many years by the founder in the film industry. This represented the fruit of several years of demanding work that was continuously updated for a very specific, limited group of customers.

In order to understand the importance of the social embeddedness of the entrepreneur and its company, we have to look at the founder's social trajectory linked to the origins and evolution of the firm. Prior to starting up the firm, the founder had been working in several different positions in the film business. At the time when the new video technology, favoring an increasing market for independent film products, emerged in the 1980s, the film studios created new positions for the acquisition of external productions. But this new function was difficult to organize and demanded an important knowledge about new film products on the market. It was even advantageous to know about film projects early enough before the finished products entered the market.

This was identified as a market niche by the firm's founder who started the firm in the late 1980s. The concept of the company is a good example for a knowledge-based business model which evolved incrementally in the context of the local film industry in Hollywood. The actual "knowledge capital" of the company has been accumulated by the firm founder and its partner – a former film producer – over years, thanks to their professional experiences in the film industry, as well as through intensive social exchange relationships with a whole range of film business people. A regular presence at numerous internationally important film festivals and the interactions with film producers, film traders and festivals represented the basic source of the knowledge stock of the company,[6] rather than the mere fact that the company sold its services exclusively through the Internet. The Internet and the electronic commerce in this case was only a tool for organizing the business relationships to the customers more efficiently, i.e. cheaper, more customer-friendly, and above all, more up-to-date, giving the customers the possibility to dispose of the most recent information without delay. That means that the company has grown incrementally from a conventional knowledge-based business service firm toward an Internet- and knowledge-based service provider. Furthermore, it still kept its very small size, its staff not exceeding a handful of people.

However, this development occurred not without major problems. The emergence of the new Internet business field during the 1990s contributed to a change of institutional environments, temporarily increasing the legitimacy of Internet-based business-models and therefore creating a high pressure on specialized, globally operating service companies to adapt to these newly emerging models. It was obvious that the company with its particular business model actually was predestined for the Internet-based knowledge economy. Thus, there was a need to think about the new technological possibilities. At this time, there were first offers from other Internet start-ups to buy the company. These Internet start-ups in general understood only the technology side of the business and lacked the industry-specific knowledge and information base that would have enabled them to offer high quality knowledge-based services through the Internet on their own. On the other hand, suddenly other Internet start-ups emerged, proposing similar services on the Internet for free.

> And then three or four companies suddenly proposed what I was doing as a service that would be on the internet, and for free. That was a huge moment for us. I knew, we needed to go on the internet, we were just databased. No, I have histories for all these films. I have how they are financed, where they have sold – they never had that – where they have been reviewed, where they have played festivalwise. All they had was: here is a market, and here is what is being sold; and here is some independent films, and here is the contact information. It was much more superficial! But it was really a huge threat! And they all wanted to buy us, because we had the content. The deals weren't very attractive, they were speculative, and none believed that the business plans would work. We were the only ones making money! They had no idea how to make money.
>
> (anonymous)

During the decisive years of 1999 and 2000 the company received numerous offers from Internet start-ups, trying to obtain its data base. But most of the offers were based on impossible or unrealistic business models, reflecting a lack of experience, competence and knowledge of its authors in the film business. In this situation, the company had two alternative possibilities: either to develop on its own the whole Internet business, the website and related marketing, or to search for a competent partner with the necessary financial power. Because of the limited financial resources of the firm and the lacking knowledge about Internet technology, it chose the latter possibility. This was an important, and at the same time very risky decision. Among the numerous offers, only one seemed to be founded on a solid and serious concept; it was the offer that finally had been accepted. It came from an Internet short-film portal, originally created in 1998 in San Francisco that later on moved to Hollywood. It was nevertheless a typical dot.com start-up, showing the same aggressive growth strategy as most of the other dot.coms of that time. Its objective was to build up a leading market position on the Internet in this field by buying and integrating a large range of different film-related services (previously offered by different, highly specialized small firms). This plan, oriented toward rapid expansion, was designed just when the boom of the Internet economy had reached its peak.

A short time after, just when the Internet film portal signed the deal with the knowledge-based service provider we studied, the business started to decline. Then the troubles started. While the Internet portal had promised to pay a huge fee for the company, as well as to keep the staff employed at competitive salaries and to expand the company, it started to trim back, to cut back the paid employees as well as the travel expenses and tried to renegotiate its deal. In fact, this endangered the basis of the recently bought company, especially travel being essential for its long-term survival. The following period was characterized by a time of high risk and uncertainty concerning the long-term perspective of the business. This period lasted for about 18 months. In order to have a chance of survival, the founder's very urgent objective during that time was to get the company out of the deal and to buy it back:

> We knew we had to get the company out or we would have been destroyed. We didn't know if they would survive, they did survive, they are here. But we really didn't know if they would survive, and if they didn't we would be dead! And I had no place to go. I mean, where do you go with my age, having done what I did, there is no more technology. Maybe I would have had some, but I didn't want to loose this! This is my annuities. So, I knew I had to get out. They didn't want to pay, because if they had payed what they owed, they would have gone bankrupt.
>
> (anonymous)

This example shows how the emergence of a whole new category of businesses can be accompanied by a (at least temporary) modification of institutional environments that affects existing companies as well. New companies, eager to increase the legitimacy of their new activity (cf. Aldrich 1999: 224ff), may have an important impact on existing companies if they succeed in convincing central actors, thus together contributing to create a kind of social incitation in favor of the adoption of the new practices. But at the same time, economic actors may resist this pressure. This is reflected by the firm's critical posture vis-à-vis the majority of the Internet start-ups that offered cooperation or that wanted to overtake this firm. This critical posture was possible thanks to the particular social embeddedness of the company in the industry, thus providing a more realistic base for a rational assessment of business models in that field. However, the company found itself in a difficult position during the early boom of the Internet economy.

On the one hand, it realized the necessity to propose its services online, especially in view of the fact that it occupied a very specific niche for knowledge-based services to the film industry *worldwide*. On the other hand, being a very small-sized firm with a staff of five (the founder and her partner, a former film producer, plus three employees), it did not really consider important investments in new technology on its own. This was caused by a lack of competency in technology matters, a lack of own capital to invest and because of unfamiliarity with external capital investments, especially those of venture capital firms.

The decision to join with an Internet start-up of the film sector therefore seemed to be the easier solution. However, very quickly it turned out to be a trap when the Internet economy declined as a whole, even affecting Internet firms with more serious concepts, which was partially a problem of missing legitimacy. Strong conflicts emerged inside the newly formed company, composed of different specialized sub-units, over resources that could not be settled down due to the important financial problems of the new company. As we have seen, it took 18 months for the small service firm to become independent and get their firm out again. The success was only relative since it represented a real development break for the firm which had to restart its business, and now independently build up and develop the Internet technology domain necessary for the services.

Conclusion

The pioneering phase of Internet-based business in knowledge- or technology-intensive sectors in California was characterized by high insecurity and uncertainty about the possibilities of value creation related to this new form of economic transaction. Above all, there existed uncertainty about how to open up new business fields that could create a space for a new category of Internet companies. At the same time, this pioneering phase was marked by a spirit of departure that developed its own social dynamic, and even allowed for the launch of immature business concepts. This tendency was particularly strong in California. In this region there was a dense environment of powerful, specialized service providers for knowledge- and technology-driven businesses that were willing to support the new Internet-based companies and mutually reinforced each other in their positive posture toward them. At the same time, high risks had to be accepted. Even though they were largely compensated by potentially high profit chances, they represented another aspect forming the perception of economic actors. Lacking prior experience in this new field, a general disposition of the influential innovation actors dominated to support unconventional, new business models that implied both high risks as well as important profit chances.

On the one hand, this lowered the threshold for experimenting with the new Internet-based business models. On the other hand, it favored behavioral patterns of lower rationality, since those new concepts could be based only on an incomplete knowledge of assured facts, instead of being based on a sufficiently large tacit knowledge, accumulated in the past. The major issue was to act quickly, hoping to profit from a time advantage over competitors in the realization of promising concepts. In that way, a small minority of long-term sustainable and continuously evolving concepts emerged that might not have been existed in the context of a more rational handling of risks. Inversely, it was virtually inevitable that an important majority of those companies had to fail. Failure as a mass phenomenon, and the diverse difficulties the companies were faced with, represented the costs of the learning process initiated at the same time. This lead to the formation of an early tacit knowledge in the field.

As we have seen in our case studies, the change in the legitimacy of Internet-related business models affected the development possibilities of the companies in an important way. The external support of the environment of the firms varied in function of this legitimacy. When the Internet bubble burst, the legitimacy of Internet start-ups was quite low, leading to the failure of numerous firms while creating more or less serious troubles for others. At the same time, there was a come-back of a much more rational-based economic behavior pattern. In the case of our first example, this meant that the accumulated debts, as well as the necessary restructuring of the business, in order to correct preceding errors, could no longer be financed, due to a suddenly restrictive attitude of investors. The company failed also because prior to the restructuring of the business, it did not get legitimacy from the central actors in the field of its activity. The large software producers were rather hostile to the idea of selling their products online through an intermediary Internet company. Thus, power relationships play a role too.

If the company failed, this does not necessarily mean that it was merely a victim of unfavorable contexts. It means only that the selected strategy was not suited to the particular context (independently from the question if there would have been the possibility for another, more successful strategy). In the second case of the small service firm working for the film industry we saw that, in fact, the firm had a certain margin of liberty to act or struggle against the effects of changing institutional environments, translated into increasing conflicts inside the overall organization. However, it was important for the entrepreneurs to see and analyze the problems in time, and to rapidly adopt a counterstrategy. In this respect, it mattered that they had a proven business concept and a considerable knowledge about the sector they were operating in, providing them with a fine perception of the problems. But even on this base, coping with the problems implied a very conflictual struggle that required assistance from a law firm, in order to defend their own position inside the new organization, and to get the firm out of the contract with the new partner, i.e. to buy it back. This was the only possibility to avoid the logic of downsizing, imposed by the effects of the legitimacy crisis of the Internet economy on the fusioned company, which would have been disastrous for the small firm, endangering its long-term perspective. In any case, it was a radical break in the firm's development, and the critical phase lasted for months (their own failure being sometimes very close). On the other hand, it shows that there was a solution and that the firm finally was able to succeed transforming itself into a modern Internet-based, knowledge-intensive service provider.

Notes

* This article is based on a research project supported by a grant of the Deutsche Forschungsgemeinschaft (DFG) and uses data collected during a stay of the author in 2001–2002 at the University of California, Los Angeles (UCLA).
1 There are already several publications available on the market about the failure of Internet start-ups, principally written from an autobiographical or journalistic perspective (Frey 2002). Examples are the books of Stephan Paternot (2001) or of David Kuo (about the ambitious e-commerce concept of Value America; see Kuo 2001). In addition, the subject has also been thematized by a documentary film in the United States ("STARTUP.COM," 2001, directed by Chris Hegedus and Jehane Noujaim).
2 For example, in 2000, the Californian service industries' share in total employment was close to 80 percent – 5 percent above the already high US level of 75 percent (US Department of Commerce, Bureau of Economic Analysis and California Employment Development Department).
3 "Due to the perception that Delaware's corporate law is 'business friendly,' many major corporations are incorporated in Delaware [...] Experts say Delaware is popular for bankruptcy filings because courts there are perceived as being faster, more predictable and friendlier to debtors. Delaware gets 60% of all major corporate filings nationwide and a third of those in Orange and Los Angeles counties since 1990" (Morin 2002: B2).
4 This development was favored by the important improvements in video game technology: " 'Ten years ago, video game characters were these crude things that were 5 pixels high, and you could compose the music on your telephone keypad' said Geoff Keighley, a journalist who has covered the industry for more than a decade. 'Now, they're using 80-piece orchestras and professional voice actors. As these new game consoles allow for more visual panache and sonic flare, there will be more demand for top creative talent to create these games. That just means more business for people here in Hollywood' " (Pham 2001: C6).
5 Most of the engineering programs of Southern Californian universities, for example, were financed by the defense industry.
6 These time-consuming social interactions are at the center of the work of the company, in order to obtain continuously new film-related information. This is reflected by the fact that the time spent by each of the entrepreneurs at different film festivals in the world easily sums up to six months a year. However, by attracting attention for its services offered and by getting in contact with potential customers, the festivals could be used at the same time as a marketing device for the company.

Bibliography

Aldrich, H.E. (1999) *Organizations Evolving*, London: Sage Publications.
Audretsch, D.B. (1995) *Innovation and Industry Evolution*, Cambridge: The MIT Press.
Bahrami, H. and Evans, S. (2000) "Flexible Recycling and High-Technology Entrepreneurship," in Kenney, M. (ed.) *Understanding Silicon Valley: The Anatomy of an Entrepreneurial Region*, Stanford: Stanford University Press.
Center for Continuing Study of the California Economy (ed.) (2001) *California Economic Growth*, Palo Alto: CCSCE.
Cooke, P., Heidenreich, M. and Braczyk, H.-J. (eds) (2004) *Regional Innovation Systems*, 2nd edn. London: Taylor & Francis.

Dickerson, M. (2002) "Unemployment Rate in California Dips to 6.3% in May but Payrolls Fall," *Los Angeles Times*, June 15: C1–C2.

DiMaggio, P.J. and Powell, W.W. (1991) "The Iron Cage Revisited: Institutional Isomorphism and Collective Rationality in Organization Fields," in DiMaggio, P.J. and Powell, W.W. (eds) *The New Institutionalism in Organizational Analysis*, Chicago: The University of Chicago Press.

Frey, C. (2002) "Closing Books on Dot-Coms – Memoirs: Dot-Com Journals," *Los Angeles Times*, January 2: A1, A32.

Hall, P.A. and Soskice, D. (2001) "An Introduction to Varieties of Capitalism," in Hall, P.A. and Soskice, D. (eds) *Varieties of Capitalism: The Institutional Foundations of Comparative Advantage*, Oxford: Oxford University Press.

Kenney, M. (ed.) (2000) *Understanding Silicon Valley: The Anatomy of an Entrepreneurial Region*, Stanford: Stanford University Press.

Kenney, M. and Florida, R. (2000) "Venture Capital in Silicon Valley: Fueling New Firm Formation," in Kenney, M. (ed.) *Understanding Silicon Valley: The Anatomy of an Entrepreneurial Region*, Stanford: Stanford University Press.

Kuo, J.D. (2001) *Dot.Bomb: My Days and Nights at an Internet Goliath*, Boston: Little, Brown & Company.

Lee, C.-M., Miller, W.F., Hancock, M.G. and Rowen, H.S. (eds) (2000) *The Silicon Valley Edge: A Habitat for Innovation and Entrepreneurship*, Stanford: Stanford University Press.

Leslie, S.W. (2000) "The Biggest 'Angel' of Them All: The Military and the Making of Silicon Valley," in Kenney, M. (ed.) *Understanding Silicon Valley: The Anatomy of an Entrepreneurial Region*, Stanford: Stanford University Press.

Morin, M. (2002) "Courts Working to Keep Bankruptcies Local," *Los Angeles Times*, March 13: B2.

National Science Board (2002) "Science and Engineering indicators," National Science Board. Available online at http://www.nsf.gov/sbe/srs/seind02/start.htm.

Numark, C. (1999) *Transition and Transformation: The Story of the South Bay Technology Community – a Study of Technology Companies and Industries in the South Bay of Los Angeles*, Los Angeles: Los Angeles Regional Technology Alliance, The South Bay Economic Development Partnership.

Paternot, S. (2001) *A Very Public Offering: A Rebel's Story of Business Excess, Success and Reckoning*, New York: John Wiley & Sons.

Pham, A. (2001) "Southland a Key Player in Game Industry," *Los Angeles Times*, November 11: C1, C6.

PricewaterhouseCoopers (2002) "MoneyTree Q1," PricewaterhouseCoopers. Available online at http://www.pwcmoneytree.com/moneytree/index.jsp.

Saxenian, A. (1994) *Regional Advantage: Culture and Competition in Silicon Valley and Route 128*, Cambridge: Harvard University Press.

Scott, A.J. (1993) *Technopolis: High-Technology Industry and Regional Development in Southern California*, Berkeley: University of California Press.

US Patent and Trademark Office (PTO) (2000) "1999 Patent Statistics Announced. Press Release #00–16," US Patent and Trademark Office, March 2.

Zucker, L.G. and Darby, M.R. (1999) *California's Inventive Activity: Patent Indicators of Quantity, Quality and Organizational Origins. A Report Prepared for the California Council on Science and Technology*, Sacramento: The California Council on Science and Technology.

11 The new economy assets of the Berlin metropolitan region

Development chances and threats

Stefan Krätke

Introduction

The "new economy" sector has been regarded as the most important growth machine of recent times as well as a big hope for many regional economies that are attempting to become centers of new growth. However, it does not yet have a precise definition. The new economy sector is frequently defined as including the broad range of information and communication industries and services as well as other "knowledge based" industries. This particularly comprises knowledge based and innovation driven sectors like the manufacturing of ICTs, the software industry (which is frequently regarded as part of the advanced producer services), the media industry with its growing sub-sector of "new media" and the Internet business and the contemporary "life sciences" sector with its sub-sectors of biotechnology and medical engineering. All these sectors recorded considerable growth in the period up to the year 2000. However, the real economic expansion of the various knowledge-based and innovation-driven industries should not be confused with the speculative exaggeration of their potential within the stock market which came to a sudden breakdown in 2000. The question "what is left of the new economy?" is related to the recent collapse of the new economy's stock market prices, in which many actors seemingly lost a tidy sum of money. However, a statement to one of those who endured considerable losses as a result of the 2000 new economy crash reveals that this is not the entire story. One of his professional colleagues said "don't worry, my friend – your money has not really *vanished*, it just belongs to someone *else!*" Indeed, those well versed actors who sold their new economy assets at the stock market's peak managed to achieve incredibly high financial returns.

Regarding the new economy's regional dimension, the most important feature of its spatial configuration is the formation of local and regional "clusters" in terms of a selective concentration of firms and supporting institutions in certain regions, particularly in the leading metropolitan regions. The concept of "regional production clusters" has assumed a prominent position in the institutional approaches which have been applied in economic geography and regional economics in recent times (Scott 1998; Scott *et al.* 2001; Krätke and Scheuplein 2001; Cooke 2002). This concept stems from the competitive advantages approach developed by Porter (1998, 2001). Talking about regional clustering of economic activities relates to the spatial concentrations of elements in a production chain (or value creating chain). The regional integration of companies and supporting institutions resulting from their transaction, co-operation and communication networks is one of the constitutive elements of clusters. Additionally, functioning production clusters rely on the cluster firm's supra-regional and international inter-links. The economic fabric of a given region might contain several different clusters with different activity profiles as well as economic branches without cluster qualities side by side. Particularly the metropolitan regions might be regarded as "superclusters" (Scott 2001b) which comprise, for example, a cluster of finance and business services, a media industry cluster, certain high-technology clusters, etc. These are not necessarily interlinked by direct transactional relations. In the light of the above mentioned differences between the regions in terms of their economic structure and the size, composition and network-ing qualities of their clusters, it becomes clear that there are various regional pathways to the new economy.

The cluster approach is highly relevant to the examination of the new economy's spatial configuration, since most sub-sectors of the new economy particularly show a clear tendency toward clustering in metro-politan regions. However, in countries with a polycentric urban and regional system (like Germany) we might identify several competing regional centers (clusters) of the new economy. Furthermore, we have to examine the competitive position of these clusters in an inter-regional comparative perspective: the development prospects of a certain regional cluster do not only depend on its own size and internal qualities but also on the development of other competing regional clusters.

This chapter examines the development of the new economy in the particular case of the Berlin metropolitan region; it focuses on the media industry as an important sub-sector of the new economy. The media indus-try is part of the knowledge- and information-intensive economic activ-ities. In Berlin it incorporates a considerably high share of firms and employees within the region's new economy assets. The first section pro-vides a short outline of Berlin's position as a center of knowledge-intensive ICTs; the second section deals with the relation between the new economy and the media industry; the third section examines the regional, national and global level of Berlin's media industry development; the last section discusses the role the new economy plays in overcoming the region's "backwardness."

Berlin's position as a center of knowledge-intensive industries and ICTs

While Berlin's reinstatement as the capital of Germany has triggered a building boom and raised great expectations of its transformation into a major economic center in the European urban system, large-scale de-industrialization (the number of industrial employees in Berlin dropped from 380,000 in 1990 to below 170,000 by 1998) has led to mass unemployment (at a rate of 17 percent in March 2002) and social polarization (Krätke and Borst 2000). The decline of Berlin as an industrial location is due to the closure of production sites in East Berlin and to the structural weakness of the industries in the western part of the city, which for decades had been able to use the special Berlin subsidies to expand the assembly line production of simple mass products. The termination of these special Berlin subsidies after 1990 led to factory closures and relocations. In the turbulent years following 1990, the city has not been able to fulfill many of the exaggerated expectations of its economic development.

Large cities and metropolitan regions are empirically characterized by major differences in their economic specialization profiles and the way their regional economies are organized. Such structural differences determine the development paths and varying competitiveness of these urban regions. The large metropoles might be regarded as a particular type of regional economy. According to the main lines of discussion in contemporary regional research, the internal differentiation, the innovative capacity and the institutional resources of regional economies are of strategic importance in determining regional futures (Storper 1997; Cooke 2002).

Since it is not possible to assess the size of Berlin's new economy directly through statistical data, we have to employ different modes of enquiry. First, the economic specialization profile of Berlin's regional economy can be demonstrated in a regionally comparative perspective; second, the size of particular sub-sectors of the new economy can be assessed. The varying regional economic specialization profiles of the metropolitan regions can be demonstrated by the number of people working in their economic sub-sectors (per 1,000 employees in the region). In comparison with Hamburg, Munich and Frankfurt-Main, in 1996 Berlin revealed a comparatively high employment in the state sector, in household-related services and in the building sector (which is related to the "capital city building boom"), along with a very low level of employment in R&D-intensive industries. Berlin also has a significantly smaller proportion of the workforce in the finance sector.

Berlin's business services and the culture and media industry sectors reveal no significant difference in the relative share of employees from other West German metropolitan regions. However, if we subdivide the business service sector, some cases of major differences in regional

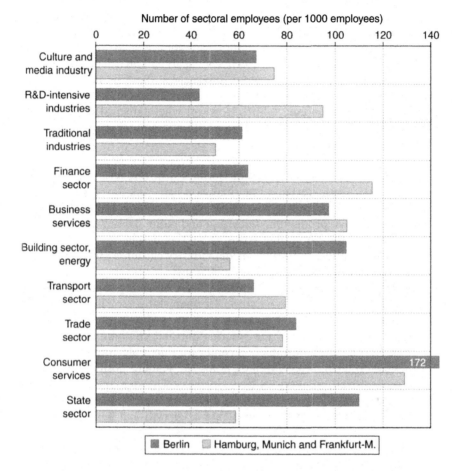

Figure 11.1 Regional economic profile of German metropolitan regions (1996): Berlin compared to Hamburg, Munich and Frankfurt.

economic specialization become apparent: in the field of enterprise-related services, Berlin today might be seen as the "capital of the cleaning squads and private security firms" (Krätke and Borst 2000). In office cleaning and security services sectors, Berlin ranks first among West German metropoles for its number of employees. However, the development potential for the regional economy rests with the much more important branches of "advanced producer services" like business consultancy, legal advice, or information and communication services.

With regard to the industrial sub-sectors, the metropolitan region of Berlin is a long way behind West German metropolitan regions in almost all branches of R&D-intensive industries. This grouping of industrial activities refers to their differing innovative capacity by using expenditure on

R&D as a criterion.[1] Berlin has only attained a strong position in the field of measuring and control engineering (including medical engineering). Meanwhile, Munich leads in manufacturing of electronic components and data processing technology; Hamburg and Munich lead in the aviation industry; the Frankfurt-Main region in chemicals and pharmaceuticals, etc.

With regard to the new economy sub-sectors, these findings at a first glance seem to indicate a comparative overall structural weakness of Berlin's regional economic fabric. However, the statistical data conceal that Berlin has reached a quite strong position in a number of sub-sectors of the new economy.

- The most important strength of Berlin lies in the culture and media industries. Thus, Berlin is regarded as a first rank "media city" (this shall be examined below in more detail). The culture and media industry include film production, television and radio, the new media, music production, the publishing trade as well as design agencies and the advertising industry. Berlin's media industry cluster is growing rapidly and today comprises more than 7,000 firms.
- Berlin has a strong position in the software industry, which is included as part of the business services in German statistics. Thus, the above indicated size of R&D-intensive industries does not comprise an important sub-sector of the information and communication industries. Berlin is not a production center for micro-electronics and data-processing technology (Munich holds the leading position beside its strong software industry; in East Germany, Dresden and Jena are the most important regional clusters). However, in the software industry the Berlin region reveals a high rate of growth and has developed a cluster of more than 1,700 specialized firms.
- Along with Munich, Berlin is a leading center of the European life-sciences sector which comprises biotechnology and medical engineering firms. In the biotechnology sub-sector, Berlin has one of the largest clusters of firms besides London and Cambridge, Paris, Zürich and Munich (Ernst & Young 1999). Altogether, the Berlin region reveals a high concentration of knowledge-intensive industries of the life-sciences sector with a cluster of roughly 300 specialized firms. These are backed by the strong presence of high ranking centers of medical services and related biomedical research institutions in Berlin. This particular strength is being concealed within the group of R&D-intensive industries because of Berlin's weak position in other sub-sectors of this group of industrial activities.

The above listing of Berlin's new economy sub-sectors indicates that in terms of a regional concentration of business establishments the *media industry cluster* represents the largest new economy asset of the Berlin metropolitan region.

The regional innovation system and economic development in Berlin

In view of the crisis in Berlin's traditional industries, urban economic development policy has focused on "innovative areas of technology," such as ICT, medical engineering, the media industry, pharmaceuticals and transport engineering (Senatsverwaltung für Wirtschaft 1997). The relatively large number of specialized firms in some of the aforementioned subsectors is regarded as being a location advantage of the Berlin economic area. However, little is known about real progress of the region's firms toward developing an innovative regional economy, including the link-up of research and production and the formation of dense transactional inter-firm links within the Berlin region.

Moves in this direction have been made by laser engineering companies in Adlershof, for instance, and in the field of medical engineering at the Zentrum Focus Mediport in Steglitz. Early in 1997, the Senate Department of Urban Development devised a new strategy (Senatsverwaltung für Stadtentwicklung 1997), which aimed at linking production activity with R&D establishments within locational integrated sites of production (local clustering of firms). The most important locational concentration of this kind is the research and technology district of Adlershof (Krätke 2000). This site is synonymous with the creation of a regional technopole, incorporating a large number of research institutions and technology-oriented, small-sized enterprises. However, the Adlershof Technology Forum has repeatedly drawn attention to the inadequate level of networking between the companies in Adlershof; most of the firms cooperate largely with other Berlin institutions outside the site itself while internal cooperation in Adlershof is on a low level. Berlin's position as a major technological research center is often documented with reference to the large number of university and non-university research institutes in the city. Relating to this, the metalworkers' union, IG Metall, has pointed to the inadequate linking-up of research and industry within the Berlin economic area; the industrial application of the research findings made in Berlin largely takes place in Stuttgart or Munich, where the manufacturing establishments of R&D-intensive industries are concentrated.

The development prospects of the previously cited innovative fields of technology in Berlin therefore significantly depend on the progress in building and maintaining regionally integrated production clusters in terms of dense inter-firm networking within the region in addition to the supra-regional and international business links (which are also highly relevant). The formation of clusters is attributed to gains in economic efficiency in the sphere of business transactions and information exchange as well as to the creation of a labor pool with special knowledge, experience and skills. Moreover, it is assumed that – in the long run – local production clusters can strengthen the companies involved as these clusters stimulate their learning and innovation capacity (Storper and Scott 1995) thanks to an informal network of information and exchange of specific knowledge. Local clustering within particular districts of a metropolis or within local technopoles can stimulate inter-firm cooperation. However, it is important to state that this says nothing about the quality and density of inter-firm relations within a local cluster.

Thus, in order to evaluate Berlin's regional innovation system, one needs to assess the quality of the institutional fabric and density of inter-firm networking within the region's innovative technology sectors. Note that a region's innovation system does not primarily refer to the presence of R&D-intensive economic sectors. Rather, it refers to the quality of the region's institutional setting in terms of the existence of production clusters with dense inter-firm relations and of the presence of (cluster-specific) supporting institutions which promote regional networking and innovation capacities as well as supra-regional linkages of the respective enterprise clusters. However, despite Berlin's economic development policy's many initiatives to promote regional inter-firm networks, the relational qualities of Berlin's innovative technology clusters have, to date, not been analyzed. One exception is the analysis of the local media industry cluster in Potsdam/Babelsberg, which is a part of the Berlin metropolitan region's media industry (Krätke 2002b).

A detailed network analysis of the film industry in Potsdam/Babelsberg comes to the conclusion that this particular media cluster matches the ideal notion of a functioning production cluster. Not only does it display an internal functional differentiation and intensive transaction and communications relations among the cluster firms, it also has a high level of supra-regional integration, i.e. a considerable amount of economic interlinks with film industry companies in other media locations at the national and international level. A dense network of relations within the cluster in combination with strong supra-regional connections can be seen as an advantage in furthering the innovative capacity of the cluster firms. In a nutshell, the structural features of the relational network represent a social capital of the Potsdam/Babelsberg cluster, which provides a dynamic impulse to the whole ensemble of cluster actors. In recent years, the Potsdam/Babelsberg film industry cluster recorded a considerable growth of employment and turnover.

Berlin's regional innovation policy has concentrated on a technology-centered approach in order to enhance the urban region's economic performance and to situate Berlin among other German regional systems within the international centers of competitive technology. In the 1990s, the city built up a variety of supporting institutions for the promotion and transfer of new technologies. These include the Technology Foundation Innovation Centre Berlin and the Berlin Technology Transfer Agency. Additionally, the city has provided innovative start-up firms with a number of financial supporting schemes. Furthermore, it has created a number of technology-oriented innovation and start-up centers which are clearly related to the above mentioned focus on promoting cluster building in innovative areas of technology.

We can distinguish two approaches to this cluster-oriented development policy. First, there are initiatives to promote regional inter-firm networking by means of spatially integrated (local) cluster building within the urban territory. These aim at creating local concentrations of complementary production and service firms together with research and development establishments. Examples of these kinds of initiatives are the Adlershof research and technology district, the Focus Mediport Centre in the urban district of Steglitz which concentrates on medical engineering firms and the Biomedical Research Campus Berlin-Buch which concentrates on biotechnology firms and research institutions. Since 1991 Berlin has established a considerable number of innovation and start-up centers. These are similar to the Berlin Innovation and Start-up Centre (BIG) in the urban district of Wedding which was created as a forerunner in 1983. In 1988, the city reported a total of 21 innovation and start-up centers (Senatsverwaltung für Wirtschaft 1998; Krätke and Borst 2000), which serve to support new start-up firms as well as the local concentration, information exchange and networking of complementary enterprises. However, it has been more and more realized among the initiators that in the local clusters too there is need for an active "cooperation management," since spatial nearness of firms and research establishments does not automatically lead to networking processes and the formation of integrated local production clusters.

Second, besides the spatially oriented approach there is an increasing number of institutionally centered initiatives toward the formation of regional inter-firm networks. Examples are the Enterprise Network for Mechanical and Transport Engineering Berlin-Brandenburg (ProNetz) founded in 1999, or the ProT.I.M.E. Enterprise Network in the fields of ICT and new media which was founded in 1996. These institutional initiatives for networking have not always been geared toward the inclusion of all the regional firms, particularly the small and medium enterprises. In some cases they primarily represent a sort of strategic alliance of the region's leading large firms. As an example, the member list of the ProT.I.M.E. network is clearly dominated by the resident big players and market leaders like Siemens, debis, Alcatel SEL, IBM and Telekom. This effect is further supported by the high annual contribution of 6,000 euro for participating firms. Nonetheless, the diversity and sheer number of initiatives that support innovation activities, regional cluster building and networking in particular fields of economic activity represent a strong point of Berlin's regional innovation system.

The new economy and the media industry

The media industry's activities include film production, television and radio productions, music production, the publishing trade, as well as design agencies and the advertising industry. All these fields of activity make use of new electronic media and the large media corporations have integrated new media such as the Internet within their extended value chains. Most of the media industry's sub-sectors are doing business with "image production" activities (Scott 1997). In today's marketing society these not only include the product images created by advertising and design agencies, but also the lifestyle images communicated via the entertainment and media industries' program formats. The content of image production activity has a particular spatial dimension in that the lifestyle images are being picked up in certain localities by the media industry's trendscouts for the purpose of commercialization. The media industry acts as a focus for the commercialization of cultural production and is also located at the heart of the "culturalization of the economy," given that its market success is based on the construction of images and extensive marketing activities.

As an information and entertainment industry, the media industry actually is part of the old economy; in the industrialized countries the media industry came into existence a long time ago and has shown a relative stable development and long-term expansion as compared to other branches of the old economy such as the textile industry. First, this is connected with a long-term expansion of media consumption and the insaturable demand for continuously new products and program of information and entertainment in terms of the content supply. Second, it is connected with the continuing innovation process in the culture and media industries which not only create their products and programs with rapidly changing contents but also integrate new ICTs and media in their production processes and distribution channels. This old – and at the same time highly innovative economic sector – particularly profits from ICT's contemporary technological innovation waves.

In contrast to this view, the media industry today is frequently regarded as an important part of the so-called new economy, particularly as many of the media firms with a stock exchange quotation are included in stock market's new economy branch. However, it is impossible to make a clear distinction between the new media sub-sector and the media industry as a whole, since there is a strong tendency of media convergence. Additionally, new media activities are to a large extent being integrated into the value chain of large diversified media corporations. Altogether, the new economy is a somewhat confused grouping of firms which run their business with ICTs, with electronic media including new media like the Internet, with new markets in the field of electronic commerce and, in the case of the life-sciences sector, with new branches of knowledge-intensive industries. At the same time it is a circumscription of management concepts which bet on a high scale of flexibility of work and employment relations and on a maximization of shareholder value.

Both new as well as long established firms of the media industry have been included into the new economy not only because of their association with information, communication and electronic media, but also for the purpose of marketing. Up to the recent collapse of the new economy's stock market prices this sector was regarded as a quite attractive growth machine which was untouchable by business cycles and crisis. Before the new economy's stock market collapsed in 2000, firms in the Internet and the e-commerce business had for years scored a tremendous rise of their (often quite fictitious) stock market prices. On this basis, they could mobilize a large amount of "fresh money" to finance their activities. However, the supporters of the new economy lacked a closer understanding of the real economy's developmental interrelations. They thus overlooked the fact that newly founded Internet services or new e-commerce enterprises in the long run really need to sell their services and goods to real world customers. This is quite similar to the railway companies, which 150 years ago could not remain in their start-up euphoria but had to really transport goods and people in order to make non-fictitious profits.

In this way there continues to exist a strong connection between the new economy and the demand coming from the old economy which stands for the majority of potential customers of its products and services. This also applies to those Internet firms, which supply information and communication services within the publicity sector of the media industry and thus rely on advertising income from old economy firms. At the same time, the old economy enterprises are themselves engaged in technological and product innovations, so that they are important clients of the ICT producers within the new economy. Thus a simple dualistic division between the "new" and "old" economy branch is highly questionable.

Additionally, it should be emphasized that new media like the Internet do not at all open up unlimited economic growth perspectives, since a large share of the investment in websites and electronic network infrastructures does not serve an overall market expansion but rather competition on individual firms' market-shares. Many firms are using the Internet as an additional advertising media besides others, which increases their information and communication expenditure but not necessarily their turnover. Regarding the future prospects of the Internet economy, the most striking problem is not to bring the firms into the Internet, but to bring the Internet into the firms.

For the media industry firms it is also relevant that many of the contents that are meant to be distributed via the Internet are being supplied by already existent content producers. These contents are at the same time provided in different kinds of media. However, this does not mean that the media consumers might arbitrarily extend the amount of time for media consumption. In 2000, the per head media consumption time in Germany already amounted to 8.5 hours per day on average, wherein television and radio held the largest share. Thus old and new media are competing with each other. In this competition the old media such as print media, broadcasting, cinema and television are not driven out of the market. Instead, on the side of producers, we are experiencing the integration of old and new media; the large media companies act in different fields of media production at the same time and particularly organize a multiple exploitation of the same content through different media channels. This is also one of the driving forces of concentration and globalization processes in the media industry.

There is still another critical point of the new economy to be mentioned: it is true that the new economy is only partially represented by media industry firms. However, concerning the flexibilization of work relations and the expanding sector of self-employed freelancers, the culture and media industries can be regarded as forerunners of a rather problematic trend which has been carried to extremes in the new economy: the pronounced polarization between the group of privileged flexible employees and the group of flexible workers with precarious employment conditions. For a large share of employees in the culture and media industries, particularly the frequently used freelancers, socially protected forms of employment had been rather irregular for many years. Within the so-called new economy, this pattern has been further extended. The privileged group of flexible employees in the media industry contained primarily the stars of the industry's entertainment branch and it has expanded to include the highly skilled specialized Internet and multimedia experts (Haaren and Hensche 1997; Gottschall and Schnell 2000).

In 2000, the big bubble of the new economy collapsed and in early 2001 there was hardly a German new economy share that had not lost 70–90 percent of its stock market value. After some years of tremendous gains not only many smaller start-ups and dot.com firms' stock market prices experienced a radical fall, but also most of the large companies in the Internet economy and the ICT sector were hit by severe losses. This radical downturn also applied to the Internet firms and their content providers within the media industry and thus the crisis also affected the large, more diversified media firms. In the big bubble's inflation phase, a sharp increase in stock market prices had been recorded for new economy firms which frequently had nothing more to offer than just a good basic idea.

However, the collapse of the new economy's stock market prices doesn't mean that the majority of the established firms in the information and communication technology sector and in the media industry have been failing. Rather, it indicates a failure of speculation in these growth sectors. Nonetheless, this has also indirectly hit the firms with a real economic base and ability to survive. This is the case because the survivors as well as the latest newcomer firms in the media and ICTs are being confronted with increasing difficulties in raising investment funds for their business on the stock market.

Berlin's position as an upcoming media industry center

Among the "media cities"[2] of the German regional system, Berlin has revealed a considerable growth in importance during the last ten years, as opposed to the comparatively weak development of its regional economy and its continuing labor market crisis. Whereas the number of firms in the German media industry grew by 6 percent between 1994 and 1998, the growth of firm numbers in Berlin amounted to nearly 10 percent (Krätke 2002a). In 1998 the culture and media industry in Berlin comprised a total of 9,103 establishments (firms and self-employed freelancers together) and thus represented a larger sub-sector of the regional economy than the advanced producer services which recorded a total number of 8,031 establishments. These results have been underlined by a recent report on Berlin's media industry (Medienbüro Berlin-Brandenburg 2001), that shows a considerable growth of the number of resident media firms in Berlin from 2000 to 2001: the advertising industry, for example, recorded a 27 percent increase, the film industry a 22 percent increase, the music industry and the publishing sector a 17 percent increase.

The new economy sub-sector of multimedia firms experienced the sharpest increase: within one year (2000–2001), their number grew by 92 percent to a total of 855 firms. Surprisingly, this growth acceleration started at the same time as the collapse of the new economy stock market. However, insiders of the Berlin multimedia branch feel that this particular development can actually be interpreted as an outcome of the new economy crisis. The collapse in 2000 also hit the Berlin multimedia firms, particularly the Internet business. The failures of firms and employees' dismissive attitude in this sub-sector were driving forces for a large number of discharged multimedia specialists to immediately establish new start-up firms. They hoped to remain in the sector and to gain success with new business concepts or to get an acquisition offer from the strong established companies in the new media sector.

However, the Berlin metropolitan region remains a strong and dynamic locational center of the media industry. In 2000, the regional chamber of commerce published a survey among the resident firms in the sub-sectors of the media and information and communication industries to evaluate the city's particular strengths and weaknesses (IHK 2000). According to this, the media industry firms regard the availability of highly qualified creative employees, the local media culture in terms of the local clustering of many specialist firms and institutions and the city's cultural attractiveness as the most important strength of the region. Meanwhile, the urban government's political support for the media sector got the poorest judgment. The resident ICT firms emphasize Berlin's R&D capacities as the region's most important strength, as well as the availability of highly qualified specialist personnel, the local clustering of many specialist firms and service providers and the high quality of the telecommunication infrastructure.

The Berlin metropolitan region (including Potsdam/Babelsberg) holds a leading position in the particular field of post-production activities of the film industry. In the year 2000, of the recorded 211 specialist firms for digital image processing and computer animation in the German film industry 25 percent were located in the Berlin metropolitan region, whereas Munich and Hamburg held a share of 13 percent respectively, Frankfurt-Main 9 percent and Cologne 7 percent (Krätke and Scheuplein 2001). The digital post-production and computer animation activities represent a field of intersection between the media and information technology industries (including software development). These activities reveal a particularly strong dynamic in those locational centers which have a clustering in both sub-sectors (which applies not only to Berlin, but also to Los Angeles etc.).

Regarding the spatial organization of Berlin's media industry, the most important characteristic is the formation of local enterprise clusters within the inner urban area of the metropolis (Krätke 2002a). This is particularly well illustrated in the multimedia sector. The Berlin media industry contains a cluster of multimedia firms of considerable size (with 424 establishments in 2000 and more than 800 recorded in 2001). Today, many well known multimedia agencies like Pixelpark, Aperto, MetaDesign and others are located in Berlin and the start-up activities are continuously strong. Against this background, Berlin is now the second largest location of Internet firms in Germany after Munich. The knowledge- and technology-intensive multimedia firms are regarded as an important sub-sector of the new economy. The recent crisis has particularly hit the multimedia sector and the Internet firms. Thus, the former growth euphoria has vanished and is being replaced by the expectation that a certain number of the currently existing firms might not be able to maintain their hold on the market. As a result, there is still a high fluctuation of start-ups and failures. Within the urban spatial fabric of Berlin, the multimedia firms are concentrated in a number of local clusters, most of which are located in the densely built and mixed use inner urban area.

The largest concentration can be found in the eastern city center and extends to the central part of the adjacent inner urban district of Prenzlauer Berg as well as to the newly built Potsdamer Platz area. Within the "City East," multimedia firms are clustered for example in the Chaussee-Street (which is popularly referred to as "silicon alley"), where the European New Media Center is being built. In the outer urban area we find a local clustering of multimedia firms within the Adlershof "technology and research district." The so-called Media City Adlershof contains 126 media

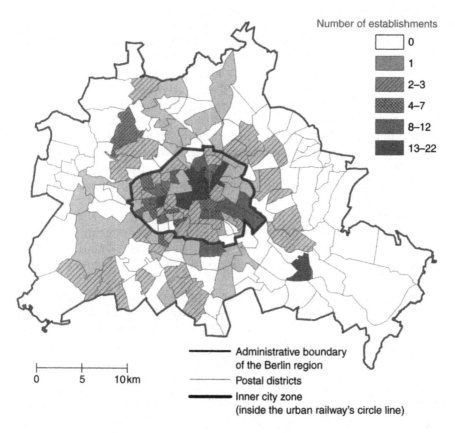

Number of establishments

□	0
▨	1
▨	2–3
▨	4–7
■	8–12
■	13–22

0   5   10 km

――――― Administrative boundary
            of the Berlin region

――――― Postal districts

▬▬▬▬ Inner city zone
            (inside the urban railway's circle line)

Figure 11.2 Local clustering of the media industry in Berlin (2000): multimedia
firms (producers and service providers).

firms (in 1998) which can set up links with the many specialized firms of
the ICT sector located in Adlershof. Another local concentration of digital
media firms outside the inner urban area of Berlin is the Media City
Potsdam/Babelsberg, located on the fringes of the metropolis.

It is important to note that most local clusters of the multimedia branch
in Berlin coincide with local concentration areas of other media industry
sub-sectors, particularly the film industry. The fact that Berlin has a
number of common local concentration areas of firms from different
media industry sub-sectors (Krätke 2002a) might indicate that the actors
involved share common locational preferences. These include the high
demand for a dense local environment of differently specialized media
industry firms, which is being appreciated in terms of a creativity-boosting
atmosphere regardless of the actual existence of inter-firm transactional
relations.

The spatial concentration of the media industry within the urban area of Berlin is related to several influencing factors. Most of the newly established media firms prefer to locate themselves in the inner urban districts in which living and working environments merge with leisure-time culture. For corporate operators and employees in the media industry the local connection between working, living and leisure time activities is an attraction factor that is in harmony with their lifestyle. These people deliberately seek out locations in a sub-cultural urban district that they can use as an extended stage for self-portrayal during working hours and in their leisure time. In the local media clusters there is thus a direct link between certain lifestyle forms and urban organization forms of production space and thus a clear overlapping of the geographies of production and consumption. Particularly in the inner urban districts (like Prenzlauer Berg) the actors of the media scene are contributing to a process of revaluation and gentrification of inner urban localities (as pioneers or real gentrifiers). However, the new economy and media industry establishments might take a location anywhere in the urban spatial fabric, wherever they can find premises for rent equipped with electricity, phone and Internet connections.

Nonetheless, the majority of these firms prefer "sexy" inner city locations. First, the actors of the media scene regard these areas as the best urban environment for a particular lifestyle which consciously combines working and leisure time activities locally within culturally attractive districts. Second, there is no scarcity of premises for rent in Berlin's inner urban districts. Third, in the inner urban districts the firms can find a supply of specialized producer services within short distance. Fourth, the close proximity of other enterprises active in the same industry is a strong pull factor of the existent local media clusters. In some local areas the actors might find the whole value chain of a particular new economy branch being represented by firms within one single building. Additionally, the local cluster formations might contribute to an intensification of communication links between the firms (without a need for formal cooperation agreements) and thus create a space of opportunities which is welcomed particularly by the start-up firms that are facing many uncertainties. Thus, the striving for risk reduction is also a quite important factor of local clustering.

Despite these inner urban location factors the overall concentration of culture and media industry firms in Berlin is an attracting factor with regard to the business opportunities being offered by a metropolitan cluster formation. The institutional infrastructures and the knowledge pool of a metropolitan cluster have to be mentioned as well. All these points underline that the media firms of different sub-sectors in Berlin can profit from socially produced locational advantages in the same way as in other large centers of this industry (Krätke 2002a).

Moreover, the city as a whole can become an attracting factor in that the symbolic quality of the specific location is either incorporated into the products of the culture and media industry or the origin of these products itself becomes a mark of quality (Scott 1997). Hence, production locations such as New York, Paris and Berlin are perceived in the sphere of culture and the media as being brand names that draw attention to the attractive social and cultural qualities of the cities concerned. This includes, in particular, the perception of Berlin as a social space in which there is a special variety of different social and cultural milieus. With regard to the content and design of their products, cultural production and media industry companies have to contend with rapidly changing trends. For that reason there is a desire to be close to the source of new trends, i.e. the sub-cultures that develop in certain metropolises, such as New York, Paris and Berlin. Cities of this kind are perceived as constituting a social and cultural potential marked by great openness. This in turn enhances their attractiveness for creative talents and makes them a source of inspiration for cultural producers. A marked social and cultural variety and openness, therefore, represents a specific cultural capital for a city, which is highly attractive for certain economic activities and players. This form of a city's cultural capital is concentrated to a special extent in large metropolises and it acts as an additional agglomerative factor in the (selective) concentration of the culture and media industries in the urban system.

Berlin's position among Germany's media cities

The German regional system contains a number of competing media cities in terms of large regional production clusters in the culture and media industries which are selectively concentrated in the large metropolitan regions (Krätke 2002a). Thus, the urban media clusters are being involved in the locational competition of metropolitan regions on the national as well as on the international scale. However, the media centers reveal a differing mix of their most important media industry sub-sectors. The leading German media cities are characterized by an absolute concentration of firms and employees in all sub-sectors of the media industry, i.e. they can make use of cross-sectoral impulses. The most important media cities in Germany might be identified by selecting the regions belonging to the ten largest centers by the number of employees in different sub-sectors of the culture and media industry.

According to this criterion, the German regional system's culture and media industry has five prime centers which are among the absolutely largest centers in all different sub-sectors. The prime centers are Berlin, Munich, Hamburg, Cologne and Frankfurt-Main. There are also some media cities which belong to the largest centers in only two media industry sub-sectors such as Düsseldorf and Stuttgart with a strong position in the sub-sectors of advertising and publishing. Thus, in a comparative perspective, Berlin is a prime center of the German media industry. However, it

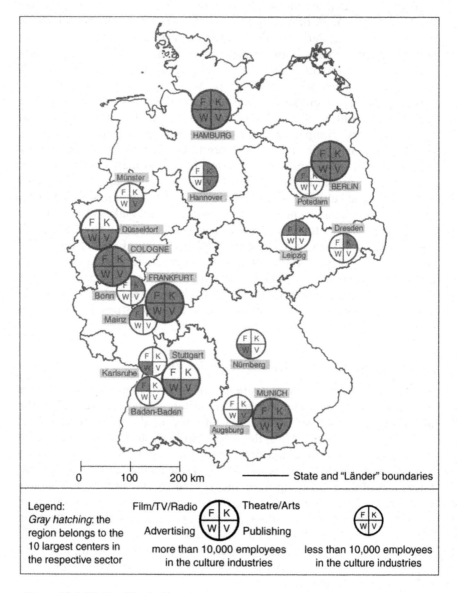

Figure 11.3 Media cities in Germany.

has strong competitors not only on the international scale, but also within the German regional system.

Note that the large firms in the media industry frequently have located their establishments in various important regional media centers. This allows them to make use of all the particular regional production and innovation capacities and to profit from the media cities' locational competition. In this way the various regional clusters of the German media industry are being interlinked in terms of the organizational networks of large media firms which strive to be present in all of the large media centers and take part in the respective local media clusters' inter-firm transaction and communication networks.

Berlin's position as a "global media city"

Like other sub-sectors of the new economy, the media industry is a prime mover for globalization processes in the urban system, in which media industry clusters act as local nodes in the global networks of the large mediá groups. New communication technologies and the emergence of large multinational groups within the culture and media industries con-tribute to a global flow of cultural forms and products (Held *et al.* 1999). Since the 1970s, the liberalization and deregulation of the telecommunica-tions and media industries have led to the globalization of the corporate media sector. However, this situation cannot be taken as indicative of a trend toward the global homogenization of cultural consumption. The global companies in the culture and media industries are obliged to take account of specific tastes and cultural preferences in other countries and regions.

The producers and market strategists employed by global media firms are well aware of the cultural variety and differentiation of their global audiences, customers and consumers and have long given their products and programs a regional touch with a view to stabilize or enhance their global market success. In other words, they have adapted their products and programs to specific regional or national tastes and cultural preferences. A good example of this is the successful global TV music broadcaster, MTV, which does not simply reproduce the content of the MTV program in the USA for consumption in all the other regions of the world, but has set up a series of regional MTV channels (including several for the European region alone), which produce and vary the program in accordance with regional tastes and preferences. At the same time, this trend toward cultural market differentiation is a driving force for the organization of global production *networks* in the culture and media industries with local anchoring points in different regions and nation-states.

The media industry is not only characterized by a growing concentra-tion on a world scale and the geographical concentration and formation of clusters in a series of metropolitan regions and global cities, but also by a marked trend toward the globalization of corporate organization (Robins 1995; Pratt 2000). The huge media groups not only occupy a prominent position in the culture industry of individual countries, but are also creat-ing an increasingly global network of branch offices and subsidiaries. This global network of establishments linked under the roof of a media group has its local anchoring points in the leading culture and media industry centers of the worldwide urban system.

First, it should be emphasized, however, that the globalization strategy pursued by media companies is primarily geared toward market development and the extension of market penetration through the establishment of a presence in the major international centers of the media industry. Second, the globalization strategy of media companies reveals a strong orientation toward enhancing their innovative capacity for the simple reason that a presence in the leading centers of cultural production gives the global media groups the chance to incorporate the cultural industry's latest fashion trends as quickly as possible through their integration into the respective local clusters of the regional economy. At the same time, it allows them to exploit the latest technological developments in the media sector (e.g. in digital image processing, special effects, transmission technologies and Internet applications). The global players in the culture industry network at the local level corporate with the small specialized producers and service providers. They thereby establish a global network of their branch offices and subsidiary companies, which links the internationally distributed urban centers of cultural production with one another. The global media groups organize the worldwide marketing of their respective cultural products and thus contribute to the global spread of media content and formats, which are generated in the production centers of the global culture industry, in particular in Los Angeles, New York, Paris, London, Munich and Berlin. Within processes of globalization, the globally operating media firms are at least as influential as the global providers of corporate services, because they create a cultural market of global dimensions on the basis of which the specialized global service providers can ensure the practical management of global production and market networks.

Most of the studies on global cities and the international urban system reveal a tendency to reduce the high-ranking world cities to their function as financial centers and centers providing specialized corporate services (Sassen 1991). In other words, they underestimate the role these cities play as locations for industrial production and as centers of the generation of knowledge and industrial innovation. The debate on new industrial spaces and technology districts, in particular, contains numerous references to the major role that global city regions continue to play in industrial development (Scott 1998; Schamp 2000). In many cases they provide central locations for new knowledge-based production chains and for highly innovative production clusters in the fields of ICT, medical engineering, biotechnology, the media industry, etc. These urban innovation centers for new and old industries are often characterized by extensive networking within metropolitan areas and by strong supra-regional connections with innovation centers in other countries' metropolitan regions. Thus, the relations between innovative companies in the high-technology clusters of

Munich and San Francisco (Silicon Valley) contribute to the worldwide networking of industrial innovation processes. The economic and functional changes in position of the global cities are today determined by processes of selective concentration of global service capacities as well as innovative industrial capacities. In their recent joint publication on "Global City Regions," Scott *et al.* emphasize the diversity of economic sectors which tend toward agglomeration in the global city regions and which together transform these centers into "regional motors of the world economy." Thus, it is important to emphasize globalization's geographical complexity which cannot be reduced to a simple hierarchy of global cities with global service providers.

An analysis of the location networks of global media groups makes it possible to trace the global structure of media cities as an interlocking network of internationally operating media firms in the same way as global city research has done with regard to advanced corporate services (Beaverstock *et al.* 1999; Taylor and Hoyler 2000; Taylor and Walker 2001). Global media firms have established a network of branch offices, subsidiaries and holding companies that are distributed worldwide across a series of cities. The creation of branch offices or subsidiary companies around the world allows for quicker and more direct linkages with potential clients in the respective region, particularly in those places where new media services are entering a phase of expansion.

The production cluster of the film industry in Potsdam/Babelsberg on the outskirts of Berlin represents an example that illustrates that cluster firms are not only closely networked on a local scale, but are also integrated into the supra-regional location networks of global media companies. In the case of Babelsberg, the local cluster firms are directly linked with the resident establishments of global media firms in Paris, London and New York and indirectly linked with other global players in the film and TV industry thanks to their business relations with the media firms that are resident in Berlin. In other words, the global players in the culture industry network locally with the small specialist producers and service providers, while at the same time they run a global network of branch offices and subsidiaries that permits global linking of the urban centers of cultural production.

Starting from this basic concept of a multi-scale interlocking network, an empirical study was conducted on the business location networks of 33 global media firms with a total of 2,766 enterprise units (Krätke 2002a). To qualify as global, a media company had to have a presence in at least three different national economic areas and at least two continents or world regions (USA/Canada/Latin America; Europe; Asia/Australia; Africa). The geographical organization of global media firms should not be interpreted as a star-shaped hierarchical structure, but rather as a network of business units (acting on their own responsibility), between which there are many different information and communication flows that enable special regional or local impulses and customer requirements to be picked up and processed in a flexible manner on a global scale. In a global media city there is a partial overlapping between the location networks of several global media firms in the urban economic space. Here, the local and the global firms in the media industry are linked in a joint development context that can foster the formation of an urban media cluster, whose international business relations are handled primarily via the present global media firms.

The result of this analysis is a ranking of cities based on the number of enterprise units (establishments) of global media firms that are located in the respective metropolitan region. The media industry's world cities were distinguished by means of two criteria and divided into three groups: alpha, beta and gamma world media cities.[3] The analysis illustrates the markedly unequal distribution of the global media firms' establishments over a small number of cities: over 50 percent of the branch offices and subsidiary companies of global media groups are concentrated in just 22 centers of the worldwide urban system. The organizational units of the globalized media industry reveal a highly selective locational concentration on a global scale. The network of global media cities as a whole is a reflection of the locational system run by the western-style media industry, which is concentrated mainly in North America and Europe.

Prominent among the alpha world media cities are New York, London, Paris and Los Angeles, which are ranked as genuine global cities in virtually every analysis of the global urban system. They are also designated here as world cities in the media industry. However, one needs to be aware that there are interesting deviations from the widely employed global city system. Based on this analysis, the alpha group of global media cities also includes Munich, Berlin and Amsterdam. In global city research, which focuses on corporate services, these cities are ranked as (third-rate) gamma world cities (Beaverstock *et al.* 1999). In the system of global media cities, by contrast, Munich, Berlin and Amsterdam are included in the top group.

Of the 33 global media groups included in the analysis between 18 and 29 are to be found in the alpha group cities, the most located in London (with a presence of 29 global firms and a total of 180 establishments), followed by Paris (26/129) and Los Angeles (25/111). Of course, New York (22/185) also assumes an outstanding position. Additionally, Munich (with 20 global firms and a total of 96 establishments), Berlin (19/70) and Amsterdam (18/64) have achieved a degree of integration into the location networks of global media firms that qualifies them as internationally outstanding centers in the contemporary media industry.

Berlin, in particular, could perceive the message spelled out by this analysis as a reason to make the media industry core area of its economic development policy and to further enhance the local creative potential of

Figure 11.4 Global media cities in Europe: classification based on local concentrations of global media firms' establishments in European cities 2001.

the culture and media sector as a world media city's important factor of attraction. The analysis indicates that Berlin is a city that is now (once again) gaining worldwide importance, especially in cultural production and the media industry. Berlin's international reputation as a cultural metropolis was an important urban development factor in the 1920s. This reputation can now be restored on the basis of *current* economic developments. However, while Berlin still does not rank as a global city defined as an economic center with global control capacities and as a center of strategic corporate services (Krätke and Borst 2000), it is a first-rank global media city with a worldwide significance and impact.

Thus, as far as the media industry is a part of the new economy, we might say that in this particular sub-sector of the new economy Berlin can be placed among the world's leading centers. As a result, its long-term regional economic development policy can build on this strength, even if the new economy's stock market crisis also affects some of the large media firms like Pixelpark which are an integral part of Berlin's media industry cluster. Concerning the German media cities' global connectivity, Berlin and Munich are in the alpha group, while Hamburg is included in the group of beta world media cities and Cologne in the group of gamma world media cities. Frankfurt, which generally appears in the first rank group in other global city research which concentrates on the finance sector and corporate services, forms part of the second-rank group in the analysis of global media cities. Altogether, an analysis of the global connectivity of regional media centers identifies the cities and regions, which function as key nodes of the global media firms' organizational networks. This analysis emphasizes that there is not one single over-arching hierarchy of world cities and thus it highlights that we have to be aware of the globalization's diversity of geographies.

The role of the new economy with regard to Berlin's development prospects

Despite the structural weakness of the city's regional economy, prominent representatives of the city do believe in a possible future of Berlin as a major European economic center and a global city and have been trying to market the city as an "international node within the world's network of growth sectors" (Ewers 1999: 68). This vision has become part of the urban governments' program of innovation and technology development in 1999 (Senatsverwaltung für Stadtentwicklung 1999). Previous sections illustrated that Berlin has attained the status of a first rank global media city today. However, the government has been primarily engaged with regional marketing and did not perceive the city's cluster formations as prosperous development prospects.

In German cities, political decision-makers have a varying knowledge of the content of regional innovation systems (Braczyk *et al.* 1998, 1999). Hence they often employ innovation as little more than a fashionable paraphrase for the well-known fixation on high technology. Nevertheless, there are innovative European initiatives regarding the development of strategies for regional and urban innovation policy. In 1999, a strategy for a competence-based economic development of urban regions was presented as part of the European "Cities' Dialogue Initiative" (Initiative für Städtedialog III 1999). The competence-based strategy of urban development focused on the quality of the urban economies' institutional fabric and it is closely bound up with strategies for knowledge-based and innovation-oriented urban development. It emphasizes that the prospects for a successful urban economic development policy are best in two cases. First, wherever local or regional *clusters* of specialized firms and related institutions can be identified (and fostered or extended); related institutions include research and education facilities, the regional state's support, the region's business and labor organizations. Second, wherever it proves possible to bring these firms and players together via networking and cooperation for an extensive exchange of knowledge, specific skills and ideas for innovation. What we are talking about here is information that is not generally available, but specialist knowledge which is frequently based on experience concentrated at the regional and local level. These clusters emerge in certain competence areas, which often go beyond the outdated statistical branch divisions of the urban and regional economy and are linked with one another in a new way; in the multimedia production competence area, for instance, certain technology producers and specialized producers from the media industry cooperate with various specialized service providers.

Similar to Berlin, many European cities are attempting to become regional competence centers in those areas which rank as future growth areas in the European and global economy. The standard list includes ICT, telematics, medical engineering, biotechnology, environmental engineering, the new media, culture and education, etc. (Initiative für Städtedialog III 1999). Individual cities frequently make a special selection from this list. First, problems arise here because the competence center strategy is mostly reduced to the same high-tech sectors. Therefore, many cities and regions tend to overlook – or fail to identify properly – the specific competence areas they could develop. Second, insufficient attention is often paid to the very different employment effects of the prominent innovative areas of growth, although the labor market situation and the social development of many European cities would indicate that priority needs to be given to a development policy which moves in this direction.

It has been established above that Berlin has a relatively strong competitive position in three sub-sectors of the knowledge-based and innovation-intensive industries which are included in the new economy. These are (in order of the respective clusters' size in terms of the number of firms) the media industry, secondly the software industry and thirdly the life-sciences sector (biomedical research and development, biotechnology and medical engineering). Berlin's regional innovation policy has also created a variety of supporting institutions to promote the development of these clusters. However, it has not presented an analysis of their particular strengths and weaknesses and of their competitiveness with regard to the respective clusters in other cities of the German and the European urban system, while putting emphasis on superficial urban *marketing* initiatives. Most importantly, by following a technology-centered approach it has widely ignored the differing employment effects of the above listed innovative areas of growth. The role of these new economy sub-sectors to overcome the backwardness of the Berlin region should be evaluated not only with regard to the number of established firms and new start-ups (cluster size) and their technological performance quality, but also with regard to their possible contribution to the growth of employment in the region. In 1999, the Berlin media industry cluster and the ICT sector (particularly the software industry cluster) together employed roughly 100,000 persons, of which nearly 25,000 were self-employed freelancers. Thus, there is a quite high contribution of these particular new economy sub-sectors to the region's labor market. On the other hand, the entrepreneurial life-sciences sector in Berlin employed not more than 3,500 persons which is a tiny number as related to the metropole's labor market situation.

However, the biotechnology cluster not only lies well behind the labor-intensive areas of the media and culture industry, most of the existent biotechnology firms in Berlin do not yet have a marketable product to offer. As a result, the development prospects of this particular new economy sub-sector cannot be judged seriously. The life-sciences sector's contribution to employment would be much higher if we include the bio-medical R&D activities and medical services, i.e. if we concentrated on the development of a regional center of competence which comprises not only biotechnology and medical engineering, but also biomedical research and medical services. This possible orientation is being hindered by the pre-dominance of a *technology*-centered approach in Berlin's innovation policy. Furthermore, a re-orientation is threatened by the new government's intention to close down one of the city's large public medical R&D centers (the Free University's clinic) as part of a policy which deals with the city's financial crisis in a very short-sighted manner.

The predominance of a technology-centered approach in Berlin's innovation policy applies also to the media industry, which proves to play a quite important role in Berlin's regional economy as regards its high share of employment and growth dynamic. Previous sections have argued that this dynamic to a large extent stems from the city's cultural capital and from its locational attractiveness in terms of being a center of cultural production in all of the cultural economy's activities, which cannot be reduced to the media industry's technology-intensive activities. Berlin is a center of competence in the culture industry as a whole, with a high degree of product differentiation, specific know-how and performance capacities. However, among the resident media firms, the urban government's support for the media has got a rather bad reputation. From a broader perspective on the city's cultural economy, other important actors of the region's cultural production cluster such as the large number of creativity boosting experimental cultural establishments are today being threatened by the urban government's policy of sharp financial cuts in order to deal with Berlin's financial crisis.

Altogether, there are many reasons for a new orientation and a more suitable focusing of Berlin's regional innovation policy in order to strengthen the existent clusters of knowledge-based economic activities. However, such a re-orientation is being hindered by the catastrophic effects of Berlin's financial crisis which has been actively produced by the former urban government in setting up a large public financial corporation (the Berlin Bank Corporation) that engaged in failed speculative real estate bonds and, leaving the city with an unexpected financial burden of several billion euro. It should be highlighted that members of Berlin's political class are continuing to make private profits from the speculative real estate bonds which are protected by public guarantees of profits and were exclusively offered to Berlin's politicians and affluent citizens. In a broader view, these speculative financial activities and the related policy are also part of the new economy in terms of an ideological conception of the new economy which bets on financial investments and deals including real estate business. This kind of new economy has the strongest support of Berlin's political class which used to confuse regional economic development with finance and real estate business (Krätke and Borst 2000) and actively took part in these activities. Today, the financial collapse stemming from this particular urban development policy is indirectly damaging the prospects of Berlin's innovative clusters and its productive new economy sub-sectors. In a nutshell, the ideological new economy has been nagging at Berlin's real new economy assets.

Conclusion

To come to a short conclusion, two points need to be emphasized. First, the comprehensive term "new economy" covers a wide range of economic activities which should not be confused with regard to their different institutional settings and development prospects. This might cause the terms to become misleading when it comes to the assessment of a region's industrial clusters and its innovation policy. Second, we need to make a distinction between four different dimensions of the new economy. One of these is the regions' real economic capacities in knowledge-based and innovation-intensive industries (the Berlin case study has concentrated on this dimension). However, the particular branches of such activity should not be lumped together under the common heading of a new economy. Rather, they should be distinguished accurately in terms of the regional production cluster approach. Another dimension is the speculation on new knowledge-based and technology-intensive enterprises, which can influence the respective sub-sectors' development positively as well as negatively (as in the case of the new economy's recent stock market crisis).

A further dimension relates to the problematic labor relations which are spreading in many sub-sectors of the new economy, where the flexibilization of employment and the growth of dependent self-employed freelancers is a main characteristic. Last but not least there is the ideological content of the new economy, which is not confined to the well-known belief in new information technology as a permanent growth machine. The ideological conception of a new economy promotes an economic culture which emphasizes the model of fast and effortless success by means of financial juggling. This can undermine and damage a region's capacity for competence-based economic development as we are experiencing in the case of Berlin. Thus, while in specific regional settings positive interrelations do exist between different sub-sectors of the new economy which enforce regional clustering, quite negative interrelations between different dimensions of the new economy might also develop.

Notes

1 Of the various approaches to a classification of industrial branches, this chapter focuses on "high-tech" industries. Given the problems raised by a distinction between high-, medium- and low-tech industries, the prevailing view now is that a grouping of industries has to take into account the varying levels R&D encountered in the various branches of industrial production. This view stems from the realization that an industry's capacity for innovation is more important for its future development than the kind of production technology it employs. The OECD, for instance, uses expenditure on R&D as a criterion to group the various branches of industry. The R&D-intensive industries include (a) the aircraft construction industry; (b) electronic components, office machines and data processing equipment; (c) measuring, control and communications engineering, medical engineering; (d) chemicals and pharmaceuticals; (e) mechanical engineering; and (f) vehicle construction. The establishment of a sub-sector comprising R&D-intensive industries enables us to distinguish a group of other industries, which are referred to as "traditional" industries. These are characterized by a comparatively low level of R&D.
2 "Media city" is a term currently used to describe centers of cultural production and the media industry operating at very different geographical levels. They range from local urban clusters in the media industry to the cultural metropolises of the global urban and regional system.
3 An *alpha world media city* had to have more than 17 of the 33 global media companies (i.e. over 50 percent of the global players analyzed here) in its location area (first threshold value). Additionally, more than 60 business units from the included global media firms had to be present (second threshold value). A *beta world media city* had to be the location for more than 11 (i.e. over a third) of the global media companies incorporated and more than 30 business *units* of these companies had to be present in its business location area. A *gamma world media city* had to be the location for more than eight (i.e. over a quarter) of the global media companies incorporated and over 20 business *units* of these companies had to be present.

Bibliography

Beaverstock, J.V., Smith, R.G. and Taylor, P.J. (1999) "A Roster of World Cities," *Cities* 16(6): 445–458.

Braczyk, H.-J., Cooke, P. and Heidenreich, M. (eds) (1998) *Regional Innovation Systems: The Role of Governances in a Globalized World*, London: UCL Press.

Braczyk, H.J., Fuchs, G. and Wolf, H.-G. (eds) (1999) *Multimedia and Regional Economic Restructuring*, London: Routledge.

Cooke, P. (2002) *Knowledge Economies: Clusters, Learning and Cooperative Advantage*, London: Routledge.

Ernst & Young (ed.) (1999) "European Life Sciences 99 Report: Communicating Value," Stuttgart: Ernst & Young.

Ewers, H.J. (1999) "Ist der Wirtschaftsstandort Berlin fit für die Globalisierung?," in Senatsverwaltung für Wirtschaft (ed.) *Konsequenzen der Globalisierung für den Wirtschaftsstandort Berlin*, Berlin: Senatsverwaltung für Wirtschaft.

Gottschall, K. and Schnell, C. (2000) "'Alleindienstleister' in Kulturberufen – Zwischen neuer Selbständigkeit und alten Abhängigkeiten," *WSI-Mitteilungen* 12: 804–810.

Haaren, K.V. and Hensche, D. (eds) (1997) *Arbeit im Multimedia-Zeitalter: Die Trends der Informationsgesellschaft*, Hamburg: VSA.

Held, D., McGrew, A., Goldblatt, D. and Perraton, J. (1999) *Global Transformations: Politics, Economics and Culture*, Cambridge: Polity Press.

IHK (2000) *Medienstandort im Aufbruch: Die Ergebnisse einer Befragung der IHK Berlin*, Berlin: IHK.

Initiative für Städtedialog III (1999) *Stadtentwicklung durch Kompetenz, Forschung und Information: Vorlage des Innenministeriums Finnland in Kooperation mit Experten aus anderen EU-Mitgliedstaaten*, Tampere: Finish Ministry of the Interior.

Krätke, S. (2000) "Berlin – the Metropolis as a Production Space," *European Planning Studies* 8(1): 7–27.

—— (2002a) *Medienstadt: Urbane Cluster und globale Zentren der Kulturproduktion*, Opladen: Leske und Budrich.

—— (2002b) "Network Analysis of Production Clusters, the Potsdam/Babelsberg Film Industry as an Example," *European Planning Studies* 10(1): 27–54.

Krätke, S. and Borst, R. (2000) *Berlin – Metropole zwischen Boom und Krise*, Opladen: Leske und Budrich.

Krätke, S. and Scheuplein, C. (2001) *Produktionscluster in Ostdeutschland: Methoden der Identifizierung und Analyse*, Hamburg: VSA.

Medienbüro Berlin-Brandenburg (ed.) (2001) *Branchenreport Medienwirtschaft Berlin*, Berlin: Medienbüro Berlin-Brandenburg.

Porter, M.E. (1998) "Clusters and Competition: New Agendas for Companies, Governments, and Institutions," in Porter, M.E. (ed.) *On Competition*, Boston: Harvard University Press.

—— (2001) "Regions and the New Economics of Competition," in Scott, A.J. (ed.) *Global City-Regions: Trends, Theory, Policy*, Oxford: Oxford University Press.

Pratt, A.C. (2000) "New Media, the New Economy and New Spaces," *Geoforum* 31(4): 425–436.

Robins, K. (1995) "The New Spaces of Global Media," in Johnston, R.J., Taylor,

P.J. and Watts, M.J. (eds) *Geographies of Global Change: Remapping the World in the Late Twentieth Century*, Oxford: Basil Blackwell.

Sassen, S. (1991) *The Global City: New York, London, Tokyo*, Princeton: Princeton University Press.

Schamp, E.W. (2000) *Vernetzte Produktion: Industriegeographie aus institutioneller Perspektive*, Darmstadt: Wissenschaftliche Buchgesellschaft.

Scott, A.J. (1997) "The Cultural Economy of Cities," *International Journal of Urban and Regional Research* 21(4): 323–339.

—— (1998) *Regions and the World Economy: The Coming Shape of Global Production, Competition, and Political Order*, Oxford: Oxford University Press.

—— (ed.) (2001a) *Global City-Regions. Trends, Theory, Policy*, Oxford: Oxford University Press.

—— (ed.) (2001b) "Globalization and the Rise of City-Regions," *European Planning Studies* 9(7): 813–826.

Scott, A.J., Agnew, J., Soja, E. and Storper, M. (2001) "Global City-Regions," in Scott, A.J. (ed.) *Global City Regions: Trends, Theory, Policy*, Oxford: Oxford University Press.

Senatsverwaltung für Stadtentwicklung (1997) *Gewerbeflächenentwicklung Berlin*, Berlin: Senatsverwaltung für Stadtentwicklung.

—— (1999) *Innovations- und Technologiekonzept*, Berlin: Senatsverwaltung für Stadtentwicklung.

Senatsverwaltung für Wirtschaft und Betriebe (1997) *Wirtschaftsbericht Berlin 1997*, Berlin: Senatsverwaltung für Wirtschaft und Betriebe.

—— (1998) *Wirtschaftsbericht Berlin 1998*, Berlin: Senatsverwaltung für Wirtschaft und Betriebe.

Storper, M. (1997) *The Regional World: Territorial Development in a Global Economy*, New York: Guilford Press.

Storper, M. and Scott, A.J. (1995) "The Wealth of Regions: Market Forces and Policy Imperatives in Local and Global Context," *Futures* 27(5): 505–526.

Taylor, P.J. and Hoyler, M. (2000) "The Spatial Order of European Cities under Conditions of Contemporary Globalization," *Tijdschrift voor Economische en Sociale Geografie* 91(2): 176–189.

Taylor, P.J. and Walker, D.R. (2001) "World Cities: A First Multivariate Analysis of Their Service Complexes," *Urban Studies* 38(1): 23–47.

Index

Printed in the United States
by Baker & Taylor Publisher Services